Women in Sufism

Exploring the diverse myriad of female religious identities that exists today within the various branches of the Moroccan Sufi order, Qādiriyya Būdshīshiyya, this book evidences a wide array of religious identities, from those more typical of Berber culture, to those characterized by a 'sober' approach to Sufism, as well as those that denote New Age eclecticism.

The book researches the ways in which religious discourses are corporeally endorsed. After providing an overview of the order historically and today, enunciating the processes by which this local *ṭarīqa* from north-eastern Morocco has become the international organization that it is now, the book explores the religious body in movement, in performance, and in relation to the social order. It analyses pilgrimage by assessing the annual visit that followers of Hamza Būdshīsh make to the central lodge of the order in Madāgh; it explores bodily religious enactments in ritual performance, by discussing the central practices of Sufi ritual as manifested in the Būdshīshiyya, and delves attention into diverse understandings of faith healing and health issues.

Women in Sufism provides a detailed insight into religious healing, Sufi rituals and Sufi pilgrimage, and is essential reading for those seeking to understand Islam in Morocco, or those with an interest in Anthropology and Middle-East studies more generally.

Marta Dominguez Diaz is Assistant Professor in Islamic Studies (Anthropology) at the University of St Gallen, Switzerland. Her research interests include North-African Sufism, Islam in Europe, ritual studies, religious healing, comparative religion and Muslim–Jewish relations. She has published a number of articles on Sufism and on ritual studies.

Routledge Sufi Series
General Editor: Ian Richard Netton
Professor of Islamic Studies, University of Exeter

The Routledge Sufi Series provides short introductions to a variety of facets of the subject, which are accessible both to the general reader and the student and scholar in the field. Each book will be either a synthesis of existing knowledge or a distinct contribution to, and extension of, knowledge of the particular topic. The two major underlying principles of the Series are sound scholarship and readability.

PREVIOUSLY PUBLISHED BY CURZON

AL-HALLAJ
Herbert I. W. Mason

BEYOND FAITH AND INFIDELITY
The Sufi Poetry and Teaching of Mahmud Shabistari
Leonard Lewisohn

RUZBIHAN BAQLI
Mysticism and the Rhetoric of Sainthood in Persian Sufism
Carl W. Ernst

ABDULLAH ANSARI OF HERAT
An Early Sufi Master
A. G. Ravan Farhadi

THE CONCEPT OF SAINTHOOD IN EARLY ISLAMIC MYSTICISM
Bernd Radtke and John O'Kane

SUHRAWARDI AND THE SCHOOL OF ILLUMINATION
Mehdi Amin Razavi

PERSIAN SUFI POETRY
An Introduction to the Mystical Use of Classical Poems
J. T. P. de Bruijn

AZIZ NASAFI
Lloyd Ridgeon

SUFIS AND ANTI-SUFIS
The Defence, Rethinking and Rejection of Sufism in the Modern World
Elizabeth Sirriyeh

SUFI RITUAL
The Parallel Universe
Ian Richard Netton

DIVINE LOVE IN ISLAMIC MYSTICISM
The Teachings of al-Ghâzalî and al-Dabbâgh
Binyamin Abrahamov

STRIVING FOR DIVINE UNION
Spiritual Exercises for Suhrawardi Sufis
Qamar-ul Huda

REVELATION, INTELLECTUAL INTUITION AND REASON IN THE PHILOSOPHY OF MULLA SADRA
An Analysis of the *al-hikmah al-'arshiyyah*
Zailan Moris

PUBLISHED BY ROUTLEDGE

1. **MUSLIM SAINTS OF SOUTH ASIA**
   The Eleventh to Fifteenth Centuries
   Anna Suvorova

2. **A PSYCHOLOGY OF EARLY SUFI SAMA**
   Listening and Altered States
   Kenneth S. Avery

3. **SUFI VISIONARY OF OTTOMAN DAMASCUS**
   'Abd al-Ghani al-Nabulusi, 1941–1731
   Elizabeth Sirriyeh

4. **EARLY MYSTICS IN TURKISH LITERATURE**
   Mehmed Fuad Koprulu
   Translated, edited and with an Introduction by Gary Leiser & Robert Dankoff

5. **INDIAN SUFISM SINCE THE SEVENTEENTH CENTURY**
   Saints, Books and Empires in the Muslim Deccan
   Nile Green

6. **SUFI CASTIGATOR**
   Ahmad Kasravi and the Iranian Mystical Tradition
   Lloyd Ridgeon

7. **POPULAR SUFISM IN EASTERN EUROPE**
   Sufi Brotherhoods and the Dialogue with Christianity and 'Heterodoxy'
   H. T. Norris

8. **THE NAQSHBANDIYYA**
   Orthodoxy and Activism in a Worldwide Sufi Tradition
   Itzchak Weismann

9. **SUFIS IN WESTERN SOCIETY**
   Global Networking and Locality
   Edited by Ron Geaves, Markus Dressler and Gritt Klinkhammer

10. **MORALS AND MYSTICISM IN PERSIAN SUFISM**
    A History of Sufi-Futuwwat in Iran
    Lloyd Ridgeon

11. **SPIRITUAL PURIFICATION IN ISLAM**
    The Life and Works of al-Muhasibi
    Gavin Picken

12. **SUFISM AND SOCIETY**
    Arrangements of the Mystical in the Muslim World, 1200–1800 CE
    Edited by John J. Curry and Erik S. Ohlander

13. **ISLAMIC MYSTICISM AND ABŪ ṬĀLIB AL-MAKKĪ**
    The Role of the Heart
    Saeko Yazaki

14. **WOMEN IN SUFISM**
    Female Religiosities in a Transnational Order
    Marta Dominguez Diaz

Women in Sufism

Female Religiosities in a Transnational Order

Marta Dominguez Diaz

Routledge
Taylor & Francis Group
LONDON AND NEW YORK

2 Park Square, Milton Park, Abingdon, Oxon OX14 4RN

and by Routledge
711 Third Avenue, New York, NY 10017

Routledge is an imprint of the Taylor & Francis Group, an informa business

British Library Cataloguing in Publication Data
A catalogue record for this book is available from the British Library

Library of Congress Cataloging in Publication Data
Dominguez Diaz, Marta (Anthropologist of religion)
Gender and Sufism : female religiosities in a transnational order /
Marta Dominguez Diaz.
pages cm -- (Routledge Sufi series)
Summary: "Exploring the diverse myriad of female religious identities that exist within the various branches of the Moroccan Sufi order, Qariyya B
Includes bibliographical references and index.
1. Sufism--Morocco--History. 2. Qadiriyah--Morocco. 3. Women sufis--Morocco. 4. Sufism--Doctrines. I. Title.
BP188.8.M6D66 2014
297.4'8--dc23
2014005385

ISBN: 978-0-415-74173-6 (hbk)
ISBN: 978-1-315-81511-4 (ebk)

Typeset in Times New Roman
by Taylor & Francis Books

Printed and bound in the United States of America by
Edwards Brothers Malloy on sustainably sourced paper

To Bruno and Lara with Love

Contents

Acknowledgements x
Arabic transliteration chart xii

1 Introduction 1

2 An Historical Overview 22

3 The Būdshīshiyya Today 40

4 Būdshīshiyya Online 62

5 *Ziyāra* 78

6 Ritual 97

7 Healing 120

8 Final Caveats 141

Appendix 1 – Būdshīshiyya's saintly genealogy 153
Appendix 2 – Būdshīshiyya's central lodge 155
Glossary 156
Index 163

Acknowledgements

So many people have contributed to this study that it would be impossible to name all of them here. I want to particularly express my gratitude to the people of the Būdshīshiyya who have made this research possible by giving me their time and explaining to me the nature of their passion and religious dedication. Through their kindness and attention, they made my fieldwork an enjoyable experience and helped me understand what is to be a member of a Sufi order today. I am particularly grateful to those female members of the order who, with sincerity and affection, have shared their faith and spiritual life with me. I am also indebted to those who had been and those who think one day they may become members of the order, and to those who know it well albeit not being part of the organization; they have all answered my queries and attentively explained to me their views, and their insights have also been central to this research.

I would especially like to express my gratitude to my PhD supervisor Dr Kate Zebiri whose continuous guidance and feedback has been both insightful and enriching; without her close and meticulous attention to work in progress this research would not have been possible. I would also like to thank her for sharing her academic expertise, which has enhanced my knowledge and understanding of contemporary Islam.

I am also grateful to Prof. Ron Geaves for his valuable feedback and continued support, and to Dr Marat Shterin for his interesting insights on the doctoral thesis on which this book is based. Prof. Brian Bocking was of particular help on issues related to the fieldwork. I appreciate enormously the preliminary guidance given me by Prof. Ferran Iniesta who first inspired the theme of this research and who helped me contact the people of the Būdshīshiyya. Thanks also to my friend Dr Fabrizio Ferrari for helping me during the initial steps of my academic career and to Dr Raphaël Voix for his insights. I am thankful to Dr Rachida Chih for all the meetings we had concerning our common research interests at the beginning of this project. Her initial advice on Modern Sufism in general and on the Būdshīshiyya in particular set me on the right track with this research. I also appreciate the exchange of ideas with Dr Tony Langlois whose approach as an ethnomusicologist made me more aware of the contextual frame of the order in

Morocco. I am also thankful to Dr Silvia Montenegro with whom I have had the chance to exchange ideas on Morocco and conducting fieldwork there. I would particularly like to thank David Stretch-Dowse whose advice has been valuable in the edition of the manuscript.

I am also grateful to the students at the University of St Gallen, whose views have made me rethink on several occasions my assumptions on matters related to religion. I would like to express my gratitude and appreciation to my family and friends for their endless patience, support and good moments. And last but not least, I am deeply grateful to my partner Bruno and my daughter Lara from whom I have learnt and continue to learn so much, and whose support is invaluable.

Arabic transliteration chart

Arabic letter	Transliteration
ا	ā,a
آ,أ	ā
ب	b
ت	t
ث	th
ج	j
ح	ḥ
خ	kh
د	d
ذ	dh
ر	r
ز	z
س	s
ش	sh
ص	ṣ
ض	ḍ
ط	ṭ
ظ	ẓ
ع	‘
غ	gh
ف	f
ق	q
ك	k
ل	l
م	m
ن	n
و	ū, w
ه	h
ى,ي	ī,y
ء	’
ة	a, at
ى	ā
◌َ	a
◌ِ	i
◌ُ	u

1 Introduction

Sufism today is a predominantly international phenomenon. This book is drawn from a doctoral 'Study of Religion' supervised by Dr Katherine Zebiri at the School of Oriental and African Studies (University of London) and defended in 2010.[1] It is an exploration of a Moroccan Sufi *ṭarīqa*, focusing primarily on its transnational dimension. In the 2008 CESNUR International Conference on New Religious Movements (NRMs), scholars pointed to the lack of research into new forms of religious life as developed in Islam. It was indicated that too much attention is often paid to so-called Islamist groups at the expense of other emerging Islamic religiosities. Among these, the ways in which some forms of Sufism have evolved and entered the arena of global religious movements raises new questions for research, some of which I try to address in this study, an exploration of one such globalizing movement.

The Sufi order Qādiriyya al-Būdshīshiyya has developed a geography of varied groups that extend across the globe, from Morocco and West Africa to Western Europe, Latin America, the United States and Canada. The *ṭarīqa* originated in the Moroccan region of l'Oriental, in the Berber-dominated north-eastern province of Berkane, a region that still contains the majority of its devotees. However, in recent decades the *ṭarīqa* has transformed itself into a transnational organization incorporating members from urban *milieux* in Morocco and abroad. In this transformation it has surpassed its traditional ethnic boundaries, coming to accept members from a variety of backgrounds.

This is a comparative study of the array of religious identities existing in the Būdshīshiyya order in Morocco and beyond. In addition to the Berber peasantry, the diversity of followers (*fuqarā'/faqīrāt;* sing. *faqīr/a*) that this study considers includes Arab populations from the Moroccan metropolis, Moroccan labour migrants who have settled in France, Belgium and Spain, European converts to Islam, and European sons and grandsons of Muslims who have seen, in this religious group, their way back to practising Islam.

This research deals with the transnational dimension of this *ṭarīqa*, focusing on the religious identities of the *fuqarā'* in Western Europe and in Morocco. I am particularly interested in examining those developments by which religious meanings, symbols and institutions are reinterpreted and modified to accommodate new social realities. Thus the book analyses the ways in which

Muslim followers of the current Būdshīshiyya *shaykh*, Sīdī Hamza,[2] participate in the supra-local discourses of the Islamic Sufi tradition, and also how their local realities and regional *milieux* shape the ways in which they participate in these discourses. I aim to approach this order as an holistic entity with a comparative perspective in which the rural enclaves of the Moroccan countryside, the urban groups in Morocco and some of the strands which exist in Western Europe (in France and Spain mainly, but also in Belgium and the United Kingdom) are considered and contrasted. The study understands the Būdshīshiyya order as affected by the internal dynamics of this *ṭarīqa* and by the contextual factors of the social *milieux* in which it has settled.

In the field

The information gathered for this book is mainly the result of multi-sited fieldwork undertaken to speak with people having first-hand knowledge of the Būdshīshiyya. The main source of information comes from members of this *ṭarīqa.* I have talked to devotees of the order from most of the Western European and Moroccan contingents and to individuals who had been attending the activities organized by the organization but had not (at least, not by the time I concluded this fieldwork) undertaken the formal commitment to become disciples – an adherence to the organization sealed by a formal ritual commonly known as 'the pact' (*bay'a*).[3] Among my informants, there were also former disciples, people who were once 'formal' devotees of this organization but who have more recently decided to abandon the *ṭarīqa*.

Of relevance to this study, also, have been the testimonies of individuals who have never been Būdshīshiyya members but live in places in which this Sufi order plays an important social role. For example, I have spoken to youngsters of the Moroccan diaspora in Europe who, despite not being Būdshīshiyya devotees, may have family and friends who are members of this order, and are familiar with their activities and know their leaders – on occasion better than some of those who, although they have formalized their allegiance, have done so very recently. In Morocco, in particular, this *ṭarīqa* holds an overt public profile with a very clear political agenda. The Būdshīshiyya has been a relevant political actor in north-eastern Morocco, with members of the Būdshīshiyya lineage having long held key positions in public administration and local government.

A jump into public acknowledgement of the political role this organization plays at the national level came in 2012 with the appointment by King Muḥammad VI of Aḥmad Tawfīq, a devotee of the order, as Minister for *Habus* (religious endowments) and Islamic Affairs, a move that has to be related to the active involvement of the *ṭarīqa* in supporting the monarchy nationwide. In Morocco, thus, there are many that have direct and prolonged contact with the organization, its leaders and/or members, although they may not consider themselves devotees of Hamza Būdshīsh. In particular, the inhabitants of the northern towns of Berkane, Nador, Ahfir and Saidia, as well as those from the neighbouring smaller villages, have been crucial in informing this research.

I have also gathered data by participating in activities and meetings held by various groups of the Būdshīshiyya in Morocco and in Europe and in the central lodge of the order in Madāgh. Some relevant data collected among rural members of this *ṭarīqa* was obtained during two trips to the region, the first in March 2008 when I attended the Būdshīshiyya's major celebration (the *Mawlid*)[4] – and the second during the summer of 2008. An international gathering held in Paris in spring 2008 was also a good place to meet devotees. I have collected opinions, perceptions, ideas and views on this Sufi organization over a prolonged period of time, from November 2006 to July 2012, by meeting people from a variety of enclaves and from the social *milieux* in which they exist. Even though I have also used written sources (articles, journals, booklets and books written by members of the order), as well as audiovisual (voice and image recordings) and digital (web pages, blogs, forums and official sites) materials, the main source of information used for this research has been personal narratives. These have been collected mostly through casual conversation and interaction in ritual gatherings and social meet-ups, mostly with women. Instead of following a reduced group of followers over a lengthy period of time, I have preferred to focus on trying to obtain a many-sided portrait, by gathering as many views and experiences on and about the order as possible – at times, conflicting views on particular issues appeared as a result of the array of informants to which I had access.[5]

Given the degree of geographical dispersion, cultural and ideological diversity that characterizes this organization, undertaking multi-sited fieldwork turned out to be a necessity. Applying a 'dislocating' method in defining the scope of the field has brought about questions on how notions of place, space and locality are to be perceived in this study. Dislocated fields like that of the transnational Būdshīshiyya impose a rethinking of the nature of the relationship between culture and territory and help us to problematize in more nuanced ways the idea that communities develop identities as manifestations of their relationship to bounded *milieux* – a criticism of the conventional ethnographic method originally advanced by Appadurai (1995) and Marcus (1995). Instead, this study places great attention on the interconnectedness of sites, on the limitless nature of social spaces and on mobility:

> Multi-sited research is designed around chains, paths, threads, conjunctions, or juxtapositions of locations in which the ethnographer establishes some form of literal, physical presence, with an explicit, posited logic of association or connection among sites.
>
> (Marcus, 1995: 105)

In the study of Sufi orders in particular, multi-sited ethnographies definitely furnish new modes of exploration. Whereas the way the study of Sufi orders was traditionally approached assumed an original 'pristine' religiosity to be found in the original contingent of each *ṭarīqa* and a series of mimetic expressions reproduced beyond this central focus, an emerging yet timidly developed perspective (e.g. Draper et al., 2006; Klinkhammer, 2009) emphasizes the model of a 'multi-centre scenario' (Beyer, 2009: 13). This means that all the branches of an order exercise a certain influence over all the others, so that enclaves become 'glocal' – settings with a worldwide exchange of social and cultural ideas that contribute to the transformation of local realities and cultural behaviour (Geaves et al., 2009: 4).

By conducting multi-sited fieldwork, my study identifies a *ṭarīqa* constituted of the characteristic eclectic religiosities typical of glocalized religious hybridity. Likewise, it has found that devotees not only develop particular ways of construing their religious identities in accordance with their personal life trajectories and cultural frames, but also that each group redefines, in accordance with its members' religious stances, the ways in which it relates to the other groups in the order and to social and political events that are well known to all members (e.g. the Arab Spring, the 9/11 attacks, issues related to Islamophobia, mass migration and so on).

Something that became apparent during the preparatory stages of fieldwork was the gender divide among members of this *ṭarīqa*. The Būdshīshiyya is a gendered organization, which means that men and women carry out their activities separately; ritual practices are always performed under these circumstances and in most locations men and women only relate to each other in quite exceptional instances. Some of the female members I met had entered the *ṭarīqa* without knowing any male devotees; and some months later they still didn't know any. This divide limited the scope of the research I was planning to undertake, the result being that the fieldwork data I collected was voiced almost exclusively by women. Access to male devotees was only occasional, so although their accounts were sometimes considered, there was not a sufficient number of them to facilitate a comprehensive study of both male and female religiosities within the *ṭarīqa.*

So the research is confined to an analysis of the religious identities of female followers of the Būdshīshiyya. As a female researcher I had access to women's groups and congregational meetings, but I was not allowed to attend the men's. The fact that my subjectivity informs this research is nowhere more evident than in this issue of gender. Meeting male members of the order was more difficult in some enclaves than in others, and as a result most of the subjects in the study are women, and most of the experiences, beliefs and ideas analysed are feminine.[6] Yet the focus on gender in this study is not only the result of an acknowledged limitation deriving from the field conditions; the pervasiveness of gendering in religious praxis and its pivotal role in shaping people's understanding of morality and normativity makes of gender an elucidating analytical tool in the study of religious life. Notably, as gender is mainly a cultural construct, this study contends it is an insightful tool for scrutinizing the cultural variances that occur transnationally within this order.[7]

Multi-sited fieldwork also makes us look at categories often used in the 'Study of Religion' in new ways. One of those, 'the insider/outsider problem',[8] needs to be specially reconsidered here. This *ṭarīqa* displays a significant degree of fluidity when it comes to membership. Thus, informants who were once members, are no longer; some others want to be tagged neither as members nor as non-members; some are considering becoming members; yet others do not understand devotion to Hamza Būdshīsh in terms of formal discipleship to a religious organization. These are some of the ambiguities typical of an order with a quite young average devotee age, a juvenile character that may contribute to determining mobility in religious commitment. In any case, the issue of intermittence in adherence transforms the terms in which we must think of the insider/outsider antithesis.

Also of importance in rethinking the insider/outsider terms is the notion of locality. Given the geographical dispersion of the organization, most devotees do only know a reduced number of *fuqarā'*, mostly from their own group, and often treat Būdshīshiyya members from other enclaves as 'outsiders' (they perceive each other as cultural strangers); this is especially, although not only, how Moroccan followers perceive non-Moroccan devotees. There seems to be a trend of scholars who are converts to Islam working on Sufism. I have always clearly stated that my interest in the order was academic, but devotees, especially Europeans, often thought that my 'academic' interest would end up being a personal journey of religious transformation. These particular circumstances also meant that I was never really treated either as an outsider or as an insider. In terms of my 'journey', they were somehow right; I was deeply transformed by the experience of this fieldwork, although not in the way in which many had expected. In this regard, I consider having immersed myself in so many Būdshīshī worlds to have been fascinating, morally educational and as moving as very few other experiences in life can be. I am aware, however, that while some will see the fact I never became part of the organization as an advantage for the rigour of the research, others will view it as having been an obstacle to attaining the 'True Knowledge' they believe only comes with discipleship and religious devotion.

I have never understood how, in the post-9/11 world, any researcher has managed to collect genuine accounts of experiences and opinions on Islam in a fairly relaxed atmosphere with a recorder in hand. I asked for permission to record conversations with my first informants, but most people refused to be recorded – even when I provided evidence of my academic credentials (business cards as well as the document provided by my university explaining that I was collecting data for a doctoral study), explained real names would not be revealed and gave assurance that the recordings would only be listened to by me and exclusively used to produce academic materials. Speaking about an order with a contested political agenda as well as with people who, as Muslims, feel they are often unjustly treated with suspicion adds to the more general fact that many informants did not really like 'being an object of research' – well, who does? As a result, I thus used the recorder only to record evidence of those instances that do not include speech, mainly ritual sessions and *samā'* concerts, for which it was not difficult to get consent, and otherwise had to rely on written personal notes – which were taken immediately after concluding each encounter – as the main source of 'raw' data. These field notes constitute the bulk of material from which this research is derived.

Throughout this book I have defended the need to re-centre the object of study in the analysis of religious phenomena by proposing a move away from the relevance traditionally attributed to religious texts and ideas in favour of the study of the situated, socially and culturally contingent scrutiny of religious embodiment(s). I argue, in line with Vásquez's theories on non-reductive materialism (2011), that religious identity is better understood by looking at the ways in which people manifest it, an argument in favour of prioritizing the scrutiny of embodiment, emplacement, practice and material culture in the 'Study of Religion', at the expense of texts and a more abstract, less dependent-upon-context approach to beliefs and ideas. The focus on situated religious *praxis* and embodiment seems to be particularly adequate when applied to the Būdshīshiyya, as this order in its entirety, from the leadership to the majority of its disciples, places far more importance on the experiential and the sensorial than it does on the textual and the intellectual.

Disciples seem to be largely unaware of the doctrine supported by the order to which they belong; nor do they know well the senses in which these differ from the teachings of other *ṭuruq*. Traditional scholarship on Islam would have argued that the popular nature of Sufism, with its unorthodox flavour, is the reason behind this lack of knowledge; on the contrary, I am of the opinion that this is not specific to Sufism or Islam; religion everywhere in its daily manifestations shows little awareness of the grand meta-discourses that sustain its foundational basis. In any case, and given the limited referral to doctrine these religiosities manifest, my interest in knowing the 'official line' and in interviewing religious authorities as a result was not a final goal *per se* in this study.

My interest in the leadership was thus 'relational', i.e. I tried to unpack what a devotee with an interest in contacting someone of the upper echelons of the organization is asked to do, and, in so doing, I learnt how religious authority functions in this order. If a *faqīra* wants to contact anyone in the upper levels of the *ṭarīqa's* leadership she will need first to ask the person in charge of her local group (*muqaddima*),[9] who in turn will pass her query to the higher ranks of the organization. I was told I would be able to speak to various higher up personalities at the various international gatherings I attended, although these ended up being minimal encounters – an occasional three minutes of casual conversation with the son of the order's leadership, Sīdī Munīr, surrounded by tens of followers eager to gain closer contact with their religious superiors.

The central concern of this study is to analyse the Būdshīshiyya in its current multifaceted expressions. Consequently, historical developments are summarily presented, understood as sociocultural drives that only partially contribute to shaping the present nature of the group. The fact that the emphasis of the study is on the everydayness of religious experiences implies that individual narratives – perceived as a 'source' of human thought and behaviour – and not historical analysis are primarily used as a matrix from which the present investigation is derived. Furthermore, in order to explore the diversity within the movement, this research focuses its interest on the 'particular'. Thus, I have only briefly considered the 'official' Būdshīshiyya discourse, and the other collective meta-discourses with which the *ṭarīqa* operates (whether from the Sufi tradition or Islam). At the same time, individual narratives are often informed by the 'collective'. For this reason we have included certain aspects of these major discourses when they appear in dialogue in individual positions. Along the same lines, 'tradition' is apprehended in its current, reconstrued, re-imagined, contested and reified forms as part of religious 'talk'.

The focus is thus placed on religious manifestations. The notion of 'corporeality'[10] as a signifier has inspired this research, serving as a thematic continuum throughout the present work. Religious meanings are stamped in the human body, to the extent, as this study suggests, that they can be elucidated by looking at the ways in which the body is 'treated'. As Jackson once argued (1998: 131), 'what is done with the body is the ground of what is thought and said'. Accordingly, I propose here to understand the Būdshīshiyya *faqīrāt*'s religiosities[11] by exploring the religious body in movement (i.e. pilgrimage), in performance (i.e. ritual) and in relation to the social order (i.e. notions of illness and health). Emplacement is also of primordial interest to this work: since bodies express identity the ways they do, because they are (at least partially) contextually determined, religiosities can be approached as part of a dynamic exchange between the subject and the surrounding social *milieu*. Thus, the accounts of members, individuals considering becoming members and ex-members are as decisive in getting a picture of this order as are those of non-members that live in social settings in which the Būdshīshiyya is a relevant actor in daily life. These voices, I contend, despite being from persons that are not part of the organization, are crucial to understanding contextual correlates.

Literature review

The scholarly interest in contemporary Sufism, despite containing a substantial number of under-researched lacunas, has seen unprecedented growth in the last decade, showing a promising and still expanding dynamism. A sign of this proliferation is the array of edited volumes that have been published, e.g. Westerlund (2004); Hinells and Malik (2006); Bruinessen and Howell (2007); Geaves et al. (2009); Raudvere and Stenberg (2009); Gabriel and Geaves (2013). Contributors to these compilations have often proposed new approaches and have been interested in themes that had been previously neglected by a scholarship traditionally more centred on the figure of the saint *per se* (e.g. Doutté, 1900; Lings, 1961) and on offering general knowledge by compiling secondary literature (e.g. Trimingham, 1971; Popovic and Veinstein, 1996). Although these former works had been extremely useful, they had contributed little evidence of Sufism as a thriving contemporary religious phenomenon with social, economic and political dimensions.

The scholarly richness added by this newer collection of case studies is, however, still incipient, as they all discuss particular aspects of Modern Sufism, but lack the analytical depth provided by monographs. These lengthier works have been primordial in the consubstantiation of my research within the field and have informed my work; in particular, Ron Geaves's *The Sufis of Britain: An Exploration of Muslim Identity* (2000) is a seminal work providing a valuable survey of the various *ṭuruq* established in the UK. It covers a wide variety of groups and movements and is useful because it is based on extensive fieldwork research. It is a pioneering study in the field, and though written over a decade ago it remains a fundamental point of reference for fieldwork conducted today, not least because it helps to elucidate the dynamic, ever changing nature of religious life among Sufi communities in the British context.

Andezian's (2001) research among the Algerian 'Issāwā of Tlemcen is a detailed analysis of this religiosity and shows interesting parallels to my own research due to the geographical proximity of her fieldsite to the Būdshīshiyya's central lodge (*Zāwiya*). Rozehnal's (2007) analysis of the Pakistani Chishtī Sabīrī *ṭarīqa* is a fascinating study on the beliefs and social manifestations of this order with informing analyses on Sufi thought, but also on its missionary dimension (*da'wa*) and ritual. Raudvere's (2002) study is an illuminating exploration of how female *dhikr* circles face the challenges of Turkey's modern urban life by discussing the symbolism and meanings of Sufi ritual among female devotees from Istanbul. The book provides an insightful perspective on ritual based on participant observation that has been an inspiring instance for comparison and contrast with my own ethnographic experience.

Taji-Farouki's latest work (2007) is a well-researched study of one non-*ṭarīqa* Sufi group in the UK. It contains extensive research into the ways in which Ibn 'Arabī's thought has been reinterpreted by individuals in Europe who regularly meet to study in devotion the works of the medieval Spanish thinker. Her insights into the particularities of this encounter between Sufism and New Age are a significant advancement in the field and have decisively informed my own perspective on some of the New Age phenomena in the European Būdshīshiyya. Werbner's (2003) analysis of a transnational order with fieldwork conducted both in Zindapir (Pakistan) and in Birmingham (United Kingdom) is so far the only work that has developed an in-depth, multi-sited transnational approach to the analysis of a contemporary order. She has explored the kaleidoscopic world of Sufi ritual, from *dhikr* to healing and miracle performance in Britain and Pakistan, and has elaborated a pioneering comparative perspective of both sites. *Pilgrims of Love: The Anthropology of a Global Sufi Cult* is a masterpiece in the anthropological study of Modern Sufism and has been a major source of reference to this research.

Morocco is one of the places for which the study of Sufism has been analysed in more depth and this body of literature has fundamentally shaped this research. The seminal works of Gellner (1969), Geertz (1971), Crapanzano (1973), Eickelman (1976), Rabinow (1977), Dwyer (1982), Hart (1984), Brunel (1988), Munson (1993), Hammoudi (1997), Ensel (1998) and Cornell (1998) have on some occasions a profundity of scrutiny yet to be paralleled by more recent works, although some of the latest contributions have also sometimes added interesting angles to well-established anthropological debates. Especially, a critique of the anthropologist's long-held assumptions that defined Moroccan society in terms of binary typological distinctions, i.e. 'Arab' versus 'Berber', 'urban' versus 'rural' communities, 'Scripturalist' versus 'Sufi' Islam, 'great' and 'little' traditions, has been masterfully articulated using innovative research (e.g. Claisse, 2003), as well as by proponents of methodological reconsiderations (e.g. Hammoudi, 2009; Dwyer et al., 2013), among others. Specific aspects of this research have found a rich frame within Moroccan studies to which they could relate. For example, on the interplay between notions of corporeality and belief systems and on understandings of health and healing, the works of Akhmisse (1984), Maarouf (2007), McPhee (2012) and Mateo Dieste (2012) have been inspiring. On ritual performance and religious music, Langlois (1998, 2009), Waugh (2005), Kapchan (2007) and El Abar (2008) deal with Sufi groups with features similar to those I studied for this research.

Despite the prolific amount of literature existing on Morocco, however, it is worth noting that the north-eastern region has largely escaped the interest not only of tourism but of scholars as well. Although the area resembles in some aspects other predominantly Berber zones that have been studied more thoroughly, some of the specificities derived from its frontier character and its dual Hispano–French colonial past give it a distinctiveness largely obliterated by academic scrutiny. In this sense, the accounts of Seddon (1973), Coon (1980) and Katan (1990), while they are interesting they are yet too old to hold current relevance; only McMurray's (2001) work offers a view on borderland communities with compelling similarities to the part of my research that deals with northern Morocco.

Existing research on the Būdshīshiyya is, given the public profile of the order, surprisingly scarce. Draper's (2002) unpublished PhD thesis, an ethnographic comparative study of the Būdshīshiyya and the Naqshbandiyya in the United Kingdom, is one of the few comprehensive works produced so far on the order. Draper tries to understand how these two *ṭuruq* have engaged with the underlying spiritual tendencies of their western adherents, which he calls 'the Glastonbury experience'; he offers valuable insights into some of the religiosities existing among British devotees. The political role of the order in Morocco has been explored by Tozy (1990, 1992, 1999) and Ben-Brahim (2012) but there still is a significant lack of comprehensive research into the

Būdshīshiyya, not only but including as a religious organization. Chih (2012) has analysed the missionary initiatives undertaken by the order in Morocco in cooperation with the *makhān*, while Sedgwick (2004), Voix (2004) and Haenni and Voix (2007) have developed initial accounts of the eclectic religious styles in Morocco and France. Besides, there is some literature produced by members of the order, which, with albeit a general subtle proselytizing flavour, are rich accounts of devotees. These texts, sometimes biographical, have been used in this study as primary source material as they sometimes present the motivation of its authors to enter this order, and often also provide helpful data to contextualize the teachings of Hamza Būdshīsh within the Moroccan Sufi tradition (e.g. Ben Driss, 2002; Ben Rochd, 2002; Malik, 2004; Qustas, 2007).[12]

Overall, albeit being part of a large body of scholarship, the present study intends to explore an existing interplay between significantly unexplored areas of research. In itself, it deals with a Sufi order that, despite its current social relevance in Morocco and among the Moroccan diaspora, has so far received scant scholarly attention. Additionally, the study seeks to address the realities of transnational Moroccan Sufism by exploring trends and communities that have received limited academic consideration, namely, the religious lifestyles of north-eastern Moroccans, the emergence of NRMs in Morocco, the phenomena of conversion to Islam[13] and of Sufi hybridity, especially in non-English speaking parts of Western Europe, and the incorporation of New Age cross-pollinations with Islam. The study of this multifaceted *ṭarīqa* has been undertaken by using anthropological research combined with theories drawn from other disciplines (religious studies, sociology, history and political sciences).

On method

The members of this Sufi order all live in rapidly changing societal environments. Despite differences in wealth, access to education and medical assistance, Būdshīshiyya devotees live in a world that is imagined and perceived beyond the mere locality of the village or the city. Rural members are often temporary workers in the greenhouses of southern Spain, and urban members are connected to the realities of globalization either through migration or cosmopolitanism. Accordingly, it would be misleading to understand their religious views, the ways in which they imagine their relationship to society and the ways in which they construe their understandings of religious authority, by presenting them as localized individuals existing in independent, isolated locations.

Whether the knowledge they have of a reality somewhere else (Europeans of Morocco and Moroccans of Europe) is an imagined construct or not is, strictly speaking, not of relevance here. What is relevant is the fact that all the followers conceptualize their religiosities in relation to a world that goes beyond their immediate space. The religious subjects that we are considering in this study perceive themselves in what we might term a kaleidoscopic way. Thus, an amalgam of discourses is incorporated, contested, reinterpreted and personified in the construction of their worldviews. Their accounts are not bounded arenas, but pervasive fields informed by a multiplicity of sources. In addition, the study of the Būdshīshiyya as a source of religious experience is mainly conveyed by its intersubjective expressions,[14] since every subject relates to other subjects, to bodies of thought, to collective experiences, and so forth.

Accordingly, this book proposes a research framework that stands in a liminal space between various bodies of scholarship. In this multidisciplinary spirit, it aims to better comprehend the complex multilayered dynamics of hybridity, typical of the religiosities of international Sufi movements such as the Būdshīshiyya. The reader will notice that sociological approaches to secularization, conversion and social movements, as well as anthropological perspectives on ritual, pilgrimage and charisma have informed the analysis. However, I have not attempted to use these frameworks either comprehensibly or in equal measure, but only discretely when they could be useful to better comprehend specific aspects of the research.

In 'the West', the Būdshīshiyya is a melange of Hermansen's (1996) categorization of Sufi transplants and hybridity.[15] In this study, additionally, I have incorporated the ethnic component into the scrutiny of religious identities by following a trend initiated by Geaves (2000). In his assessment of Sufism in Britain, he aligns Hermansen's classification of *ṭuruq* in 'the West' with an underlying ethnic factor that also crucially contributes to determining how particular groups behave and how branches and sub-branches are organized. Ethnicity is pivotal in understanding the adherence of devotees to one particular *ṭarīqa,* he argues, and what may end up determining schismatic divisions within the same *ṭarīqa*.

Is the Būdshīshiyya a New Age group or a NRM? This book argues that to a certain extent it is both. However, given the ambiguity often ascribed to these terms I suggest the order I have studied evidences a specific collection of NRM features that need to be discussed more precisely. In his seminal essay on new forms of religious life, Wallis (1984) identified three types of NRM. First, the 'world-rejecting movements' are those that see society as having departed from God's commands and which tend to demand from members absolute and exclusive loyalty. The lifestyle characteristic of members of these groups is – despite appearances to the contrary – that of being remarkably organized and controlled (Wallis, 1984: 14). These movements often imbue in their members a sense of 'deindividuation', and, when people join the group, a feeling of being 'reborn' which encourages them to break with their past life (1984: 19). 'World-rejecting' groups often advance critiques of modern greed and materialism, which are portrayed as negative phenomena with potentially devastating consequences. As we will see in the course of this research, there is within the Būdshīshiyya something of a tendency towards these features, notably among members in some of the European groups (particularly converts). Remarkably, however, other characteristics of Wallis's 'world-rejecting movements' (e.g. communal life, millennialism and authoritarian leadership) are not to be found in this Sufi order. In fact, it would seem that the European groups of the Būdshīshiyya represent the 'world-accommodating' pattern rather than the 'world-rejecting' one.

Second, the 'world-accommodating movements' make a distinction between the spiritual and the mundane. Religion is not linked with social matters, but instead constitutes a source of personal solace and nourishes the interior life (Wallis, 1984: 35). However, as Fichter has argued, this does not necessarily indicate a lack of social concern, since 'the conviction is that a better society can emerge only when people have become better' (see Fichter in Wallis, 1984: 36). It is particularly striking that when a movement of this type has been inspired by, or has its genesis in, Islam, religion disappears from the public realm (where it typically manifests itself in the Muslim world) and situates itself in the private sphere. As we will see in the course of this study, this is very often the case with the European Būdshīshiyya. Adherence to 'world-accommodating' movements does not necessarily have profound consequences for the devotee's routines and lifestyle, as such movements do not set forth a strict code containing precise details of how to live – only that their followers should behave in a more or less religiously inspired way. Devotees, by and large, carry on with their conventional lives as accountants, shopkeepers, housewives, students and so on. Hence, these movements adapt to the world rather than affirm or reject it. While belief and ritual performance are presented as being of potential benefit to the individual, religious practice and worship are performed collectively (Wallis, 1984: 36). According to the majority of their members, movements of this type restore an experiential element to the spiritual life and replace certainties which are perceived as having been lost; these movements are common in societies with a perceived sense of religious institutions having become increasingly relativized (Wallis, 1984: 37). And third, 'world-affirming movements' are loosely institutionalized groups, without a fixed set of rituals or official discourse. Indeed, Wallis argues, they may even lack most of the features of religious groups.

There are certain aspects of all three types to be found within the Būdshīshiyya, and distinctions need to be made in this regard. By and large, the characteristic behaviours of most members of the Būdshīshiyya authorities would point towards defining the European branches of this Sufi order as being of the 'world-accommodating' type. However, it should also be noted that certain characteristics of the 'world-rejecting' as well as of the 'world-affirming' movements are certainly noticeable among some of its members. This denotes the vast plurality of approaches that exists within this *ṭarīqa*, a remarkable attribute and one that will be explored throughout the course of the present research.

Equally of paramount significance is the use this study makes of the term 'New Age'. I am aware of the problematic and highly contested nature of the term – different scholars have used it to mean different things, making its usefulness somewhat questionable. Heelas famously categorized New Age as being a 'hotchpotch of disparate ideas' (Heelas, 1996: 2). In addition, it has been argued that New Age is a self-category not often found at the *emic* level (Sutcliffe, 2003). This is certainly attested to by the present study in which hardly any members of the Būdshīshiyya whom we have described as New Age would have defined themselves in this way. However, despite these reservations, this study uses the term New Age to refer to a highly distinctive set of beliefs. Accordingly, I use it to characterize a person's belief or interest in (a) channelling; (b) healing and spiritual growth; and (c) transpersonal psychology.

The Būdshīshiyya evidences some of these practices and beliefs; in some cases, *all* of these together.[16] I define channelling as a belief based on the conviction that some people act as a 'channel' for information from sources typically identified as 'entities' living on higher levels of being (New Age followers of the Būdshīshiyya will accept not only Sufis, but also people of other religious and non-religious backgrounds as channellers, and as the channelled entities, be they alive or dead).

In terms of healing and spiritual growth, I understand this to be the view that both body and psyche are aspects of one encompassing reality, understood to be spiritual rather than physical. When it comes to healing, this means that psychological problems are reflected on the physical level, for example, in the form of 'energy blockages' in certain parts of the body resulting in physical dysfunctions of various kinds. According to this view, the process of healing is closely linked with the idea of spiritual development. Psychological and physical problems ultimately result from a lack of spiritual harmony, and, conversely, their effect is to block natural development towards such harmony. Healing in the broadest sense of the word is thus a necessary part in the process of spiritual development to achieve complete inner harmony.

In the case of Būdshīshiyya's New Age followers, the practice of Sufism constitutes such healing, although other healing therapies and spiritual techniques – e.g. shiatsu, yoga, homeopathy, shamanic practices and so on may also be considered. Finally, this study conveys that transpersonal psychology is the belief based on the conviction that a holistic view of the human psyche is only possible by including for consideration so-called transpersonal experiences (which may include ecstatic experiences, paranormal perceptions and 'altered states of consciousness'), which are perceived as superior stages of psychological functioning.

It may be argued that these three areas of activity and belief are to be found, to some extent, within the Sufi tradition (in the historical sense of the term), and I would suggest that broadly speaking this is certainly the case. What has been and in fact still is characteristic of Sufism is the belief that the saints show us signs of an otherworldly nature, and the use of medical treatments that fall beyond the scope of the Western medical tradition. Finally, ecstatic experiences have been and are held in high esteem by many Sufis. However, I would argue that 'extreme eclecticism'[17] lends to the New Age followers in the Būdshīshiyya a distinctive quality which is not to be found – at least not to the same extent – in Islamic mysticism. For example, Sufis who are not New Age believe that the only valid channelling is that which is carried out by *awliyā' 'Allāh*, 'the friends of God', which on some occasions might include not only Muslims, but also special Christian and Jewish personages and even certain Hindus (in the case of South Asian Sufism).

The point is that this group does not include individuals who belong to traditions that are perceived as culturally or religiously alien or exotic. By contrast, New Age members of the Būdshīshiyya will refer to a wide variety of sources and individuals, many of them possibly being perceived as 'foreign' (some Sufi, but many others as well) in an approach which this study holds to be more characteristic of the 'pick and mix' religious culture typical of 'post-modern' Western European *milieux* than of Sufism as it developed historically in the Muslim world.

On the contents of this book

This research is an attempt to understand Būdshīshiyya *faqīrāt*'s religiosities by looking at the ways in which religious discourses are corporeally endorsed. In a sense, it is a journey through embodied expressions of Sufism. Chapter 2 provides an historical introduction to the order that will help us to better understand the processes that support the changes in religious doctrine needed for the geographical expansion by which this local *ṭarīqa* from the region of l'Oriental has become the international organization that it is today. Chapter 3 is an overview of the order. It situates this *ṭarīqa* geographically, by mapping the diverse enclaves considered in the study. Further, it assesses 'officialdom' within the order, by introducing the leadership of this *ṭarīqa* and the texts that constitute the 'authorised' discourse. The chapter also discusses the diverse types of members that constitute the order, a preliminary picture of the religiosities that are further explored in relation to specific issues in subsequent chapters.

Chapter 4 analyses the 'unbodied' expression of religiosity by exploring the presence of the Būdshīshiyya online. It compares and contrasts different types of digital materials with ethnographic accounts. The chapter assesses the impact of the internet in promoting proselytization (*da'wa*), the emergence of new types of *shaykh*–disciple relationship, and the enhancement of new forms of charisma as a result of the devotee's access to new forms of information and communication. It also explores the transformation of ritual praxis by the influence of the digital and the advantages and disadvantages that the Būdshīshiyya presence online poses for the order's leadership and how the internet contributes to concretizing/diluting the feeling of belonging to the order.

Chapter 5 explores pilgrimage and aims to identify patterns of continuity and transformation in relation to the impact that ideas and manifestations of religious travel and pilgrimage have in constructing religious identities. It assesses various aspects of the annual visit that followers of Hamza Būdshīsh make to the central lodge in Madāgh, in north-eastern Morocco. It addresses the importance given to *ziyāra* by Hamza's devotees and the sense of communal solidarity that constantly appears in *faqīrāt*'s narratives. It critically assesses whether this *camaraderie* dilutes economic, social and cultural differences – as is commonly claimed – or whether, by contrast, it is culturally and socially framed. The chapter also examines diverse cultural conceptualizations of *ziyāra* in relation to notions of social etiquette, solidarity and hospitality, and it sheds light on the economic dimensions involved in this mass event, thus focusing on their practical implications.

Chapter 6 discusses bodily religious enactments in ritual performance. The chapter first discusses the central practice in Sufi ritual, *dhikr*, in its collective and individual forms. It also addresses issues related to the performance of other prayers and explores how ritual has been adapted to the diverse understandings of Islam and the personal circumstances of various *faqīrāt*. Further, it analyses the symbolic meaning attached to food and the diversity of attitudes towards fasting that exist within the order in Europe and the changing position that music has had in the Būdshīshiyya.

Chapter 7 scrutinizes Būdshīshī diverse identities as they find expression in practices and understandings related to health issues. The chapter first explores the historical development of healing practices within the Qādiriyya tradition (of which the Būdshīshiyya is part). This serves to elucidate how two crucial *personages* in the order today relate themselves to a broader tradition of miracle performance: the guardian of today's tombs' complex and *Zāwiya,* Sīdī Bābā, and the head of the *ṭarīqa*, Hamza Būdshīsh. It also explores the stance adopted by Hamza in relation to *shifā'* and to the specificities of Moroccan Sufism in this regard. Besides, it discusses the official position of the order on *shifā'*, and compares it with several followers' interpretations and practices of healing. The chapter delves into the practical implications of such interpretations; particular attention is given to matters related to mental health issues. Finally, it analyses how the *ṭarīqa*'s official discourse has been adapted by followers in European and Moroccan urban *milieux* in an attempt to accommodate New Age understandings of body and self. Intra-*ṭarīqa* tensions derived from the appearance of competing narratives on those issues are also assayed in this chapter.

A concluding chapter reflects upon the main lines of thought developed throughout the book by revisiting some of the facts exposed in the research, as well as the most significant areas of theorization. It also suggests potential areas for future research and the ways in which these studies can contribute to extend previous research on Modern Sufism as well as to my own work.

Notes

1 The original thesis entitled 'Revisiting Moroccan Sufism and Re-Islamicizing Secular Audiences: Female Religious Narratives in the Tarīqa Qādiriyya Būdshīshiyya in Morocco and Western Europe Today' was defended in February 2010 to a Board of Examiners composed of Dr Marat Shterin (King's College, London) and Prof. Ron Geaves (Liverpool Hope and Director of the Centre for the Applied Study of Muslims and Islam in Britain).

2 Sīdī is the Arabic term used before the name to refer to male members of the group and it expresses affection. For females, the term used is Lālā. I have not used the real names of my subjects in order to protect their identities. For a more detailed description of the rationale used to name public personalities in the order see note 28 of Chapter 3.

3 *Bay'a* is considered paramount by members of the organization outside the region where the order originates, but discipleship is understood altogether differently by north-eastern Moroccans; this aspect is discussed in more detail throughout the book, particularly in Chapter 6 which is devoted to the analysis of rituals.

4 Celebration to commemorate the birthday of the prophet Muḥammad. It is also known as *Mawlid an-nabī* and it occurs during the third month of the Islamic calendar (*rabi' al-awwal*). In the Būdshīshiyya, the *Mawlid* is considered a major festival consisting of an entire week of celebrations; followers from all over the world go to Madāgh to visit Hamza Būdshīsh.

5 An interesting volume on the challenges of participant observation is Hume and Mulcock's (2004) edited volume from which I gleaned valuable advice.

6 Much has been written about gender issues when conducting ethnographical research, but I found particularly insightful the perspective developed by Hackney and Warren (2000).

7 A stimulating collection of essays on gender and religion that has informed the theoretical underpinnings of this book is the volume edited by King and Beattie (2005).

8 Reflections and theoretical perspectives on the insider/outsider debate can be found in the volume edited by McCutcheon (1999). Some of these issues have also been raised by Rozehnal (2007: 10–12) in his study of the Chishtī Sabīrī order in Pakistan.

9 A more detailed exposition of the order's leadership echelons is provided in Chapter 3.

10 The study of how meanings are expressed bodily can furnish insights for any research; it is a field that increasingly appeals to both social scientists and scholars of religious studies. See, for instance, Giddens (1992), Shilling (1993), Falk (1994), Turner (1996, 2003), Arthur (1999), Baudrillard (2004), Bordieu (2004) and Douglas (2004). Of particular relevance is the comprehensive study of Feyer (1989). The studies that deal with bodily perspectives within Islam are scarcer. See, for instance, Malti-Douglas (1991, 1995), Winter (1995), Rida (1998), Katz (2002) and Kugle (2007).

11 A distinction is drawn in this research between the notions of 'religiosity' and 'religion'. What I call 'religiosity' in this study is often equated with 'religiousness'. We are referring to the idea of 'personal faith' – that is, individual and subjective ways of feeling, perceiving, apprehending and expressing religious feelings, beliefs and thoughts. By contrast, we use the term 'religion' when referring to the institutional aspect of such practice. So 'religion' indicates a set of beliefs and practices generally subscribed to by a group of people, and also the organizations that support, institutionalize or formalize them (e.g. Islam, Christianity and so on). On occasion we have used the term 'religion' in a more generalized, theoretical way, when speaking of it in relation to 'social phenomena' (e.g. religion and the body, religion and consumption and so on).

12 A more detailed exploration of their contents has been discussed in Chapter 3.
13 This study relates to a significant body of scholarship on religious conversion, particularly within Islam (e.g. Köse, 1996; van Nieuwkerk, 2006; Zebiri, 2007).
14 The idea of religious experience being intersubjective was first proposed by Bruner and Turner (1986). Since then, scholars have been increasingly interested in exploring the intersecting nature of religious experience as composed of lived experience and told experience and informed by the experiences of others.
15 Hermansen's (1996) threefold typology of Sufi groups in the West identifies the following categories: (a) Hybrid, groups that link themselves with a larger Islamic tradition and are generally composed of members of Muslim origin and converts; (b) Perennials, which are groups that do not relate Sufism to Islam and tend to be classified among New Age Movements; and (c) Transplants, which are *ṭuruq* whose followers are migrants living in western contexts, and which tend to reproduce the structure, organization and rituals of the original *ṭarīqa*.
16 In general terms our definition follows that of Hanegraaff (2007), although there are certain aspects (e.g. 'Neo-Paganism') that he highlights that are not to be found among members of the Būdshīshiyya, and which we have therefore omitted.
17 We refer to 'extreme eclecticism' as we assume that a certain degree of eclecticism derived from receiving outer influences is a natural and common process within religions, including Sufism. The term 'extreme' refers to the fact that the degree of 'mixing tendencies' is far more acute than in the general pattern.

References

Akhmisse, M. 1984. *Rites et secrets des marabouts à Casablanca*. Casablanca: SEDIM.

Andezian, S. 2001. *Expériences du divin dans l'Algérie contemporaine: Adeptes des saints de la région de Tlemcen*. Paris: Centre national de la recherche scientifique (CNRS).

Appadurai, A. 1995. 'The Production of Locality', in R. Fardon (ed.) *Counterworks: Managing the Diversity of Knowledge*, 204–25. London: Routledge.

Arthur, L. B. 1999. 'Introduction: Dress and the Social Control of the Body', in L. B. Arthur (ed.) *Religion, Dress and the Body*, 1–8. Oxford: Berg.

Baudrillard, J. 2004. 'The Finest Consumer Object: The Body', in M. G. Fraser and M. Greco (eds) *The Body: A Reader*, 277–82. London: Routledge.

Beattie, T. and King, U. 2005. (eds) *Gender, Religion and Diversity: Cross-cultural Perspectives*. London: Continuum.

Belal, Y. 2011. *Le cheikh et le calife: Sociologie religieuse de l'Islam politique au Maroc*. Lyon: ENS Éditions.

Ben-Brahim, N. 2012. 'La boutchichiyya au Maroc: Entre l'Islam randiste, "le Makhzenisme" et l'Islamisme', unpublished Masters dissertation. Oslo: Universitetet i Oslo.

Ben Driss, K. 2002. *Sidi Hamza al-Qadiri Boudchich. Le renouveau du soufisme au Maroc*. Beirut: Albouraq.

Ben Rochd, E. R. 2002. *Le soufisme. Patrimoine universel méthode d'épanouissement et doctrine d'harmonie*. Casablanca: Dechra.

Beyer, P. 2009. 'Globalization of Religions. Plural Authenticities at the Centres and at the Margins', in R. Geaves, M. Dressler and G. Klinkhammer (eds) *Sufis in Western Societies. Global Networking and Locality* 13–25. London; New York: Routledge.

Bordieu, P. 2004. 'Belief and the Body', in M. G. Fraser and M. Greco (eds) *The Body: A Reader*, 87–91. London: Routledge.

Bruinessen, M. and Howell, J. D. (eds). 2007. *Sufism and the 'Modern' in Islam*. London: Tauris.

Brunel, R. 1988. *Essai sur la confrérie religieuse des aissaouas au Maroc*. Casablanca: Afrique Orient.

Bruner, E. M. and Turner, V. W. 1986. *The Anthropology of Experience*. Urbana, IL: University of Illinois Press.

Chih, R. 2012. 'Sufism, Education and Politics in Contemporary Morocco', *Journal for Islamic Studies* 32(1): 24–46. Rondebosch: University of Cape Town Publications.

Claisse, P. A. 2003. *Les Gnawa marocains de tradition loyaliste*. Paris: L'Harmattan.

Coon, C. S. 1980. *A North Africa Story: The Anthropologist as OSS Agent, 1941–1943*. Ipswich: Gambit.

Cornell, V. J. 1998. *Realm of the Saint: Power and Authority in Moroccan Sufism*. Austin, TX: University of Texas Press.

Crapanzano, V. 1973. *The Ḥamadsha; A Study in Moroccan Ethnopsychiatry*. Berkeley, CA: University of California Press.

Crawford, D. and Newcomb, R. 2013. *Encountering Morocco: Fieldwork and Cultural Understanding*. Bloomington. IN: Indiana University Press.

Douglas, M. 2004. 'The Two Bodies', in M. G. Fraser and M. Greco (eds) *The Body: A Reader*, 78–81. London: Routledge.

Doutté, E. 1900. *Notes sur l'Islâm maghribin, les marabouts*. Paris: E. Leroux.

Draper, M. 2002. 'Towards a Postmodern Sufism: Eclecticism, Appropriation and Adaptation in a Naqshbandiyya and a Qadiriyya Tariqa in the UK', unpublished PhD thesis. Birmingham: University of Birmingham.

Draper, M., Nielsen, J. and Yemelianova, G. 2006. 'Transnational Sufism. The Haqqaniyya', in J. Hinnells and J. Malik (eds) *Sufism in the West*, 103–14. London: Routledge Curzon.

Dwyer, K. 1982. *Moroccan Dialogues: Anthropology in Question*. Baltimore, MD: Johns Hopkins University Press.

Eickelman, D. F. 1976. *Moroccan Islam: Tradition and Society in a Pilgrimage Center*. Austin, TX; London: University of Texas Press.

El Abar, F. 2008. *Musique, rituels et confréries au Maroc les 'Issāwā, les Ḥamādcha et les Gnawa*. Lille: Atelier National de Reproduction des Thèses.

Ensel, R. 1998. *Saints and Servants: Hierarchical Interdependence between Shurfa and Haratin in the Moroccan Deep South*. Amsterdam: Universiteit van Amsterdam

Falk, P. 1994. *The Consuming Body*. London: Sage.

Feyer, 1989. *Fragments for a History of Human Body*. 3 vols. Cambridge, MA: MIT Press.

Gabriel, T. P. C. and Geaves, R. (eds) 2013. *Sufism in Britain*. New York: Bloomsbury.

Geaves, R. 2000. *The Sufis of Britain: an Exploration of Muslim Identity*. Cardiff: Cardiff Academic Press.

Geaves, R., Dressler, M. and Klinkhammer, G. 2009. 'Introduction', in R. Geaves, M. Dressler and G. Klinkhammer (eds) *Sufis in Western Societies. Global Networking and Locality*, 1–12. London; New York: Routledge.

Geertz, C. 1971. *Islam Observed: Religious Development in Morocco and Indonesia*. Chicago, IL; London: University of Chicago Press.

Gellner, E. 1969. *Saints of the Atlas*. Chicago, IL: University of Chicago Press.

Giddens, A. 1992. *The Transformation of Intimacy*. Stanford, CA: Stanford University Press.

Hackney, J. K. and Warren, C. A. 2000. *Gender Issues in Ethnography*. Thousand Oaks, CA: Sage Publications.

Haenni, P. and Voix, R. 2007. 'God By All Means … Eclectic Faith and Sufi Resurgence among the Moroccan Bourgeoisie', in M. Bruinessen and J. Day Howell (eds) *Sufism and the 'Modern' in Islam*, 241–56. London: Tauris.

Hammoudi, A. 1997. *Master and Disciple: The Cultural Foundations of Moroccan Authoritarianism*. Chicago, IL: University of Chicago Press.

——2009. *Being There: The Fieldwork Encounter and the Making of Truth*. Berkeley, CA: University of California Press.

Hanegraaff, W. J. 2007. 'The New Age Movement and Western Esotericism', in D. Kemp and J. R. Lewis (eds) *Handbook of New Age*, 25–50. Leiden: Brill.

Hart, D. M. 1984. *The Ait 'Atta of Southern Morocco: Daily Life and Recent History*. Cambridge: Middle East and North African Studies Press.

Heelas, P. 1996. *The New Age Movement: The Celebration of the Self and the Sacralization of Modernity*. Oxford: Blackwell.

Hermansen, M. 1996. 'In the Garden of American Sufi Movements: Hybrids and Perennials', in P. B. Clarke (ed.) *New Trends and Developments in the World of Islam*, 155–78. London: Luzac.

Hinnells, J. and Malik, J. (eds) 2006. *Sufism in the West*. London: Routledge Curzon.

Hume, L. and Mulcock, J. (eds) 2004. *Anthropologists in the Field: Cases in Participant Observation*. New York: Columbia University Press.

Jackson, M. 1998. *Minima Ethnographica: Intersubjectivity and the Anthropological Project*. Chicago IL: University of Chicago Press.

Kapchan, D. A. 2007. *Traveling Spirit Masters: Moroccan Gnawa Trance and Music in the Global Marketplace*. Middletown, CT: Wesleyan University Press.

Katan, Y. 1990. *Oujda, une ville frontière du Maroc (1907–1956): Musulmans, juifs et chrétiens en milieu colonial*. Paris: L'Harmattan.

Katz, M. H. 2002. *Body of Text: The Emergence of the Sunni Law of Ritual Purity*. Albany, NY: State University of New York Press.

——2008. 'Cleanliness and Ablution', in Jane Dammen McAuliffe (ed.) *Encyclopaedia of the Qur'ān*. Brill Online. School of Oriental and African Studies (SOAS), available online at www.brillonline.nl/subscriber/entry?entry=q3_SIM-00081 (accessed 9 May 2008).

King, U. and Beattie, T. 2005. (eds) *Gender, Religion and Diversity: Cross-cultural Perspectives*. London: Continuum.

Klinkhammer, G. 2009. 'The Emergence of Transethnic Sufism in Germany. From Mysticism to Authenticity', in R. Geaves, M. Dressler and G. Klinkhammer (eds) *Sufis in Western Societies. Global Networking and Locality*, 130–47. London; New York: Routledge.

Köse, A. 1996. *Conversion to Islam: A Study of Native British Converts*. London: Kegan Paul.

Kugle, S. A. 2007. *Sufis and Saints' Bodies. Mysticism, Corporeality and Sacred Power in Islam*. Chapel Hill, NC: University of North Carolina Press.

Langlois, T. 1998. 'The G'nawa of Oujda: Music at the Margins in Morocco', *The World of Music* 40(1): 135–57. Paris: International Music Council.

——2009 'Music and Politics in North Africa', in L. Nooshin (ed.) *Music and the Play of Power: Music, Politics and Ideology in the Middle East, North Africa and Central Asia*, 207–27. London: Ashgate.

Lings, M. 1961. *A Moslem Saint of the Twentieth Century: Shaikh Ahmad al-'Alawī, his Spiritual Heritage and Legacy*. London: Allen & Unwin.

Maarouf, M. 2007. *Jinn Eviction as a Discourse of Power: A Multidisciplinary Approach to Moroccan Magical Beliefs and Practices*. Leiden: Brill.

McCutcheon, R. T. (ed.) 1999. *The Insider/Outsider Problem in the Study of Religion: A Reader*. London; New York: Cassell.
McMurray, D. A. 2001. *In and out of Morocco: Smuggling and Migration in a Frontier Boomtown*. Minneapolis, MN: University of Minnesota Press.
McPhee, M. J. 2012. *Vulnerability and the Art of Protection: Embodiment and Healthcare in Moroccan Households*. Durham, NC: Carolina Academic Press.
Malik, A. 2004. *Qu'Allah bénisse la France*. Paris: Albin Michel.
Malti-Douglas, F. 1991. *Woman's Body, Woman's Word: Gender and Discourse in Arabo-Islamic Writing*. Princeton, NJ: Princeton University Press.
——1995. 'Faces of Sin. Corporal Geographies in Contemporary Islamist Discourse', in J. M. Law (ed.) *Religious Reflections on the Human Body*, 67–75. Bloomington, IN: Indiana University Press.
Marcus, G. E. 1995. 'Ethnography in/of the World System: The Emergence of Multi-sited Ethnography'. *Annual Review of Anthropology* 24(95): 95–117. Palo Alto, CA: Annual Reviews.
Mateo Dieste, J. L. 2012. *Health and Ritual in Morocco: Conceptions of the Body and Healing Practices*. Leiden: Brill.
——2013. *Health and Ritual in Morocco: Conceptions of the Body and Healing Practices*. Leiden: Brill.
Munson, H. 1993. *Religion and Power in Morocco*. New Haven, CT: Yale University Press.
Popovic, A. and Veinstein, G. 1996. *Les voies d'Allah: Les ordres mystiques dans l'Islam des origines á aujourd'hui*. Paris: Fayard.
Qustas, A. 2007. *Nibrās al-Mudīr*. Marrakesh: al-Ahmadi.
Rabinow, P. 1977. *Reflections on Fieldwork in Morocco*. Berkeley, CA; London: University of California Press.
Raudvere, C. 2002. *The Book and the Roses: Sufi Women, Visibility, and Zikir in Contemporary Istanbul*. Istanbul: Swedish Research Institute in Istanbul.
Raudvere, C. and Stenberg, L. 2009. *Sufism Today: Heritage and Tradition in the Global Community*. London: Tauris.
Rida, M. A. 1998. 'Norms and Values', in A. Boudhiba (ed.) *The Different Aspects of Islamic Culture. The Individual and Society in Islam*. Paris: UNESCO.
Rozehnal, R. T. 2007. *Islamic Sufism Unbound: Politics and Piety in Twenty First Century Pakistan*. New York: Palgrave Macmillan.
Seddon, J. D. 1973. 'Local Politics and State Intervention: Northeast Morocco from 1870 to 1970', in E. Gellner and C. Micaud (eds) *Arabs and Berbers: From Tribe to Nation in North Africa*, 109–39. London: Duckworth.
Sedgwick, M. 2004. 'In Search of the Counter-Reformation: Anti-Sufi Stereotypes and the Budshishiyya's Response', in M. Browers and C. Kurzman (eds) *An Islamic Reformation?*, 133–41. Lanham, MD: Lexington Books.
Shilling, C. 1993. *The Body and Social Theory*. London: Sage.
Sutcliffe, S. 2003. *Children of the New Age: A History of Spiritual Practices*. London: Routledge.
Taji-Farouki, S. 2007. *Beshara and Ibn 'Arabi: A Movement of Sufi Spirituality in the Modern World*. Oxford: Anqa.
Tozy, M. 1990. 'Le prince, le clerc et l'état: La restructuration du champ religieux au Maroc', in G. Kepel and Y. Richard (eds) *Intellectuels et militants de l'Islam contemporain*. Paris: Seuil.
——1992. 'L'Islam entre le controle de l' état et les debordements de la societé civile. Des nouveaux clercs aux nouveaux lieux de l'expression religieuse', in

J.-C. Santucci (ed.) *Le maroc actuel. Une modernisation au miroir de la tradition?*. Paris: Editions du CNRS.

——1999. *Monarchie et Islam politique au maroc*. Paris: Presses de la Fondation nationale des sciences politiques.

Trimingham, J. S. 1971. *The Sufi Orders in Islam*. Oxford: Oxford University Press.

Turner, B. 1996. *The Body and Society: Explorations in Social Theory*. London: Sage.

——2003. 'The Body in Western Society: Social Theory and its Perspectives', in S. Coakley (ed.) *Religion and the Body*. Cambridge: Cambridge University Press.

van Nieuwkerk, K. (ed.) 2006 *Women Embracing Islam: Gender and Conversion in the West*. Austin, TX: University of Texas Press.

Vásquez, Manuel A. 2011. *More than Belief: A Materialist Theory of Religion*. Oxford: Oxford University Press.

Voix, R. 2004. 'Implantation d'une confrérie marocaine en France: Mécanismes, méthodes, et acteurs', *Ateliers* 28(1): 221–8. Nanterre: Maison René-Ginouvès Archéologie et Ethnologie.

Wallis, R. 1984. *The Elementary Forms of the New Religious Life*. London: Routledge.

Waugh, E. H. 2005. *Memory, Music, and Religion: Morocco's Mystical Chanters*. Columbia, SC: University of South Carolina Press.

Werbner, P. 2003. *Pilgrims of Love: The Anthropology of a Global Sufi Cult*. Bloomington, IN: Indiana University Press.

Westerlund, D. (ed.) 2004. *Sufism in Europe and North America*. London: Routledge Curzon.

Winter, M. 1995. 'Islamic Attitudes toward the Human Body', in *Religious Reflections on the Human Body* 36–45. Bloomington, IN: Indiana University Press.

Zebiri, K. P. 2007. *British Muslim Converts: Choosing Alternative Lives*. Oxford: Oneworld Publications.

2 An Historical Overview

The Būdshīshiyya is often depicted by its own members as a kaleidoscopic amalgam of people of diverse economic and cultural backgrounds who, although understanding religion in very different ways, share an ultimate goal and an infinite love for their *shaykh*, Sīdī Hamza. The order has groups of followers in the Muslim World (especially in Morocco, where it is the biggest *ṭarīqa* in the country) as well as in predominantly non-Muslim countries.[1] The impressive geographical diffusion of the Būdshīshiyya's disciplehood, and its resulting staggering linguistic, cultural and religious diversity, can only be understood as the result of its recent history. We will thus trace back the processes of transformation by which this young *ṭarīqa* (only born in 1942) has in less than half a century transformed from being the cult to a local Sufi saint (*awliyā' 'Allāh*) and his lineage with a mainly Berber following of a local reach to an international organization with devotees in more than ten countries and across four continents.

A branch of the Qādiriyya

The Sufi order Qādiriyya al-Būdshīshiyya is made up of the followers of the living *shaykh* Hamza al-Qādirī al-Būdshīsh. He is the spiritual master of the order and belongs to a family of *shurafā'* – in the Moroccan Islamic tradition, those believed to be direct descendants of the Prophet.[2] Hamza Būdshīsh is, by his followers, thought to be genealogically connected to 'Abd al-Qādir al-Jīlānī (b.1078),[3] a pious man originally from the Persian Gilan province who lived most of his life in Baghdad and who is generally regarded as the founder of the Qādirī lineage – yet it seems that the first organized group that evolved around his teachings is to be ascribed to two of his sons and not to him (Trimingham, 1971: 40f). Today, there are two branches of the Qādiriyya in Morocco. One of them was established by the descendants of *shaykh* Ibrāhīm, one of the sons of al-Jīlānī, who first settled in Andalusia; but the group moved from Granada to Fes after being expelled from the Iberian Peninsula in 1492. The second of the branches of the Moroccan Qādiriyya entered the Maghribi region at the end of the seventeenth century. They were the descendants of *shaykh* 'Abd al-Razzāq, the eldest of Jīlānī's sons, who had settled on the borders of the Ottoman Empire – present-day Algeria – and had eventually moved into the areas bordering Morocco along with the Ottoman expansion into Western Maghreb (Draper, 2002: 172).[4]

This branch of the Qādiriyya, however, only reappears in the sources much later. Almost twenty years before the French occupation of Oujda in 1844,[5] the family was identified by the Europeans as one of the most influential in the region (Ben Driss, 2002: 106) and the family had established Qādiriyya shrines in Taghjirt (near the city of Oujda) used by the Berber populations of the Béni-Snassen.[6] It was in these *zāwiyāt* that they began to propagate the teachings that only later became identified with the *ṭarīqa*. Similarly, some historical figures that were by later generations associated with this order had relevance in the political accounts of the late nineteenth/early twentieth century. Sīdī Mukhtār al-Kabīr (d. 1914) of the Būdshīshiyya's lineage went down in history as a fighter against French colonization, and his grandson Sīdī Mukhtār al-Būdshīsh was captured and killed by the French during the last occupation of Oujda in 1907 (Ben Driss, 2002: 106; Draper, 2002: 104). However, the first accounts in which the Būdshīshiyya appears to have a recognizable *ṭarīqa* structure only date from 1942. It was founded by the Berber notable Sīdī Abīmadyan Ibn Munawwar Qādirī al-Būdshīsh and, being one of the newest orders in the country, first appeared as a local *ṭarīqa* with an exclusive rural base in the north-eastern – mainly Berber – region of l'Oriental.[7] Since its beginnings the *ṭarīqa* has served as a religious–political institution within the region, one among the many spread across rural Morocco, using its widely accepted religious legitimacy to act as a political broker between local Berber populations and the central urban powers.[8]

Although it is true that the advent of independence in 1956 in the first instance signified a great challenge to the Sufi structures of Morocco, the *maraboutic* code was so embedded in society that it soon managed to adapt to the post-independence *milieu*. The *ṭuruq* rapidly permeated the newly emerging political structure, informing attitudes in public service, ministerial circles and trade unions, as well as the business world (Hammoudi, 1997). The *maraboutic* code has even permeated Islamist organizations, which have generally been recognized as antithetical to Sufism (e.g. Sirriyeh, 1999). Illustrative of this is the movement led by 'Abd al-Salām Yāssīn, a former member of the Būdshīshiyya who left the order and founded the Islamist organization al-'Adl wal-Īḥsān (Justice and Spirituality [JS]). The JS movement and the Būdshīshiyya represent at least in theory diametrically opposed religious–political stances. Although this is true in relation to their positioning *vis-à-vis* the monarchy and the state apparatus, Islamist groups in Morocco have been largely influenced by the *ṭuruq* system.[9] Thus, Sufi ideas are incorporated into Yāssīn's discourse and the JS formation reproduces organizational practices governed by criteria typical of the *maraboutic* system (Pennell, 2000: 363).

By the end of the 1960s, and as a result of being one of its most notorious disciples,[10] Yāssīn was preparing himself to become the successor to the by then master of the order, Ḥājj al-'Ābbās, father of the current leader Hamza Būdshīsh. At that time, the order had been influenced by the burgeoning popularity of 'Modernist' ideas – still today early reformists such as Muḥammad Rashīd Riḍā or Muḥammad 'Abduh are mentioned in some of the order's texts as having ideologies akin to the Būdshīshiyya's ethos.[11] Actually, the fact that Yāssīn (not related by blood to the Būdshīshiyya lineage) was even being considered as a possible successor illustrates the extent to which reformism was being embraced by this predominantly Berber *ṭarīqa* at the end of the 1960s. Yet its flirtation with reformist ideologies made the state declare the Būdshīshiyya illegal between 1969 and 1971 (Elahmadi, 2006: 19), a period of clandestineness, however, that did not last long: the order had returned to legality when Ḥājj al-'Ābbās passed away and his son Hamza was appointed as the new leader of the order. His enthronement meant the triumph of the more traditional line; from this succession followed a *silsila*-based criterion over that of the Yāssīnite trend and this determined thereafter an acute differentiation by which two lines split and became polarized. On the one hand, the Būdshīshiyya was thereafter to consolidate a public image of *apolitisme* that has been maintained until recently – although, below the surface, the order never lost its influential political role at a regional level. On the other hand, Yāssīn became the leader of what is generally held to be the largest Islamist group in Morocco, the JS.[12]

Yāssīn's departure

Soon after leaving the order, Yāssīn published two books (in 1972 and 1973) calling for the implementation of an Islamic state in Morocco (Pennell, 2000: 353) – writings that were, surprisingly, authorized. It has been suggested that the king feared turning him into a martyr, while trying to use his figure to gain popular support against the by then growing popularity of the left (Tozy, 1987: 111). Only a year later, when in 1974 Hassan II understood that this tactic was not going to be effective, and after Yāssīn had published an open letter to Ḥassan II denouncing his rule as un-Islamic, Yāssīn was shut up in a mental hospital for three years (Munson, 1993: 162–7) and thereafter spent large periods of his life in prison – the fact that the movement largely centred on his person meant that any potential challenge to the *makhzan* he represented was removed during these periods in jail (Willis, 2007: 151).

The organization he led until his death in 2012 has never attained official state recognition despite its always having 'rejected the use of violence to reach power (nor given birth to any known radical splinter groups) and accept [ed] – at least in theory – working within the framework of legal institutions' (Masbah, 2013). The period of political containment that characterized the group during the 1970s and 1980s diluted when in the 1990s they entered the arena of political participation – since the organization is not a political party, candidates stand as 'independent'. In the 2002 election, contenders close to the organization's ideology became the third largest force in Parliament (Willis, 2007: 150), and in the 2009 municipal elections most of the constituencies of the north-eastern part of the country – the locus where the Būdshīshiyya also exercises most of its influence – have seen candidates sympathetic to Yāssīn's group winning.[13]

In the 2011 parliamentary elections the legal Islamist Justice and Development Party (JDP) became the ruling party, the first time an Islamist formation has obtained a victory of such scale. Despite the ideological differences between the JDP and the JS formation, this victory may be at least partially responsible for the relative loss of relevance of independent candidates, who have dropped from third to fifth position. In any case, the group once headed by Yāssīn and nowadays led by Muḥammad 'Abbadī retains the reciprocal mistrust that has characterized formation–*makhzan* relations since its beginnings; it rejects direct political participation and instead prefers to remain formally apart from the political system. Despite the loss of seats in 2011, it keeps its grassroots vitality and maintains widely popular support throughout Morocco, and especially within the northern region of the country where both Yāssīn and the Būdshīshiyya are originally from.

The Būdshīshiyya reformed

The Būdshīshiyya Yāssīn's desertion and Hamza's investiture marked the birth of a new *mode d'être*, a dramatic reform by which the new leader attempted to turn the order into a more inclusive organization, open to society, particularly centred on attracting urban audiences and more conciliatory towards the monarchy. Although primary sources suggest that this transformation began during the 1960s, when Yāssīn was still part of the *ṭarīqa*, the first evidence of the reform's fruits did not come until the 1980s. The former *tabarrukiyya* character that previously distinguished the organization implied that initiation was highly selective, a process in which the commitment of the aspirant to the order was continually tested (Ben Driss, 2002: 139–40). If the *faqīr* withstood the process he entered an elitist group, entirely dedicated to religious instruction. According to the locals' account, this group of students received the respect of the surrounding populations, and the local *Zāwiya* was not regularly open to visits, but only on special occasions. While for the religious pupils the lodge was an educational centre, for the people of the region it was and remains a place of social gathering on days of major religious celebrations. Emic narratives do not present the disciplehood of locals in the same terms as those of the young religious learners, as locals have never been subjected to any initiatory process (*bay'a*), still today a remarkable difference between locals and *fuqarā'* from elsewhere.

During the 1980s, the *ṭarīqa* tried to surpass its almost exclusively Berber character by adopting a new orientation towards a more diverse disciplehood.

This move, an exercise of *da'wa* (religious proselytization), is often portrayed as an 'educational' (*tarbawiyya*) endeavour – as it aimed to make Sufism 'accessible to everybody' (Tozy, 1990; Ben Driss, 2002; Draper, 2002; Sedgwick, 2004b; Voix, 2004; Haenni and Voix, 2007; Chih, 2012);[14] what it meant in practical terms was that the organization began to publicize itself among university students and secondary school pupils. It also changed its recruitment criteria: in the new Būdshīshiyya, anyone – regardless of their gender, background and/or previous knowledge or commitment to Islam – could undertake the rite of *bay'a* and become a *faqīr/a*; the number of followers steadily rose,[15] and the body of devotees diversified – a reduced group of highly committed local religious novices converted into a wider following made up of students, young professionals and peasants. Contrary to the devoted, full-time commitment of the *faqīr* prior to the reform, new disciples maintained the lifestyle they had prior to joining the order, meeting with other members only once or twice a week. Accordingly, the *ṭarīqa*'s leadership began to discourage ascetic and largely cloistered lives in favour of commitment to family and community:

> Work is paramount in this world because Divine Law requires that one has to provide for one's family, spouse and children. One also has to remain well focused on working for the Path. One therefore has to reconcile these three areas which constitute the hallmarks of one's life.[16]

In doctrinal terms, the main results of this change were threefold. First, the importance hitherto attached to a personalized mode of transmitting religious knowledge was replaced by a new ideal in which spiritual love (*maḥabba*) became the tool for acquisition of spiritual *savoir*.[17] Second, ritual has taken on an unprecedented relevance. In the absence of a physical setting in which doctrine could be taught by the master, it is ritual action, led by a secondary authority (*muqaddim/a*), that has become predominant. Religious knowledge has in a way been substituted by religious practice.[18] Last, but not least, miracle performance (*karāma*) – once an authenticating proof of the leader's sanctity, which lent legitimacy to the practices and discourses of the group – lost relevance, through the highlighting instead of the importance of genealogy (*silsila*) in validating saintly authority.[19] The notion of a direct genealogical connection between Sīdī Hamza (b.1922) and the founder of the Qādiriyya, and the Prophet, was thus to gain force as a validating element that would implicitly keep the Būdshīshiyya – despite innovations – anchored to Sufism and to Moroccan Islam. This new emphasis, grounded in doctrinal legitimacy, gave a Quietist character to the organization, making it as a result more acceptable to wider segments of society and to the palace. Overall, these doctrinal changes have been crucial in exporting the order beyond the province of l'Oriental and turning it into not only the most sizeable *ṭarīqa* in today's Morocco, but also one with a significant transnational dimension.

Būdshīshiyya's Quietist Sufism and 'New Age'

Crucial to the expansion beyond the north-eastern part of the country has been the adoption of what I have termed a 'Quietist' approach to Sufism. The term denotes a 'contemplative' understanding of religion characterized by intellectual stillness over a more vocal position on societal matters, a form of piety that is not only sober in ritual terms but also advocates the adoption of a similar stance in society and politics.[20] This is indeed a seemingly oxymoron, not only because the order has always had (and maintains) a relevant role in the local politics of the Berkane region, but because in 2002 a devotee, Aḥmad Tawfīq, became the Minister of *Habus* (Religious Endowments) and Islamic Affairs, which turned the Būdshīshiyya into the 'official' version of Islam in Morocco, given the role of the institution within the *makhzan*:

> State religious officials are the elite that represent official Islam in Morocco and act as custodians of religious authority. Religious officials are co-opted in the state apparatus comprised of the various religious city councils, grand Muftis and religious establishment under the aegis of the High Council of the Ulama and the Ministry of Habous (Religious endowments) and Islamic Affairs. The raison d'être of the religious establishment remains the promotion of the state's official religious discourse.
> (Daadaoui, 2013: 25)

Thus, promoting an image of religious Quietism was meant to promote devotees' *apolitisme*, in contrast to the political style of Islamism. However, the irony of this is that by doing so the *ṭarīqa* has gained significant political power – culminating in an overt recognition of its role in national politics when in 2011 the order organized a public march in Casablanca in favour of the new constitution proposed by the king. The 'Būdshīshiyya's Islam' the monarchy pretends to convey to the public is that defined as a distinctively Moroccan religiosity, supportive of the monarchy, 'modernist' in that it incorporates ideas of early reformist thinkers, yet 'traditional' enough in that it wants to be perceived as normative, scriptural and grounded in *Mālikī* jurisprudence, definitely 'anti-Islamist' as it wants to stands as *the* antithesis to both the JDP and the JS grassroots movement, and 'modern' in that it wants to be seen as tolerant and respectful of diversity and human rights – although its critics argue it supports anti-democratic strategies in its 'crusade' against Islamism.

The quietist ethos helped the Būdshīshiyya gain support, particularly among the younger, rapidly growing urban populations of the country.[21] At the university, academic subjects that previously attracted hardly any attention have mushroomed, including Islamic subjects which an increasing number of students are choosing to study in 'lay' institutions such as universities instead of in traditional religious centres (Tozy, 1992: 410); the Būdshīshiyya has been particularly successful in recruiting members from these university circles.

Central to the expansion of the order within Morocco was what can be viewed as a process of *de-Berberization* of the *ṭarīqa.* As part of this project, of particular relevance were the efforts to homogenize ritual praxis by 'cleaning' it of its more 'exalted' elements (e.g. the playing of music that leads to ecstasy, healing practices associated with spirit possession) – features often ascribed to Berber culture and often perceived by non-Berbers as questionably Islamic.[22] Equally relevant in this move towards attracting audiences beyond the immediacies of Madāgh was an added emphasis on the scripturalist side of Hamza's formation and his mastering of *Mālikī* jurisprudence specifically:

> Learning the Qur'ān at the age of thirteen (…) In 1936 he enrolled in a branch of the Fes' University-Mosque of Quarawīyin in Oujda, where he deepened his knowledge of religious sciences, he studied law and Arabic grammar between 1937 and 1940, and *tafsīr* from 1939 to 1943, [a] year in which he returned to the *Zāwiya* in Madāgh. During his studies he dealt with texts such as the Alfiya[23] (…) and the Ajārūmiya[24] (…), [and authors such as] Ibn 'Ashir,[25] (…) Ibn Ajiba (… [26]) all these documents are part of the official corpus of teachings of the Quarawīyin as well as in other madrasas in Morocco. Sīdī Hamza was devoted since he was very young [to the study of] morphology, grammar, Qur'ānic exegesis, *Mālikī* law and the interpretations and science of the Ḥadīth. The teaching program in Morocco is not limited to the sciences on the *sharī'a;* in addition to the disciplines mentioned above he learnt theology, metrics, rhetoric, and logic. Only when he considered that he had acquired sufficient knowledge, did he return to help his father in the fields and began to focus on a different type of knowledge, after being initiated at the hands of Sīdī Boumediene Qādirī Būdshīsh.[27]

The Būdshīshiyya's expansion has not only been possible because of the accomplishment of its quietist ethos: its success is also crucially embedded in a proactive *da'wa* attitude. Since the 1980s devotees have come to know of the Būdshīshiyya for the modern networks and new channels of diffusion of religious ideas utilized by the order. Conferences, courses, weekend 'retreats' and a strong media presence are all part of a range of choices offered to an emerging middle class that is gradually seeing religion less as a taken-for-granted issue and more as the result of choices made based on thoughtful reflection on one's own identity. For many among the Būdshīshiyya youngsters, 'what kind of Muslim do I want to be?' (as one Moroccan *faqīra* once framed it when speaking to me) has been a question that lies at the core of their decision to join the order.[28] Besides, the *ṭarīqa* partly owes its success to its *laissez-faire* style which, despite supporting normative Islam, has no mechanisms in place to ensure devotees observe *sharī'a.* As a result, it is typical of this *ṭarīqa* to find devotees with other approaches to religion, illustrated for instance in that a trend of New Age spirituality is flourishing among some of Morocco's urban followers.

Studies of religious revivalism have generally taken into account the emergence of new religious fervours of a rationalist, modernist or Islamist inclination in the Muslim World (e.g. Abdo, 2000; Mahmood, 2005), however, they have tended to ignore the perhaps more discrete emergence of New Age religiosities, a development that in the case of the Būdshīshiyya follows a feeling of political disillusionment. Among this kind of devotee, many are from an elite who were once part of leftist and nationalist movements, students and young professionals from enfranchised and largely secularized environments, reluctant to abandon the French language and culture (Pennell, 2000: 383). With largely no prior knowledge of religion, they have tended to perceive the *ṭuruq* as hierarchical organizations that demand uncritical submission to the *shaykh* and see in Sufism a backward superstitious religiosity of the masses.[29] As an economically well-positioned minority, commercial ties with France meant that the group's francophile character could be periodically renewed through visits, studies abroad and friendship.

This lay minority, always in contact with a world abroad and with the European expatriate community in Morocco, became pioneers in importing New-Age-inspired 'alternative' religiosities to Morocco (Haenni and Voix, 2007). Būdshīshiyya's 'New Agers' tend to be older than those supporting quietist Sufism and they evince typical New Age attitudes in that, for instance, a stronger emphasis on individualism is common (with less importance being given to the notion of companionship among fellow *fuqarā'* typical of the *ṭarīqa*),[30] and also a prevalence of belief in free will instead of the more common belief in predestination characteristic among other *fuqarā'*. 'New Agers' seem to evince a less culture-bound, more universalist, approach to Sufism, similar to the eclectic leaning that Westerlund has defined as a 'pick and mix' attitude among New Age Sufi groups in the West (2004: 30–2), and they often argue against any organized or institutionalized form of religion or religious authority.[31] Some among them see the Būdshīshiyya more as a group than as a Sufi *ṭarīqa* (in the traditional Moroccan sense of the term)[32] but some others defend the idea (as one devotee put it) of a 'return to the traditional legacy of Moroccan Sufism'.

The prevalence of the *maraboutic* system

For its part, the Būdshīshiyya's influence in its original enclave has been maintained and goes beyond the popularity given by a wide religious following. In this region, the Būdshīsh family still retains its remarkable social and political presence. Most rural members in this region still see in Hamza the type of Sufi leader common in the Moroccan Berber areas described in earlier scholarship (Gellner, 1969; Bidwell, 1973; Crapanzano, 1973; Eickelman, 1976; Berque, 1978; Brett and Fentress, 1996): one that heals the sick, gives assistance to the poor, helps youngsters to find better jobs[33] and mediates between local leaders and national authorities.[34] Sources attest that the influence of the Būdshīsh family goes back several generations (Katan, 1990), its members, notably, playing the roles not only of social arbitrators but of landowners (Ben Driss, 2002: 129). Although only Hamza is believed to possess saintly *baraka*, other members of the family contribute to the consolidation of the social and political power associated with it. His daughters are well known among women in the region. Besides, Hmida Būdshīsh (one of his sons and probably the next leader of the order) was a civil servant in the local administration up until 2005 and the mayor of the administrative area and town of Berkane up to 2009.[35]

When he was in office the region received the economic support of the central government to create new jobs by promoting schemes such as the creation of a multimillion-euro holiday complex on the coast near Saidia and an urban development in Berkane of 333 million dirhams (almost 30 million euro). As a result of these investments, this part of the country is becoming wealthier than ever before. In addition, a construction of a dam on the River Mūluyya has brought significant improvement to agriculture in a region that had been badly affected by episodes of drought.[36] The influence of the Būdshīshī family even extends into the judiciary; signs could be seen in Berkane and Oujda back in 2010 publicizing the services of '100% Būdshīshī lawyers. Success in your trial guaranteed!'[37] However, the Būdshīshiyya's popular support coexists with a growing discontent about the order. Among accusations of corruption and non-democratic leanings (e.g. that Hmida Būdshīsh was appointed as a representative of the monarch in the area, 'Governor of His Majesty'[38]) there is also widespread belief in their abuse of power: 'I have previously heard about the *Zāwiya*, but the day I went there, I was almost driven crazy. Enough is enough. Even the pope has no right to such treatment.'[39] These opinions epitomize the growing polarization between supporters and detractors of the Būdshīshiyya family.

Within the immediacies of the central lodge in Madāgh, Hamza Būdshīsh and the network of social relationships represent the persistence of a social model based on a patronage system that predates 1956, which is based on the perpetuation of a political culture arising out of an agricultural economy overseen by rural notables and landowners. Thus, Hamza is not only the leader of a religious community, but the patron of the agricultural communities of Madāgh and Naʿīma.[40] The model was established by the French and Spanish Protectorates (Seddon, 1973) that 'had ruled the countryside largely through local notables who were given official positions as qaids and allowed to develop their wealth through landholdings' (Pennell, 2000: 319) and was used by the *ṭuruq* system to negotiate with the powers that emerged with the birth of nation states. Today, the degree of cordiality of relations between the inhabitants of Naʿīma and Madāgh and the Būdshīshiyya remains unclear. They live in the lands of the *shaykh* and work for him, but when I asked nobody wanted to give an opinion about the Sufi family. They did, however, tell me that those living in Madāgh and Naʿīma do not attend ritual celebrations at the lodge ('it has been years since the last time I entered the *zāwiya*', a man told me), although most of the food eaten on these occasions has been cultivated by them.[41] The order discourages relationships between devotees and inhabitants from Madāgh;[42] European *fuqarā'* are often also discouraged to visit Berkane, but this may also be related to the Būdshīshiyya's overzealous sense of hospitality and protectiveness – particularly towards foreign guests.[43]

The origins of the order in Europe: Moroccans and Traditionalists[44]

The order took root in France during the 1990s via two different pathways, on the one hand through a group of Moroccan labour migrants who settled in the suburb of Argenteuil (Paris) and, on the other, through a later group of Traditionalist intellectuals at the Sorbonne. The group of migrants in Argenteuil pioneered the emergence of new transnational geographies within the order, generating international networks of relations across different countries and creating spaces of shared sociality between individuals who were previously strangers – not all the members of the Moroccan strand of the Būdshīshiyya in Europe are from the north-eastern part of the country, and many had not had previous links with the region and its communities. Yet religion seems to be a crucial element for many people in the diaspora as they adapt to new societal environments, and congregational religious meetings provide valuable opportunities to socialize in an atmosphere that is relatively familiar compared with the social environment of the new country of residence (McLoughlin, 2005: 544). In the European Būdshīshiyya, personal relationships develop between Moroccan individuals who would never have been part of the same congregation back home. These Moroccan groups appear to be distinctively 'Moroccan' (e.g. members may eat only traditional Moroccan food, come to the meetings in traditional *jilābāt*, and most of the time speak either Berber or Moroccan Arabic). This expressed *marocanité* contrasts with that back in the homeland, where traditional food and dress is less common.

Studies of this type of diaspora Sufism tend to represent these orders as 'transplants' (Hermansen, 2006: 29), identical reproductions of the religiosities in the pre-migration setting,[45] whereas the Būdshīshiyya diaspora communities display distinctive religiosities not to be found in any of the contingents in Morocco. Part of this distinctiveness is the somehow more 'exacerbated' *marocanité*, which affects its relations with other devotees of the order in Europe; the Moroccan strand of the European Būdshīshiyya is not really inclusive of 'cultural strangers' who, when they go to the gatherings, thus rarely end up joining the group and integrating.[46] As a result, the Būdshīshiyya in Europe is a 'hybrid' (Hermansen, 2006) organization made up of groups of followers of Moroccan origin on the one side, and groups of members raised in Europe on the other. The relationship between the two strands is minimal and they only occasionally conjointly congregate.

Back in the 1990s, and having little contact with these Moroccan groups, a mixture of French and Moroccan students and intellectuals began to meet to discuss the writings of René Guénon and Traditionalist ideas. Many were former Freemasons,[47] others were already Muslims, all would then turn to

Sufism as a way of realizing their 'return to Tradition'. Guénonianism was decisive in the establishment of the Būdshīshiyya in Europe, and although it continues to characterize the outlook and ideological dimension of a substantial part of this *ṭarīqa* in the continent, it seems to progressively be losing the importance it once had. The influence of new generations (mainly Muslim-born members of Moroccan origin) not interested in Traditionalism is diluting the force that this ideology once exerted within the order. There are also few Guénonians among the wealthier followers in Morocco, though including some of its most influential figures.[48]

Overall, the historical circumstances that have seen the Būdshīshiyya transform from a local cult to an organization with significant weight at the national and international levels, relate both to the doctrinal changes the order has been able to undertake in adapting to new circumstances as well as to the societal features of the cultural and societal *milieux* it has entered. In this, the Būdshīshiyya is an illustrative case of the social malleability and adaptation that often characterizes Sufi orders around the world, past and present.

Notes

1 A more detailed description of the groups' locations is provided in Chapter 3.
2 See Glossary for a general description of Sharifism.
3 His original Persian name is better transliterated as Abdolgāder Gilāni (عبد القادر گیلانی) but in most Arabic sources he appears as 'Abd al-Qādir Jīlānī (عبد القادرجيلاني), and he is generally known as such.
4 At the beginning of the sixteenth century, the Saadi dynasty joined the leaders of some of the strongest *ṭuruq* to attack the Spanish and Portuguese military outposts on the north coast, and held back the Ottoman Empire; research into that period can be found in Yahya (1981).
5 The French first occupied the city in 1844, then again in 1859 and in 1907 when they imposed colonial rule. In 1912 it was transferred to the Spanish Protectorate until 1956. Katan (1990) offers an interesting study of the city in this last period.
6 The Béni-Snassen is a mountainous region in the north-eastern part of the country and gives its name to the Berber peoples that live in the region, with towns such as Ahfir, Tafoghalt, Fezouane, Ain Reggada and Berkane. A historical introduction to these groups in the colonial period can be found in Bidwell (1973: 311–12).
7 This region of about two million inhabitants and with its capital in Oujda is one of the sixteen territorial divisions into which the country is administratively divided. The northern part of L'Oriental, where the vast majority of Būdshīshiyya *fuqarā'* live, is also the most densely populated with predominantly Berber towns such as Berkane or Nador. For an overview of the region, see Guitouni (1995). Appendix 2 of this book is a Map showing the Būdshīshiyya central lodge's location, in Madāgh.
8 As we will see in this chapter, the role of social arbitrator would not only persist but would gain prominence due to the fact that the Moroccan monarchy has catapulted the order into a prominent position – to the extent that the Moroccan authorities seek help from the Būdshīshiyya to try to counteract the increasing popularity of Islamist trends. For a classical study of the broker function of local

(Berber) saints and their relation with larger political powers, see the anthropological approach of Gellner (1969). A historical account of these power relations during the Marinid period is provided by Cornell (1998). For a general overview of the relations between the political and sacred domains in Morocco, see Munson (1993).

9 Cases that attest the inspiration that political groups and organizations have taken from Sufism can be found around the Muslim world (e.g. the early Egyptian Muslim Brotherhood), yet the markedly anti-Sufi content of their political discourses constitutes an interesting paradox. Further analysis can be found in Sirriyeh (1999); a recent volume exploring the cross-pollinations between Sufis and religious actors often considered as their 'adversaries' (e.g. Salafis) is Ridgeon (forthcoming), which also includes Idrissi's research on the political participation of the Būdshīshiyya in Morocco. A comprehensive approach to Sufi–Islamist political activism in Morocco is provided by Zeghal (2008a, 2008b, 2009) and Mohsen-Finan and Zeghal (2006).

10 He was a prominent civil servant at the ministry of education when in 1967 he was diagnosed with a terminal illness. His poor health interrupted his professional career and led him to embark on a life of 'intense spiritual activity' that would prepare him for the moment of death (Elahmadi, 2006: 18). He recovered and entered the Būdshīshiyya when it was still a localized *ṭarīqa* (Tozy, 1990).

11 See the order's booklet *Nabadat 'an al-ṭarīqa al-Qādiriyya al-Būdshīshiyya*. n.a. n.d. n.p.

12 His personal webpage is available online at http://Yāssīne.net/en/ (accessed 8 May 2009). His daughter Nadia Yāssīn is the founder of the first Islamist-cum-feminist Moroccan organization, a sub-branch of her father's party, which gained a seat in Parliament in 2009. Her personal webpage is available online at http://nadiaYāssīne.net/en/index.htm (accessed 8 May 2009). See also Dilday (2007) and Steinvorth (2007). For a full account of Yāssīn's earlier activism see Shahin (1997: 181–8, 193–5) and Mohsen-Finan and Zeghal (2006).

13 See Cembrero (2009).

14 For further discussion of the written output about the order, see Chapter 3.

15 An estimate of the number of disciples can only be an approximation; a discussion on the number of disciples is provided in Chapter 3.

16 Hamza's sayings translated into English by a British member of the order, available online at www.tariqa.org/qadiriya/texts/sayings.html (accessed 2 July 2009).

17 In this, the Būdshīshiyya seems to follow a pattern typical of certain Sufi movements born in the twentieth century (e.g. the Gülen movement) in which the idea of direct initiation has disappeared along with the teaching role of the *shaykh* (Hermansen, 2009: 29). There are also similar predecessors, for example, in the pre-colonial Indian Naqshbandiyya (Buehler, 1998).

18 The leadership of the order, however, adopts a *laissez-faire* attitude when considering expressions of ritual exhilaration, and the attempt to undermine popular interest in *karāmāt* has not entirely succeeded. This is analysed in Chapters 6 and 7. There are other cases in which processes of reform bring unexpected results; one of the most extreme is that of a *ṭarīqa*'s leader who failed to convince its members about the doctrinal changes he wanted to introduce (in light of approaching new urban audiences), a case analysed by Sedgwick (2000).

19 The Būdshīshiyya – as a branch of the wider Qādiriyya – follows the classical al-Mīrghanī category of Sufi religious authority (Karrar, 1992: 126), according to which Hamza Būdshīsh is a *shaykh al-tabarruk* – literally the one attaining *baraka* (Al-Mīrghanī in Karrar, 1992: 127). Accordingly, he is generally believed to be divinely guided and incapable of sin and his attributes are transmitted by descent.

20 The term is borrowed from a Catholic theological school of the late seventeenth century that defended a stance of self-annihilation which resulted in the mind's

withdrawal from worldly interests in favour of an exclusive contemplation of God. Despite marked differences, the term here is useful to identify the apolitical attitude proposed by the Būdshīshiyya. On Catholic Quietism, see Ward (2011).

21 Morocco's rapid process of urbanization, the emergence of a new middle class and increased access to university education for young people (Vermeren, 2001; Cohen and Jaibi, 2006; Sater, 2007) have led to the opening up of a new 'religious market', giving voice to new religious actors and institutions.

22 Scholarship on religion and ethnicity in Morocco has tended to oversimplify the complexity of social life by reducing it to a set of typological distinctions (e.g. Arab *vs* Berber, urban *vs* rural, Scripturalism *vs* Sufism, 'official' *vs* 'folk' Islam). While such ideal types are related to existing distinctions, they often appear less clearly divided and somehow intertwined, as Silverstein (2012) has noted.

23 It refers to the *al-Khulāsa al-alfiyya* by Ibn Mālik (d.672 AH).

24 It refers to the *al-Muqadimma al-Ajārūmīya fī Mabadī al-Arabiya* by the Moroccan grammarian Ibn Ajārūm (d.723 AH).

25 It refers to the *Mālikī* jurist and *ash'arite* theologian commonly known as al-Matn Ibn 'Ashir (d.1040 AH).

26 It refers to the eighteenth-century Moroccan *walī 'Allāh*, who belonged to the Darqawiyya (d.1224 AH).

27 For my own translation of a forum containing views critical of the order as well as apologetic ones, see http://forum.oujdacity.net/zaouia-boutchichia-a-madagh-fete-de-la-bourgoisie-t2411–210.html (accessed 17 October 2013). The same educational trajectory is described in other order materials targeting Moroccan audiences where formation in the Mashreq is also mentioned so as to denote the 'legitimacy' of his trajectory: see *Nabadat 'an al-ṭarīqa al-Qādiriyya al-Būdshīshiyya.* n.a. n.d. n.p.

28 In an effort to make the order seem attractive to the burgeoning middle class a new type of leadership, not formally recognized but *de facto*, has developed, an aspect analysed in Chapter 3.

29 One of them has written a book that contains an autobiographical section which epitomizes the opinion of this type of adherent; see Ben Rochd (2003).

30 The importance of companionship is distinctive of the *ṭarīqa* and is often understood to be a spiritual duty of the *faqīr/a* (Ben Rochd, 2000, 2002; Ben Driss, 2002).

31 For example a Moroccan *faqīra* told me in June 2009 that she did 'not find appropriate this blind devotion for Sīdī Hamza [in reference to the emotional devotion evidenced by rural members of the order]', although she defined herself as a member of the *ṭarīqa.* Similar challenges to 'traditional' understandings of religious authority are typically found in Sufi New Age religious groups such as the Sufi order Inayat Khan: see for example Genn (2007: 265).

32 Regarding New Age members, the Būdshīshiyya, which otherwise I define in Godlas's (2009) terms as an 'Islamic Sufi order' (that is, one that avows adherence to Islam), could be associated with a 'Quasi-Islamic Sufi Organisation' (that is, an organization where the practice of Islam is not made a condition for receiving instruction on following the Sufi Path). Although these categories are focused on the phenomenon of Sufism in the West (notably, the United States), the New Age approach of these Moroccan members can be easily equated to those categories originally used for 'Westerners'.

33 Langlois has carried out research in the region and has suggested that locals commented that membership is an asset to career development in the local civil service, and that it facilitates other matters, such as obtaining building permission and even access to services (email communication with Dr Langlois, 10 March 2008).

34 Similar cases occur in other parts of the Muslim world: see for example Chih's (2004) research on the Khalwātiyya of Upper Egypt.

35 Morocco is divided into 45 provinces of which Berkane is one. Berkane is a town of around 80,000 people in Thrifa (the north-eastern region on the border with Algeria). The province belongs to the *wilāya* of Oujda.
36 Personal communication with locals from Berkane, August 2008. More information about the dam can be found at www.berkane.cjb.net/ (accessed 3 March 2008).
37 I saw this sign during a fieldwork trip in August 2008.
38 My own translation from French (Ramdani, 2007).
39 My own translation from French (Ramdani, 2007).
40 Only 67 kilometres south of Madāgh lies Na'īma, the second residence of the Būdshīshiyya family. Like Madāgh, it is an agricultural real state, mainly producing apricots (which are dried for selling) and citrus fruits. The client–patron relationship between devotee and *walī 'Allāh* typical of Morocco (Hammoudi, 1997, 1999) can also be found in other parts of the Muslim World (e.g. Chih, 2004).
41 For further information about these celebrations and the sacred meanings attached to the food provided by the order for the attendees, see Chapter 4.
42 A European *faqīra* who had attended the *Mawlid* for a number of years used also to visit a Madāghian family; when the people of the order realized that she was doing this, they immediately prohibited the visits. The prohibition was soon extended to the rest of the European *fuqarā'*.
43 I was told that the order does so to minimize the risk of anything untoward (i.e. harassment or robbery) happening to visitors, consonant with the courteous gesture of sending a local devotee taxi driver to pick up foreign visitors at the point where they enter the country, be it the border or an airport.
44 By 'Traditionalism' we mean the contemporary esoteric philosophy, critical of modernity, which is based on a reinterpretation of the concept of 'Philosophia Perennis'. According to this view, the 'Philosophia Perennis' is something that has been apprehended and incorporated into the wisdom of peoples of every region in the world since the origins of humankind, but has only been articulated in a more sophisticated way by what the English writer Aldous Huxley (1894–1963) called 'the higher religions' – meaning the main world religions: the three monotheistic creeds, Buddhism and Hinduism. Accordingly, the plurality of religions of the world is, in this view, only a kaleidoscope of diverse manifestations of one unique Divine Truth, generally referred to by the term 'Tradition'. Tradition is for Traditionalists the core of religion; it is eternal, infinite, and unaffected by contextual variables, independent of culture and ahistorical.
Although Huxley had already made use of the term to formulate a criticism of the 'modern world', it was the French thinker René Guénon (1886–1951) who popularized it as a term of critique. Although one might argue that some subtle distinctions can be observed between the terms 'Perennialist', 'Traditionalist' and 'Guénonian', they are used in this study interchangeably, for the sake of clarity. On 'Traditionalism', see Dominguez Diaz (2013). More specifically, on Guénon see Laurant (2006) and Sedgwick (2004a). More generally, Traditionalism has notably contributed to the emergence of Sufism in the West. This is so to such an extent that Hermansen (1996: 155–78), in her typology of Sufi orders in the West, identifies Perennialists (Traditionalists) as one of three existing forms of Sufism in North America.
45 Geaves has shown this *mimesis* in his analysis of Sufism in Britain: 'Sufism in Britain remained tightly bound up with ethnic identity […] Sometimes these traditions are duplicated so effectively in the diaspora situation, providing a mirror image of village customs and practices' (2009: 97). However, Geaves has also suggested that this attitude is gradually being replaced by a more outward-looking position.
46 A European woman who is married to a Moroccan joined, but she quit soon afterwards. See Chapter 3 note 7 for further information on the case. The lack of

'cultural mixing' seems to be a common feature of migrant Sufi groups in the diaspora, whether South Asian (Werbner, 2006), Turkish (Jonker, 2006), Persian (Lewisohn, 2006) or North African.

47 The relationship between European Freemasonry and Islam can be dated back to the nineteenth century, when various European Masonic Obediences set up lodges throughout the Ottoman Empire (in today's Turkey and the Levant). For further information on the subject, see Dumont (2005).

48 Faouzi Skali is an illustrative example in this regard; see Chapter 3 for further information.

References

Abdo, G. 2000. *No God but God: Egypt and the Triumph of Islam*. New York: Oxford University Press.

Ben Driss, K. 2002. *Sidi Hamza al-Qadiri Boudchich. Le renouveau du Soufisme au Maroc*. Beirut: Albouraq.

Ben Rochd, E. R. 2000. *Lecture soufie contemporaine dans le coran. Pour comprendre notre époque et faire face a ses défis*. Casablanca: Dechra.

——2002. *Le soufisme. Patrimoine universel méthode d'épanouissement et doctrine d'harmonie*. Casablanca: Dechra.

——2003. *Le soufre rouge*. Casablanca: Dechra.

Berque, J. 1978. *Structures sociales du Haut-Atlas*. Paris: Presses Universitaires de France.

Bidwell, R. L. 1973. *Morocco under Colonial Rule: French Administration of Tribal Areas 1912–1956*. London: Frank Cass.

Brett, M. and Fentress, E. 1996. *The Berbers*. Oxford: Blackwell.

Buehler, A. F. 1998. *Sufi Heirs of the Prophet: The Indian Naqshbandiyya and the Rise of the Mediating Sufi Shaykh*. Columbia, SC: University of South Carolina Press.

Cembrero, I. 2009. 'Cuatro Alcaldías del Marruecos 'Español', en Manos Islamistas. Veto Real a que el PJD Domine los Ayuntamientos de Rabat y Casablanca', *El Pais*, available online at www.elpais.com/articulo/internacional/alcaldias/Marruecos/espanol/manos/islamistas/elpepiint/20090702elpepiint_10/Tes (accessed 2 July 2009).

Chih, R. 2004. 'The Khalwatiyya Brotherhood in Rural Egypt and in Cairo', in R. Hopkins and N. Saad (eds) *Upper Egypt: Identity and Change*, 157–68. Cairo: American University in Cairo Press.

——2012. 'Sufism, Education and Politics in Contemporary Morocco', *Journal for Islamic Studies* 32(1): 24–46. Rondebosch: University of Cape Town Publications.

Cohen, S. and Jaibi, L. 2006. *Morocco: Globalization and its Consequences*. London: Routledge.

Cornell, V. J. 1998. *Realm of the Saint. Power and Authority in Moroccan Sufism*. Austin, TX: University of Texas Press.

Crapanzano, V. 1973. *The Ḥamadsha: A Study in Moroccan Ethnopsychiatry*. Berkeley, CA: University of California Press.

Daadaoui, M. 2013. 'The Monarchy and Islamism in Morocco: Ritualization of the Public Discourse', in B. Maddy-Weitzman and D. Zisenwine. (eds) *Contemporary Morocco: State, Politics and Society under Mohammed VI*, 24–36. London: Routledge.

Dilday, K. A. 2007. 'Nadia Yassine's Journey', *Open Democracy*, available online at www.opendemocracy.net/globalization-village/nadia_yassine_journey (accessed 18 October 2013).

Dominguez Diaz, M. 2013. 'Traditionalism', in *Encyclopedia of Psychology and Religion* (2nd ed.), 912–13. New York: Springer.

Draper, M. 2002. 'Towards a Postmodern Sufism: Eclecticism, Appropriation and Adaptation in a Naqshbandiyya and a Qadiriyya Tariqa in the UK', unpublished PhD thesis. Birmingham: University of Birmingham.

Dumont, P. 2005. 'Freemasonry in Turkey: A By-product of Western Penetration', *European Review* 13. London: Birkett Press, available online at http://edoqs.com/pdf/paul-dumont-bfreemasonry-in-turkeyb-a-by-product-of-western–c90df679550dbbde6ed563152e99f5af (accessed 11 January 2014).

Eickelman, D. F. 1976. *Moroccan Islam: Tradition and Society in a Pilgrimage Center.* Austin, TX; London: University of Texas Press.

El Mansour, M. 1990. *Morocco in the Reign of Mawlay Sulayman.* Wisbech: Middle East & North Africa Studies Press.

Elahmadi, M. 2006. *Le mouvement yasiniste.* Mohamadia: Moultaka.

Geaves, R. 2009. 'A Case of Cultural Binary Fission or Transglobal Sufism? The Transmigration of Sufism to Britain', in R. Geaves, M. Dressler and G. Klinkhammer (eds) *Sufis in Western Societies. Global Networking and Locality*, 97–112. London; New York: Routledge.

Gellner, E. 1969. *Saints of the Atlas.* London: Weidenfeld & Nicholson.

Genn, C. A. 2007. 'The Development of a Modern Western Sufism', in J. D. Howell and M. Bruinessen (eds) *Sufism and the 'Modern' in Islam*, 257–78. London: Tauris.

Godlas, A. 2009. 'Sufism, the West, and Modernity', available online at http://islam.uga.edu/sufismwest.html (accessed 18 October 2013).

Guitouni, A. (1995). 'Le Maroc oriental de l'établissement du protectorat à la décolonisation: Les mutations d'un carrefour ethnique frontalier', available online at http://horizon.documentation.ird.fr/exl-doc/pleins_textes/divers08–09/010014865–29.pdf (accessed 18 October 2013).

Haenni, P. and Voix, R. 2007. 'God by All Means … Eclectic Faith and Sufi Resurgence among the Moroccan Bourgeoisie', in M. Bruinessen and J. Day Howell (eds) *Sufism and the 'Modern' in Islam*, 241–56. London: Tauris.

Hammoudi, A. 1997. *Master and Disciple: The Cultural Foundations of Moroccan Authoritarianism.* Chicago, IL; London: University of Chicago Press.

——1999. 'The Reinvention of Dar al-Mulk: The Moroccan Political System and its Legitimation', in R. Bourqia and S. Gilson Miller (eds) *In the Shadow of the Sultan: Culture, Power and Politics in Morocco.* Cambridge, MA: Harvard University Press.

Hermansen, M. 1996. 'In the Garden of American Sufi Movements: Hybrids and Perennials', in P. B. Clarke (ed.) *New Trends and Developments in the World of Islam*, 155–78. London: Luzac.

——2006. 'Literary Productions of Western Sufi Movements', in J. Malik and J. Hinnells (eds) *Sufism in the West.* London: Routledge Curzon.

——2009. 'Global Sufism. "Theirs and Ours"', in R. Geaves, M. Dressler and G. Klinkhammer (eds) *Sufis in Western Societies. Global Networking and Locality*, 26–45. London; New York: Routledge.

Jonker, G. 2006. 'The Evolution of the Naqshbandi-Mujaddidi: Sulaymancis in Germany', in J. Hinnells and M. Jamal (eds) *Sufism in the West*, 71–85. London: Routledge Curzon.

Karrar, A. S. 1992. *The Sufi Brotherhoods in the Sudan.* London: Hurst.

Katan, Y. 1990. *Oujda, une ville frontière du Maroc (1907–1956): Musulmans, juifs et chrétiens en milieu colonial.* Paris: L'Harmattan.

Laurant, J. P. 2006. *René Guénon: Les enjeux d'une lecture.* Paris: Dervy.

Lewisohn, L. 2006. 'Persian Sufism in the Contemporary West: Reflections on the Ni'matu'llahi Diaspora', in J. Malik and J. Hinnells (eds) *Sufism in the West*, 49–70. London: Routledge Curzon.

McLoughlin, 2005. 'Migration, Diaspora and Transnationalism', in J. R. Hinnells (ed.) *The Routledge Companion to the Study of Religion*, 526–40. London: Routledge.

Mahmood, S. 2005. *Politics of Piety: The Islamic Revival and the Feminist Subject.* Princeton, NJ: Princeton University Press.

Masbah, M. 2013. 'In Yassine's Footsteps', Sada, Carnegie Endowment for International Peace, available at http://carnegieendowment.org/sada/2013/01/10/in-yassine-s-footsteps/f0nj (accessed 18 October 2013).

Mohsen-Finan, K. and Zeghal, M. 2006. 'Opposition islamiste et pouvoir monarchique au Maroc: Le cas du parti de la justice et du développement', *Revue Française de Science Politique* 56(1): 79–119. Paris: Presses Universitaires de France.

Munson, H. 1993. *Religion and Power in Morocco.* New Haven, CT; London: Yale University Press.

Pennell, C. R. 2000. *Morocco since 1830: A History.* London: Hurst.

Ramdani, R. 2007. 'Soufisme ou idolâtrie? Voyage au royaume du Cheikh Hamza', Tel Quel, available online at www.mafhoum.com/press10/298S28.htm (accessed 18 October 2013).

Rézette, R. 1955. *Les partis politiques marocains.* Paris: A. Colin.

Ridgeon, L. (ed.) (forthcoming). *Sufis and Salafis in the Contemporary World. Partners in Purity.* London: Bloomsbury Continuum.

Sater, J. N. 2007. *Civil Society and Political Change in Morocco.* London: Routledge.

Seddon, J. D. 1973. 'Local Politics and State Intervention: Northeast Morocco from 1870 to 1970', in E. Gellner and C. Micaud (eds) *Arabs and Berbers: From Tribe to Nation in North Africa*, 109–39. London: Duckworth.

Sedgwick, M. 2000. 'The Primacy of the Milieu: The Dandarawiyya's Unsuccessful Attempt to Change its Identity', in D. G. Rachida Chih (ed.) *Le saint et son milieu ou comment lire les sources hagiographiques,* 203–13. Cairo: Institut Français d'Archéologie Orientale.

——2004a. *Against the Modern World: Traditionalism and the Secret Intellectual History of the Twentieth Century.* Oxford; New York: Oxford University Press.

——2004b. 'In Search of the Counter-Reformation: Anti-Sufi Stereotypes and the Budshishiyya's Response', in M. Browers and C. Kurzman (eds) *An Islamic Reformation?,* 133–41. Lanham, MD: Lexington Books.

Shahin, E. E. 1997. *Political Ascent: Contemporary Islamic Movements in North Africa.* Boulder, CO: Westview Press.

Silverstein, P. A. 2012. 'In the Name of Culture: Berber Activism and the Material Politics of "Popular Islam" in Southeastern Morocco', *Material Religion* 8(3): 330–53. Oxford: Berg.

Sirriyeh, E. 1999. *Sufis and Anti-Sufis: The Defence, Rethinking and Rejection of Sufism in the Modern World.* Richmond: Curzon Press.

Steinvorth, D. 2007. 'Interview with Moroccan Islamist Nadia Yassine: "Our Religion is Friendly to Women"', *Spiegel Online,* available online at www.spiegel.de/international/world/0,1518,492040,00.html (accessed 18 October 2013).

Tozy, M. 1987. 'Islam and the State', in I. W. Zartman (ed.) *The Political Economy of Morocco,* 130–42. New York: Praeger.

——1990. 'Le prince, le clerc et l'état: La restructuration du champ religieux au Maroc', in G. Kepel, Y. Richard (eds) *Intellectuels et militants de l'Islam contemporain*, 71–90. Paris: Seuil.

——1992. 'L'Islam entre le controle de l'état et les debordements de la societé civile. Des nouveaux clercs aux nouveaux lieux de l'expression religieuse', in J.-C. Santucci (ed.) *Le Maroc actuel. Une modernisation au miroir de la tradition?*, 407–23. Paris: Editions du Centre national de la recherche scientifique (CNRS).

Trimingham, J. S. 1971. *The Sufi Orders in Islam*. Oxford: Oxford University Press.

Vermeren, P. 2001. *Le Maroc en transition*. Paris: Découverte.

Voix, R. 2004. 'Implantation d'une confrérie marocaine en France: Mécanismes, méthodes, et acteurs', *Ateliers* 28(1): 221–8. Nanterre: Maison René-Ginouvès Archéologie et Ethnologie.

Ward, P. A. 2011. 'Quietism', in I. McFarland (ed.) *The Cambridge Dictionary of Christian Theology*, 112–13. Cambridge: Cambridge University Press.

Werbner, P. 2006. 'Seekers of the Path: Different Ways of Being Sufi in Britain', in J. Hinnells and J. Malik (eds) *Sufism in the West*. London: Routledge Curzon.

Westerlund, D. 2004. 'The Contextualization of Sufism in Europe', in D. Westerlund (ed.) *Sufism in Europe and North America*, 13–35. London: Routledge Curzon.

Willis, M. 2007. 'Justice and Development or Justice and Spirituality?: The Challenge of Morocco's Non-violent Islamist Movement', in B. Maddy-Weitzman and D. Zisenwine (eds) *The Maghrib in the New Century: Identity, Religion and Politics*, 33–40. Gainesville, FL: University of Florida Press.

Yahya, D. 1981. *Morocco in the Sixteenth Century: Problems and Patterns in African Foreign Policy*. Harlow: Longman.

Zeghal, M. 2008a. 'Réformismes, islamismes et libéralismes religieux', in M. Zeghal (ed.) *Intellectuels de l'Islam contemporain: Nouvelles générations, nouveaux débats*, Revue des mondes musulmans et de la Méditerranée, 123. Aix-en-Provence: Edisud.

——2008b. 'Appropriations étatiques et dérégulations de l'Islam: Autoritarismes, ouvertures politiques et religion en Tunisie et au Maroc', in S. Vaner, D. Heradstveit and A. Kazancigil (eds) *Sécularisation et démocratisation dans les sociétés musulmanes*, 165–86. Brussels: Peter Lang.

——2009. 'On the Politics of Sainthood: Resistance and Mimicry in Post-colonial Morocco', *Critical Inquiry* 35(3): 587–610. Chicago, IL: Chicago University Press.

3 The Būdshīshiyya Today

After covering the historical dimension of the Būdshīshiyya in the previous chapter, I turn in this chapter to the look of this *ṭarīqa* today. In order to do so, I will describe the geographical distribution of the order worldwide; identify a sociological model of the Būdshīshiyya's religious experiences; and, finally, discuss 'structural aspects' of the organization. Although this research is more concerned with the study of emplaced and embodied religion[1] than with its more 'formal' aspects (i.e. institutional, doctrinal and textual dimensions), I aim to sketch those issues in a brief detour, with the goal of giving the reader contextualizing tools to better comprehend those religious manifestations covered in subsequent chapters.

Mapping the Būdshīshiyya

For reasons I will discuss in the next section, A diverse discipleship, it is difficult to identify clearly defined groups of Būdshīshiyya devotees in north-eastern Morocco. Congregational meetings are held weekly in numerous towns including Ahfir, Berkane, Nador, Oujda, Saidia, Taourirt, Taza or Zaio, but they are not perceived to be exclusively Budshīshi, despite the professed devotion of its attendants for the family of Berber *shurafā'*.[2] In the rest of Morocco, the Būdshīshiyya has groups in most of the bigger cities: at least two groups have been identified in Salé, two in Rabat, three in Casablanca, one in Agadir, one in Tétouan and one in Ouarzazate; and followers do also exist in places such as Goulmina, Khenifra, Midelt and Taroudant, although I could not verify whether the *ṭarīqa* holds weekly gatherings in these localities.

In France the Būdshīshiyya has five groups in Paris, and also has groups in the cities of Agde, Aix-en-Provence, Avignon, Bayonne, Bordeaux, Grenoble, Lyon, Marseille, Montpellier, Nantes, Nice, Strasbourg, Toulouse and Vauvert (near Nimes). In Belgium there are two groups based around Brussels and in Spain there are two groups in Barcelona and one in Girona. In Britain there are groups in Birmingham, Bradford, London, Manchester and Nottingham. I have also known of the existence of followers in other parts of France, Spain and Britain, in addition to others in Germany, the Netherlands, Italy,

Romania and Switzerland, but further research would be needed to determine whether these members have developed stable contingents with weekly gatherings for the performance of *waẓīfa* as do the aforementioned groups.

The order also has a substantial following in Canada, the United States,[3] Mali and Senegal, and some interviewees speak of followers in Brazil, Chile and China, although information on the latter could not be independently verified. I have gathered accounts from members of an Algerian group that claim to be devotees of the 'Būdshīshiyya 'Alawiyya', a group that stems from the combination of the teachings of both *ṭuruq*, but that is recognized by neither of these two orders as legitimate. I have also met *fuqarā'* from the Emirates, although they were not willing to present themselves as 'formal' Būdshīshiyya members but preferred to be called 'Sīdī Hamza sympathisers'.[4]

A diverse discipleship

The Būdshīshiyya is made up of small groups of followers scattered all over Morocco and beyond. Among these groups there is a varying degree of 'homogeneity': in other words, in some enclaves 'in-group' members are more similar to one another than to those in other contingents. Among the more 'homogeneous' are most of the Būdshīshi communities located in north-eastern Morocco. These groups typically contain members born and raised within a certain geographical proximity and are among the most ethnically, religiously and ideologically similar within the order. Most members are of Berber – and, in most cases, of rural – origin; quite often they are from agricultural communities or small towns in which agriculture plays a central role, in economies dependent on the border to survive.[5]

In these enclaves, most devotees are 'born' in the order (i.e. they have never taken the conscious step of 'becoming' part of this organization) and, due to the relevance of this *ṭarīqa* in the region, it is often difficult to draw a clear line between the religious and the social; since the congregational activities of the Būdshīshiyya are part of the social life of many towns, it remains unclear how many of those attending consider themselves Būdshīshiyya's *fuqarā'*. When asked, most do not ascribe allegiance to Hamza in terms of membership to a religious organization; in fact, the mere idea that the Būdshīshiyya is an organization feels odd to many. Instead, they refer to themselves simply as Muslims and they would very rarely call themselves Sufis or *fuqarā'*, as do many others in this *ṭarīqa*; they tend to be less inclined to identify themselves along 'sectarian' lines of a religious kind; they would rather use ethnicity and/or social class to define their social identity.

Another, quite 'homogeneous', type of group is that formed by Moroccan migrants in Europe. These disciples tend to maintain a tight relationship with their homeland, to the extent that such Būdshīshi communities can be viewed as 'Moroccan hubs':[6] *dārija* (the Moroccan dialect of spoken Arabic) and Berber are more used than French or other European languages; the food eaten is Moroccan; and traditional *jilābāt* are worn daily by some, and by many more for ritual performances. For some of the women in these groups the weekly gatherings are the main source of socializing, an amicable refuge from the isolation of migrant life; as a *faqīra* described it 'these meetings are a home away from home'. These communities have little interaction with groups attended by non-Moroccans, and 'cultural strangers' rarely enter this kind of group,[7] due to its conceptualization of religious identity intertwined with culture, which appears disentangled in other members' self-representations. Besides, as happened with the Berber devotees from northern Morocco, these *faqīrāt* do not undertake any rituals to mark their allegiance to the order, and neither are they interested in pursuing proselytization. Despite the two aforementioned types of groups being the ones with the inclination to produce more sizeable contingents, thus constituting the majority of the order's discipleship, they are the 'less visible' side of the order, a silent majority that do not participate in the production of the *ṭarīqa*'s public image.

Contrasting with these relatively 'uniform' groups, there is a plethora of enclaves in Morocco and Europe that can be defined as 'hybrid';[8] that is, groups made up of members with diverse backgrounds. Religiously speaking, one of the very few features shared by all those who are part of hybrid groups is a particular understanding of 'religious affiliation' that, contrary to that held by devotees in those groups discussed above, implies that they either have taken the conscious decision to join this *ṭarīqa,* a choice ritually symbolized by performing the rite of *ba'ya,*[9] or see themselves in the process of acquiring the 'spiritual maturity' (in one *faqīra's* words) to do so. These devotees have a more institutional understanding of what the Būdshīshiyya is; they see the order as an 'organization' of which they are part, and have knowledge of the existence of devotees from other cultural provenances. Members in non-hybrid enclaves, by contrast, often do not deem non-Moroccan disciples to be real followers of Hamza, but see them just as 'religious tourists' (as a Moroccan woman once described foreigners who visit the central *Zāwiya*)[10] and often not as 'real' Muslims. Doubts about the authenticity of non-Moroccans' devotion contrasts, nonetheless, with the view of other Moroccan devotees who see, in the 'capacity' of the *shaykh* to make non-Muslims turn to Islam, yet another proof of his divine grace.[11]

The variety of religious paths followed by the devotees of hybrid groups can be broadly divided into the following categories: first, converts to Islam, by which we mean non-Muslims (religious and non-religious) who formally join the Būdshīshiyya by undertaking the Islamic rite of conversion (*shahada*). Many will prefer to be called reverts[12] (in French often referred to as *reconverties*). Similar to that which happens with other converts, they emphasise a belief that all humans are naturally born with *fitra,* an innate 'feeling' of God's existence. As a result, they view their acts of conversion as a 'return' to this original state of instinctive belief.[13] For some of these convert *fuqarā'*, however, the order turns out to be their 'springboard' to Islam: having converted to Islam to join this *ṭarīqa*, some leave it after a time but remain practising Muslims. When still in the Būdshīshiyya they are to be found in

European contingents (obviously, given that less than one per cent of the native population in Morocco is non-Muslim).[14]

Second, the Būdshīshiyya holds a significant proportion of 'revert' Muslims: those who were born Muslim and, after a period of religious disengagement, returned to the practice of Islam.[15] In the case of this particular *ṭarīqa*, these devotees are either (a) based in Moroccan cities – being upper-class Arabs raised *à la française*, within a secular minority largely uninformed about Islam; or (b) disciples based in European metropolises[16] – being European-born devotees, the daughters and sons (and grandchildren) of Moroccans who have migrated to Europe over the past thirty years, with a varying degree of knowledge on Islam yet mostly uninterested in the Muslim faith prior to entering the order.

Finally, the order contains a large proportion of 're-affiliated' Muslims. Re-affiliation within the Būdshīshiyya is characteristic of Moroccan and British groups. Re-affiliated Muslims are those who leave one particular denomination or sect in order to join another within the same religion. In the case of the Būdshīshiyya, re-affiliated members are typically based either in urban Morocco – being Moroccans who had been raised religiously but have only joined the order in their teens or early adulthood through university circles; or in the United Kingdom – being British-born youngsters whose South Asian parents and grandparents (largely of Pakistani origin) migrated to the United Kingdom during the last three decades. 'Re-affiliated Muslims' were born and brought up as Muslims, and can be differentiated from 'reverts' in that they deem themselves to have believed continuously in the tenets of the Islamic faith.

Sometimes, due to the marked differences in how members from 'hybrid' and 'non-hybrid' groups understand Islam, several groups coexist geographically relatively close to one another (i.e. because hybrid and non-hybrid groups do not congregate together). In general, non-hybrid groups are more uniform and tend to be bigger, whereas hybrid groups tend to be smaller and there are more of them.

Būdshīshiyya's youthful and popular character

There are some features the order evidences transnationally – characteristics shared by a significant proportion of members. The most prominent of these is the intense devotional love all devotees profess for Hamza and his family, a signal in itself, for some, of 'the authenticity of the Būdshīshiyya path' and a demonstration of his *walaya* (Godly granted authority). All the *fuqarā'* pay their utmost respect and devote 'spiritual love' (*maḥabba*) to Hamza – a sentiment that is evoked in personal narratives and which motivates drastic life changes as well as being a motif of abundant artistic expressions (songs, books, even a film!).

There are also some noticeable similarities in the types of people who join the order. In Europe, for example, the *ṭarīqa* have tended to consolidate in poor urban areas. Although a significant proportion of the hybrid groups were founded by middle- and upper-class people with an initial intellectual drive for Sufism[17] (both in Morocco and in Europe), over the years it has been the less well-off members who have kept the order running, particularly in Europe. In Morocco, despite its markedly popular character,[18] the better-off social strata are still well represented within the *ṭarīqa*, such as in cities like Fes where the organization has a significant number of devotees from the bourgeoisie and the intellectual elites. These instances would give the impression of an order that allows for an economic and ethnic melange, where the rich and poor, the Berber and Arab, meet; although a closer analysis of intra-*ṭarīqa* relations presents a rather less idyllic picture (see Chapter 5 for further discussion).

In any case, the location of the lodges in Europe is indicative of the economic background of most devotees. The *ṭarīqa* has a three-storied house in the borough of Argenteuil (Paris),[19] considered by members to be the centre, the *Zāwiya*, of the order in Europe. Followers from Birmingham also have established their own lodge in the borough of Small Heath, catering for the religious and community life of its British devotees.[20] Both are located in ghettoized urban areas; Argenteuil is the second most populous area among the so-called *villes de banlieue* of Paris, one of the poorest *banlieues* of the French capital; Small Heath is also a typical under-privileged area where high concentrations of council housing and unemployment rates are the norm rather than the exception.[21] Most of the devotees in these two cities live relatively near to each other. Similarly, groups in smaller cities also congregate in poor urban areas – usually in private homes where the followers live.

The order evidences a largely similar profile worldwide in terms of the age of its members: according to my own calculations, more than half of the *ṭarīqa*'s membership is constituted of under thirties, with a small number (in most locations around one in ten) below the age of eighteen, and very few, although among the most influential, being over fifties. Perhaps as a result of its youthfulness, commitment to the order tends to be very strong, constituting the centre of most devotees' social lives – a *fuqarā'*'s friends are usually made up of peer members of the group – although in many instances short-lived: more than half of the *fuqarā'* I have met have been in this *ṭarīqa* for fewer than two years, and when I visited the same *faqīrāt* on more than one occasion few people attending the group were there on both occasions,[22] which implies that any estimation of the number of disciples can only be an approximation.[23] I would even say that it is highly possible that some of the smaller groups that I have mapped previously in this chapter may have disappeared, while new ones may have been created since I finished gathering data in 2012. I still suggest we can approximately situate the size of the movement: in Morocco the number of disciples would be nearly 400,000, with around three quarters of this following being located in the north-eastern region, whereas in all the European countries together its discipleship would be between 500 and 1,000, with more than three-quarters being in France.

On religious authority

Transnational *ṭuruq* like the Būdshīshiyya often consist of culturally diverse and geographically dispersed groups that ultimately share respect and religious devotion for a *walī 'Allāh*[24] and perform rituals in the same way.[25] However, they seem to share little more than that, as this book illustrates. There is consensual respect for religious authority, which follows the pyramidal pattern characteristic of North African orders.[26] At the top is Sīdī[27] Hamza (b.1922), *shaykh al-tabarruk* of the *ṭarīqa* – literally, the one attaining *baraka*.[28] Accordingly, he is generally believed to be divinely guided and incapable of sin. Hamza was born in Madāgh, in a Berber rural family of *shurafā'*, the grandson of Sīdī al-Mukhtār al-Būdshīshī (d.1914)[29] and son of Sīdī Ḥājj al-'Abbās ibn al-Mukhtār al-Qādirī al-Būdshīshī,[30] who was the landowner of the agricultural plot of Madāgh where a Qur'ānic school that would later turn into today's *Zāwiya* had existed for a (difficult to determine) number of years. It was there that Hamza first studied religious sciences; he is said to have memorized the Qur'ān[31] by the age of thirteen, guided by his cousin Sīdī Mūhīdīn, and studied *uṣūl al-fiqh* and *uṣūl at-tafsīr* with his uncle – by then the person in charge of the lodge Sīdī al-Makkī (d.1936).[32] Between 1937 and 1942 Hamza received formal religious education at the Oujda branch of the Fes' al-Quarawīyin University (often deemed to be one of the oldest institutions of learning in the Muslim World and an emblem of religious 'normativity' within Moroccan Islam); in 1942 he returned to Madāgh to officially become a *faqīr* following his initiation at the hands of Sīdī Abīmadyan Qādirī al-Būdshīsh (d.1955), who granted him the *sirr* (spiritual secret) needed to obtain the godly authorization (*idhn*) to become a Sufi teacher (Ben Driss, 2002; Ben Rochd, 2002; Draper, 2002; Qustas, 2007).[33]

The Būdshīsh[34] family

Below Hamza, the second-highest echelon of religious authority within the order is formed by some of his offspring.[35] Hamza's younger son is Sīdī Mūrad, who holds no role in the religious hierarchy of the organization. He is perhaps the least-known male member of the family, and his Facebook page shows in its cover picture a Sufi procession with musicians in what looks like the streets of a Moroccan city, topped off with the image of Leo Messi with his son (!) as a profile picture.[36] Apart from his being a fan of the FC Barcelona, the little we know about him is that locals from the area consider him a charming person; many know he works as a teacher at Madāgh's nearby village of Zaio and that he studied at the University Muḥammad I in Oujda. More prominent is another of Hamza's sons, Sīdī Hmida, who also holds no role in the organization's religious pyramid, although he epitomizes the connection between religious and political power in Morocco: people know him well as, after being a civil servant for a number of years, he became governor of Berkane, the municipality where the central *Zāwiya* sits, and was in office until the spring of 2012.[37]

Hamza's eldest son Sīdī Jamāl is the prospective successor to Hamza to be at the head of the organization, believed, therefore, to be the one that will inherit the *walī*'s *baraka*. He is regularly seen leading *waẓīfa* sessions at the central lodge. He is already deemed to have a saintly aura, one that devotees believe he emanates physically, in performance, through ritual, and that can be 'reproduced' (in a young disciple's own words). Accordingly, I have met *faqīrāt* who share podcasts of him chanting *qasā'id*[38] and young boys in Morocco who try to imitate his style of performance; these sound artefacts are commonly believed to attract godly verve and to benefit disciples. Jamāl's visits to devotees in various Moroccan as well as European locations (when members from nearby locations are generally contacted and asked to come to see him personally),[39] or people's visits to Madāgh, allow *fuqarā* to 'meet' him – perhaps it is more accurate to say 'physically see' him, since most have never held a conversation lasting more than five minutes, fieldwork data suggests, with the one-day-to-become *walī*. Jamāl lives within the premises of the *Zāwiya* in Madāgh, and his house is often used to host the most prominent disciples and invitees. He is the father of Sīdī Mūnir, who leads the European branches of the *ṭarīqa*.

Contrasting with Jamāl's notorious public reticence (especially in view of what it seems is going to be his future role in the order), his son Mūnir represents a more visible face of the organization. It is not that people know much about him, but some, I would contend, selectively chosen information about him has reached the public and is *vox populi* within the *ṭarīqa*.[40] Munīr represents the highest authority of this *ṭarīqa* in Europe, a very relevant position occupied by a young man always portrayed as representing a cultural mix of Morocco and France. For example, the 'blended' character of his Moroccan and French education is used by the order's leadership to brand the organization with an 'inclusive', 'modern yet traditional', 'normative yet progressive' character attuned with the religious identity of some of the younger, urban generations of devotees in Morocco and abroad. Representative of the kind of biographical data widely accessible about him is this Būdshīshiyya's website excerpt:

> Sidi Mounir Qadiri Boutchich was born in Morocco. He grew up in the family of the Qadiri Boutchich and his earliest education was obtained from this Pure source. He graduated from Oujda University in Literary Science in 1994, and completed his Degree in Law at the Dar al Hassania Institute, Rabat, in 1996. His search for knowledge brought him to France where he has studied for a wide range of Degrees, followed by a Masters in Social Anthropology at the Europe-Maghrib Institute in Paris 2001. He recently completed his Doctorate in Islamic Law at the Sorbonne-Paris, where he researches Communication and Sufism. He is also known for his many publications on Sufism, the latest being 'The Sufi presence in an age of Globalisation (2004)'.[41]

Whereas Hamza acquired his religious learning at al-Quarawīyin University, a 'traditional' centre of religious learning, Munīr has opted for studying both religious and non-religious subjects at a 'secular' institution, the Sorbonne – and in fact, in these he resembles a somehow well-represented minority within the *ṭarīqa*'s younger ranks of devotees within which the study of Islam at 'secular' universities, either in Rabat, Casablanca, Montreal or Paris, is well represented. In terms of communicating with disciples, Hamza very rarely leaves the central *Zāwiya* and seldom speaks to his followers – an attitude legitimized by a particular understanding of spiritual knowledge and instruction central to the transnational expansion of the organization.[42] Munīr, by contrast, regularly visits disciples and 'engages in conversation' with *fuqarā'*, or at least this is the common perception. The outsider can be shocked at how brief these exchanges often are: none of those who are of low position among the devotees whom I met in my fieldwork have ever spoken to Munīr (nor to Jamāl) for more than five minutes, yet he is perceived to be the member of the leadership in whom 'to confide' (intra-*ṭarīqa* issues, as well as individual dilemmas, especially among European followers, are often addressed either to him or to Skali, of whom I will speak in the next section of this chapter, entitled Non-consanguineal religious authority.)

Munīr's visibility is also illustrated in his literary output and role as a preacher. Whereas Hamza has authored only a short collection of 'sayings',[43] Munīr is the author of various articles, most of which are available online,[44] and he regularly delivers speeches at conferences organized by the order.[45] All in all, he, it may be argued, represents a new form of Sufi religious authority that involves not only 'traditional' bodily saintly power, but also dialectical persuasion. As an *orateur* he articulates a more 'analytical' approach to Sufism, used to address the 'spiritual needs' of more 'intellectualized' urban followers. The oratorical component constitutes an actually quite successful *da'wa* strategy: fieldwork data suggests that his speeches and articles are among some of the order's materials first accessed and best remembered by potential *fuqarā'*.

Non-consanguineal religious authority

Denoting the modern, almost 'corporate' character of this *ṭarīqa* is the fact that some of the people who hold authority within the order are not related by blood to the Būdshīsh family, something uncommon in most Sufi orders. Sīdī Aḥmad Qustas is the highest authority of this *ṭarīqa* in the US and, although he lives in Fes, he regularly visits the States. The order often refers to the clichéd discourse that places in opposition Islam *vs* the West, Tradition *vs* Modernity, to present him as a 'cultural broker' (*vis-à-vis* Munīr and Skali), authentically Moroccan in his perception of Islam, yet able to 'translate' Sufism to western disciples:

> Sidi Ahmed brings his teachings to us with their traditional sufic [sic] truth intact. Thanks to his long experience and impeccable scholarship,

> he is able to make them fully accessible to the Western mind and way of perception.[46]

He studied theology and Islamic sciences at the Fes' branch of al-Quarawīyin, and Ḥadīth studies at al-Ḥassaniyya in Rabat. The fact that he lived in the US and taught at the University of Maryland in 1998 is often highlighted as proof of, as one *faqīra* put it, 'his ability to navigate between the two worlds'. The blended American–Moroccan character of his education means devotees see him at the same time as 'traditional' – with healing capabilities exerted through 'old-fashioned' bodily rituals – and 'modern': a writer, an academic and a preacher. He has authored a book about the *ṭarīqa* (Qustas, 2007), and was the editor of the Moroccan Sufi journal *al-Murīd* (no longer published or in print) that used a pseudo-academic format to publicize the kind of religiosity promoted by the order and its leadership. Together with Sīdī Faūzi Skali (b.1953), he is part of the team that annually organizes the world-renowned *Fes Sacred Music Festival.*

Another relevant personality within the order not related by blood to the Būdshīsh family is Skali. Like Qustas, he has Hamza's authorization *(idhn)*[47] to lead male *dhikr* sessions and initiate *fuqarā'*. Along with Qustas and Munīr, but perhaps even more acutely, Skali represents the more visible image of the organization, by again using an archetypal 'East–West' narrative of conciliation the *ṭarīqa* wants to convey as part of its transnational identity. His Wikipedia page defines him thus: '*Francophone writer, who is between Orient and Occident and works for the dialogue between peoples and cultures*'.[48]

As happened with Qustas and Munīr, the cultural brokerage that defines him is acquired, so the *ṭarīqa*'s narrative goes, by the 'blended' character of his education. Raised in Morocco, he graduated in anthropology and the study of religion at the Sorbonne with a thesis on Sufism in Fes and has authored a number of academic books on Sufism (e.g. Skali, 1985, 1996, 1999, 2004),[49] most of them promoting the 'kind' of Sufism that is characteristic of the Būdshīshiyya (like the *al-Murīd* journal edited by Qustas). Director of the *Fes Sacred Music Festival*[50]and public exponent of the 'multicultural oratory' that defines the event, Skali has become a representative of a 'Muslim inclusivism' proposed as antidote to the growing 'anti-West' sentiment typical of some post-9/11 Muslim rhetoric, as well as against Islamophobic perspectives by which Islam is equated with 'fundamentalism'. A website that addresses the Festival and him offers this praise:

> [The Festival is] a great meeting place for musicians of all countries and all religions, (…) [R]un by Faouzi Skali, it became a way of realizing his Sufi teachings. This spirituality [Sufism] at the heart of the religion of listening and tolerance that is Islam is far from the [commonly held]

> clichés about Muslims and their fundamentalism. [In Skali you will] encounter a man of dialogue. (Escaffit, 2001)[51]

On the inclusivist rhethoric he defends, a group of French *faqīrāt*, for example, recalls the story Skali explains:

> [A]bout a saint that was approached by a Muslim who was shocked by how a group of men did not behave as religiously as they should, he said to the saint 'please, ask God to save them!' to which God spoke through the saint and said 'why should I? Didn't I create them?'
>
> personal communication

In Morocco, as well as among circles of people interested in Sufism in Europe, he is famous, a 'spiritual celebrity' who takes religious charisma to a whole new dimension, through his appearances on TV and interviews given to newspapers. I have met non-Moroccan 'outsiders' that know about the existence of the Būdshīshiyya because of him; also, I have encountered young women 'interested in Sufism' who have been attending *waẓīfāt* for short periods of time and who know about him, but not necessarily about 'more traditional authorities' like Hamza or Jamāl.

Overall, Skali, Qustas and Munīr epitomize the most visible side of the order's leadership and, one might argue, represent a new type of religious charisma more concerned with 'ideology' and 'rational' argumentation and less centred in bodily practices. Their message seems to be proving its effectiveness in helping the *ṭarīqa* to garner new adherents, younger and more literate, particularly in urban areas of Morocco and Europe. Overall, the Būdshīshiyya's success beyond its original enclave seems to be partly related to these new ways of conceptualizing religious authority, one that may end up challenging the monopoly that *baraka*-driven charisma used to have; today, already some among the younger followers manifest a stronger devotion for Munīr or Skali than for the leading *shaykh,* Hamza.

Immediately below Qustas and Skali, the hierarchy of the order has a series of *muqaddimūn*, or secondary authorities, who are the emissaries of the central leadership of this *ṭarīqa* in diverse locations.[52] Each enclave, therefore, consists of a local *muqaddim/a* and a group of devotees. The *muqaddim/a*'s role mainly consists of deciding location and time for holding weekly *waẓīfāt* and leading the actual ritual performance of *dhikr*. There have to be two *muqaddimān* (one male, one female) for each enclave, as ritual performance of the weekly *waẓīfa* is gender-segregated.[53] The pyramidal structure is, overall, highly respected, which means that queries are most of the time first directed to the local *muqaddim/a*, who in turn pass(es) the message upwards; direct contact between people separated by one echelon of authority within the order is very rare.

Female authority

Although most of the female members of the Būdshīshiyya family do not hold any significant religious or political role, there is one woman among the *ṭarīqa*'s top-ranked, the eldest of Hamza's daughters, Lālā Asiya. She is the person in charge of 'running' the *Zāwiya* in Madāgh, a big house that, during major celebrations like the *Mawlid*, hosts hundreds of guests at the same time. During these occasions, Asiya coordinates a group of always extremely busy women who take care of keeping the premises clean and cooking for the 'crowds' of guests. Different shifts for eating and sleeping space allocation for all the various groups of visitors are organized by her. She also 'runs' the *Zāwiya* the rest of the year, at times when, still, there are always occasional visitors, invitees, students of the 'summer university' held annually there, and more infrequently casual tourists.

Since hospitality is considered a religious duty in Morocco and central to the behavioural model proposed by the order,[54] Asiya is viewed with special esteem by many members, especially women. In religious terms, she is the woman who holds the highest position of power within the *ṭarīqa*, which means that she is responsible for leading female *dhikr* sessions at the central lodge. However, the hierarchy of the order is based on a masculine line of descent, and therefore she will certainly never become the head of the *ṭarīqa*; however, she holds the kind of 'informal' influence typical of charismatic female Sufis.[55] Considered exceptional by many, she is always seen affectionately welcoming *faqīrāt* at the lodge, and with those who have been in the *ṭarīqa* for longer, asking them about their relatives and about other female disciples in their contingents. She will remember people with painstaking detail: a devotee once said 'her impressive memory has been carved with meticulous training over the years', to which another replied, 'no, it is the fruit of her connection to Sīdī [Hamza]'. I have often met disciples who see in her a role model of how a righteous Muslim woman should behave.

Although some, though very few, devotees, particularly women, do know some other female members of the Būdshīshiyya family, Hamza's female relatives remain largely anonymous. Notwithstanding, in an order which is part of a culture organized around kin groups, women, as central to the family structure, are considered 'essential'. Accordingly, the *ṭarīqa*'s leadership asks for public recognition of these ladies in their 'exemplary' role of wives or daughters of relevant Būdshīshiyya personalities. For example, when Lālā Thaus, wife of Jamāl, passed away on 1 May 2008, an email was sent to all members:

> Salam alaikum fuqara and faqirat,
>
> With great sorrow we announce that Lala Thaus has passed away today. In order to honour her, we ask you to recite Fatiha 50.[56] In this very painful time for her family and for all the faqirat [notice that no mention is made of fuqarā'], we ask our Lord to support her family, our

Master Sidi Hamza, Sidi Jamal, Sidi Mounir, Sidi Hmida and also Lala Asiya and her sisters for the loss of our beloved lala Thaus.[...]
I send you a hug, dearest faqirat,
Salam Alaikum[57]

It is noticeable that, although the letter, written by a high-ranked woman within the order, is addressed to both male and female devotees (which in turn could be potentially viewed as an exception to a gender divide according to which women can listen to and see men, although not address them, and not vice versa), and devoting ritual remembrance to the deceased is asked also of all members regardless of their gender, the letter does not consider the possibility of mourning pain being experienced by male devotees unrelated to the deceased, but only by *faqīrāt* and members of Hamza's family. Of those, explicit mention is given to descendants with a prominent role within the order – those males and the only woman that play a role in the organization. Thence, it is worth noticing that other daughters of Hamza with no official function within the *ṭarīqa* are referred to simply as 'Lālā Asiya's sisters'.

Anti-textualism, literary output and *da'wa*

In today's Būdshīshiyya the practice of rituals together with a particular etiquette of social behaviour (defined by courtesy, generosity and 'suspension of judgement')[58] are placed as the central spiritual duties of the *faqīr/a,* which has meant that the order is attempting to diminish the rationalistic approach to Sufism common among many devotees. In line with this policy, no written materials produced by this *ṭarīqa* are considered part of the 'learning curriculum' of the devotee. Indeed, when one asks about 'the texts of the order' the most common experience is to be addressed not to texts themselves but to excerpts that summarize the 'anti-textual' stance the *ṭarīqa* adopts on learning (and which will be more thoroughly discussed in Chapter 4). Devotees of Sīdī Hamza (who has authored only a short compendium of aphorisms) argue this 'prompts *fuqarā'* to "experience" Sufism instead of "reading" about Sufism, that is why [together with the fact that the order's leader is alive] as opposed to other *ṭuruq* the Būdshīshiyya is [regarded as] a 'living' Sufism (*Soufisme vivant*)'. The intellectual and the experiential are often portrayed as antithetical approaches to pursuing the spiritual quest, the intellectual being commonly viewed as an obstacle to the attainment of the experiential,

> [A]s our guide Sīdī Hamza has said (may God be proud of him) 'Sufism is not a science of papers [referring to the common notion of modern positivist-minded science] it is a science of tastes' [referring to a discipline based on feelings]'.[59]

This being the reason why Hamza 'instructs' devotees by 'transforming their hearts not by [using] words'. By departing from a verbally transmitted and/or text-reliant spiritual instruction, this *ṭarīqa* gains the capacity to surpass cultural and linguistic barriers and attract disciples worldwide, a successful (and probably necessary) mechanism of religious proselytization. But such 'anti-textualism', far from being uncontested, is ambiguously defended and the same people that advocate for 'experiencing' Sufism instead of 'reading' about it, turn out to be eager consumers of written materials (mainly online texts) on Sufism produced by other devotees.[60]

Ambiguous also is the relationship between 'textuality' and *da'wa*; whereas abandoning a text-based method of religious instruction has facilitated the Būdshīshiyya's international expansion, some specific texts are crucially utilized as a means to attract new devotees. Although proselytizing literature is nowadays mainly digital (an issue addressed in Chapter 4) there is also one 'old-fashioned' paperback which was the first appeal to the order to some of the *faqīrāt* I encountered, and that is *Qu'Allah bénisse la France* (2004) by *banlieue*-boy-turned-hip-hop-singer and Būdshīshiyya devotee Abd al Malik (b.1975).

Hailing from a Strasbourg ghetto, the singer of rap band NAP (New African Poets) and son of Congolese *émigrés,* Malik converted to Islam in his youth amid a climate of police riots and violence. The book describes the religious 'options' available to the young Muslim in the poor neighbourhoods of the city, and his initial sympathizing with groups such as the *Tablighī Jamā'at,* the Muslim Brotherhood and preachers or intellectuals such as Dīdat and Ramadan. After several years of spiritual searching, the narrative goes, Malik recognizes in these types of religiosity 'an aggressive Islamism at the margins of society'[61] (Abd al Malik, 2004) and decides to enter the *ṭarīqa* Būdshīshiyya. Since then, Malik has launched four albums as a musician: *Le face à face des cœurs, Gibraltar, Dante* and *Château rouge,* which have made it to the top of the charts. They contain, among others, songs that tell of his love for Hamza and lyrics that speak out against the politicized Islam of the *banlieues.*

Malik's (2004) biography is a narrative of 'salvation'[62] on how to survive the hardships of life in the ghetto; succinctly, the book argues that you can either support the incendiary rhetoric of '*integriste*' Muslim preachers or follow Islam's path of love by joining the Būdshīshiyya. I argue that part of the *da'wa* effectiveness of what Skali or Malik argue stems from the fact that they represent ways of coping with Islamophobia. They present experiences of exclusion that can feel close to some Muslim readers and offer a way of framing a 'presented-as-positive' response to such prejudice. Thus, when Skali criticizes the bold assumption 'Islam is fundamentalism', he appeals to the Muslim who has felt categorized by non-Muslims as a 'terrorist' and tells him/her to respond to discrimination by replacing 'reactiveness' with 'exemplarity' (i.e. show them yours is a religion of tolerance). 'Celebrity-*fuqarā*" such as Skali or Malik publicly and constantly declare their adherence to the order, and make use of their fame to engage in proselytization.

Attuned also with the pluralistic and inclusive discourse typical of Skali, Malik's lyrics take inspiration from a variety of sources, from the medieval

Moroccan Sufi author Ibn 'Aṭā 'Allāh,[63] to Albert Camus or Jean-Paul Sartre,[64] a stylistic eclecticism that has been defined by BBC reporter Polly de Blank as 'an original mix of hip-hop, slam poetry and French philosophy'.[65] When discussing with disciples who Malik is and what he means to them, various *faqīrāt* highlighted how much they like and could relate to his multi-faceted inspiration: 'we are a copy and paste generation, we learn from everybody and from everywhere' said one, to which another added 'I find stupid this Islamic purism by which you are only supposed to read Muslim authors and Islamic philosophy and have to learn Arabic, when actually you can learn a lot from everybody, not only Muslims'. This view is echoed by revert and convert devotees who, when becoming members of the *ṭarīqa,* do not want to altogether abandon their previous interests to avoid being considered 'un-Islamic', but who at the same time do not want to do anything that is against the principles of Islam.

Malik's narrative of 'salvation', which details how by joining the Būdshīshiyya he could make sense of the deaths of many friends who were the victims of overdoses, police abuses and knife and gun crime, could serve others who could relate to similar experiences to reframe their own trajectories of social deprivation. What is often said of the ethnographer – that, by getting closer to 'the biographies of others, we are engaged in biographical work of our own' (Coffey, 1999: 123) – also holds true for some of Malik's readers. In terms of proselytization, this empathy may induce young Muslims in the deprived areas of European cities to join the *ṭarīqa*, making the Būdshīshiyya seem a 'positive' alternative to the perceived-as-'hatred' forms of Islam available to them. Even if the *da'wa* success of Malik's story may have been largely proven in the ten years that have passed since the book was first published, by the number of copies sold as well as by numbers joining the order after reading it, in 2014 (a year after I am writing this) it may well acquire an entirely different dimension, when *Qu'Allah bénisse la France* will reach the cinemas as a film.

Notes

1 I adopt a stance similar to that proposed by Vasquez (2011), which urges scholars to replace the importance traditionally given to the study of 'texts' and 'doctrine' with a more dedicated analysis of religion as it is lived and expressed in specific contexts. Further discussion on these methodological aspects is provided in Chapter 1.

2 *Shurafā'* (ar. pl.) and *Sharīf* (sing.) are terms used to designate nobility: in Morocco, a descendant of the Prophet of Islam. For a more complete definition, refer to the Glossary.

3 US groups include contingents in California (Charlottesville, Virginia and San Francisco), Athens, Atlanta, Los Angeles, Chicago, Florida, Georgia, Kansas City, New York, Orlando, Philadelphia and San Diego.

4 None of the American or the non-Moroccan African followers' religiosities have been comprehensively analysed in this research; a study of those groups would nonetheless be central to obtaining a truly comprehensive picture of the Būdshīshiyya worldwide.

5 Life in these regions revolves around the border: whereas in some families I have encountered there is a mixture of 'seasonal' migrants in Spain's fields and those who stay in Morocco and take care of the 'home-grown' production, some others make their living out of activities typical of the Borderland economy. Cross-border commercial exchanges between Morocco on the one hand, and Sībtā (Ceuta, in European languages) and Mīlīlīā (Melilla, in European languages) on the other, are a pillar of the economy on both sides of the border. For an excellent ethnography on how the border economy works in Oujda, see McMurray (2001).

6 The Moroccan diaspora is a very significant emigrational phenomenon in European demographics – it is expected to become the biggest non-European diaspora group in Europe in the next decade; for further information, see Bilgili and Weyel (2009).

7 The case of a European woman who, after marrying a Moroccan, began to attend the gatherings is illustrative of the inaccessibility of 'outsiders' to these groups: she ceased to attend these meetings soon after joining the order as she felt questioned and excluded. She recalled knowing of other European wives of Moroccans in a similar situation: they convert to Islam to join this *ṭarīqa* and are introduced into their husband's Būdshīshiyya group, but after a while they tend to leave (although remaining Muslim) because they never feel part of the group. The phenomenon of keeping a cultural character seems to be common among migrant groups in the diaspora, whether South Asian (e.g. Werbner 2005), Turkish (e.g. Jonker 2006), Persian (e.g. Lewisohn 2006) or North African (e.g. Dominguez Diaz 2010a).

8 I am borrowing here Hermansen's terminology (1996), further exposed in Chapter 1, note 15.

9 *Ba'ya* is an initiatory ritual which most of the Būdshīshiyya's European members refer to as *the pact*. See the Glossary for a more complete definition of the term. This rite denotes 'voluntarism' and is more typical of Islam in 'the West' than in the Muslim World, a key distinctive feature developed by Islam as a result of its encounter with the secular systems of the western world. For further information on European Islam's voluntarism, see Cesari (2004: 128).

10 Term used in the Būdshīshiyya and other Moroccan Sufi orders to refer to the central lodge where the highest authorities of the order reside. It might also be used in a more generic way to designate any of the places where a group of followers gather together to perform collective ritual sessions and is considered as the centre of various congregations – for example, the one in Argeteuil, the one in Birmingham. The *Zāwiya* of the Būdshīshiyya is located in the town of Madāgh (north-eastern Morocco), see Appendix 2.

11 The notion that non-Moroccans are not 'real' devotees of Sīdī Hamza, but just people with a curiosity, had been put forward by various Moroccans interviewed in Morocco, in France and in Spain. On three occasions, when I told respondents there were people converting to Islam to become devotees of Hamza, they doubted the degree of 'sincerity' of these conversions and how long this 'interest' would last.

12 This phenomenon of reversion is in French generally referred as *reconversion religieuse* and not as *reversion*, as an English reader might expect; it however refers to the same discourse described above and it follows the same sort of rationale.

13 An account of this kind of rationale within the Būdshīshiyya can be, for example, found in the narrative of this French follower, available online at www.saveurs-soufies.com/forum/6-T%C3%A9moignage-et-coins-des-convertis%28e%29s/2018-cheminement-et-reconversion#2021 (accessed 20 July 2012).

14 According to CIA World Factbook, 99% of Moroccans are Muslims: https://www.cia.gov/library/publications/the-world-factbook/geos/mo.html (accessed 25 November 2013).

15 Observation of reversion throughout the Būdshīshiyya indicates that if conversion is to be defined as an act that involves 'not just adopting a set of ideas but also converting to and from an embodied worldview and identity' (Sachs Norris, 2003: 171),

then we should infer that religious reversion as it occurs in the Būdshīshiyya is indeed a form of religious conversion, as some authors have already argued in relation to religious conversion and reversion in general (Gilliat-Ray, 1999).

16 No reverts are to be found in the British groups, perhaps because rates of Moroccan migration to the UK seem to be much lower than to the rest of Western Europe. For more data on the features of Moroccan migration to the UK, see Bakewell, de Haas and Kubal's (2011) report, available at www.imi.ox.ac.uk/pdfs/research-projects-pdfs/themis-pdfs/themis-scoping-study-morroco (accessed 25 November 2013). For a comparative perspective of British and Continental European groups within the Būdshīshiyya, see Dominguez Diaz (2010b, 2013).

17 This is in consonance with other studies of religious conversion – people first feeling attracted by the intellectual side of religion and only turning to a more bodily oriented approach after an initial phase (Zebiri, 2007).

18 Once, discussing the economic condition of devotees with a *faqīra*, she joked by saying the term *faqīr* in the Būdshīshiyya has a literal meaning. The word *faqīr* means poor in Arabic, and is the term devotees use to refer to each other with affection (like sister, or brother, is often used by many Muslims). In Sufism the word refers to the idea that people should be modest and not show ostentation before God. But since many members of the order are quite short of money the *faqīra* meant that the term, instead of meaning 'modesty before God', may actually denote a socio-economic condition – that is – being poor in the monetary sense.

19 The order in Belgium and Spain is not big enough to be able to pay for buildings of its own; meetings there are more informal and are held at a follower's home. The choosing of the home often rotates, as there are sometimes problems finding a person willing to offer his/her house for the gathering. It is not clear whether the number of British devotees is substantial enough to explain the availability of a separate lodge, or whether this is evidence of a certain degree of autonomy and differentiation from the rest of European enclaves.

20 The British lodge is run by a charity called the *Amina Trust*, set up by some of the first members of the order in the UK. Their website is indicative of the thriving social life of the centre, available online at http://thezawiya.co.uk/ (accessed 1 August 2012).

21 In the Birmingham borough of Small Heath, 63.33% of the population are 'South Asian' or of 'South Asian' descent. This ethnic group comprises 18.49% of the population of the city of Birmingham and 4.09% of the population of England, according to the 2001 National Census, available online at www.neighbourhood.statistics.gov.uk/dissemination/LeadTableView.do;jsessionid=ac1f930d30d6e1e0fec2349f4998bf26bf2dd7124a78?a=7&b=560960&c=Small+Heath&d=14&e=13&g=372561&i=1001x1003x1004&m=0&r=1&s=1272463089123&enc=1&dsFamilyId=47&nsjs=true&nsck=true&nssvg=false&nswid=1003 (accessed 2 May 2012).

Similarly, Argenteuil has a notable population of North Africans or people of North African descent. It would be difficult to provide accurate statistical figures because of the lack of relevant data of this kind in France. Data available from 2010 suggests that unemployment rates in Argenteuil peaked at 16% compared to the national average of 10%. Similarly, the unemployment rate in Small Heath in 2010 was 17.9% – making it the constituency with the highest rate after Ladywood – whereas the national rate is almost half that, at 8%. For further information, visit *L'encyclopédie des villes de France*, available online at www.linternaute.com/ville/ville/accueil/1459/argenteuil.shtml; and residence-based unemployment rates by parliamentary constituency, United Kingdom, January 2010, available online at www.parliament.uk/commons/lib/research/rp2010/rp10–013.pdf (both accessed 3 May 2010). A dramatic increase in these figures is to be expected due to the ongoing economic crisis, yet accurate figures are not currently available.

22 Accordingly, many see the Būdshīshiyya as being at the centre of their lives and the most important thing that has ever happened to them; they often attach a sense of predestination to their joining. In this sense, the Būdshīshiyya exhibits some – yet not all – of the features attributed by Wallis (1984) to New Religious Movements of the 'world-rejecting' type: they imbue in people a sense of 'deindividuation' and a feeling of being 'reborn', which encourages them to break with their past life (Wallis, 1984: 19). Remarkably, however, other characteristics of Wallis's 'world-rejecting movements' (e.g. communal life, millennialism and authoritarian leadership) are not to be found in this *ṭarīqa*. In fact, it would seem that the European groups of the Būdshīshiyya represent the 'world-accommodating' pattern rather than The 'world-rejecting' one. Devotees, by and large, carry on with their conventional lives; these movements adapt to the world rather than affirm or reject it. Religious practice and worship are performed collectively (Wallis, 1984: 36). According to the majority of their members, movements of this type restore an experiential element to the spiritual life and replace certainties which are perceived as having been lost; these movements are common in societies with a perceived sense of religious institutions having become increasingly relativized (Wallis, 1984: 37). Further discussion on this issue is provided in Chapter 1 and in Dominguez Diaz (2010a).

23 It also requires undertaking fieldwork in a rather atypical way, not only for the multi-sited geography of the field researched but also because of the often highly volatile, transient nature of the commitment to the order of a significant proportion of devotees. On the process of fieldwork, see Chapter 1, as well as Dominguez Diaz (2011).

24 *Walī 'Allāh* (sing. ar.) or *awliyā' 'Allāh* (pl.) is a term used to refer to those otherwise popularly known as 'Sufi saints'; a more detailed definition is given in the Glossary.

25 It is generally translated into English as 'remembrance': a ritual commonly (but not exclusively) performed by Sufis; a more detailed definition is given in the Glossary.

26 The same pattern of religious authority is characteristic of North African Sufism, as Geertz (1971) once observed. See also an example of a *ṭarīqa* with the same authority structure in Karrar's (1992) study of a Sudanese branch of the Qādiriyya.

27 Sīdī is the Arabic term used before the name to refer to male members of the order and it expresses spiritual commitment and affection. For females, the term used is Lālā. In this book, I use the terms Lālā/Sīdī the first time a Būdshīshiyya personality referred to by his/her name appears, to make it clear they are members of the order. Members of Hamza's family are often referred to by their forename (since they all have the surname Qādiri Būdshīsh,which would therefore be unnecessary); whereas those without a consanguine relation to Hamza are referred by their surname (e.g. Qustas, Skali). Throughout this book I only use real names for public personalities whereas the anonymity of lower-ranked devotees' accounts has been preserved.

28 A term generally translated as 'blessing', it refers to the spiritual potency or power that holy individuals, places and/or objects are believed to have. A more detailed definition is given in the Glossary.

29 Their names may be spelt differently in different sources. I have kept to a transliteration that is consistent with that used throughout the book and it responds to a way of transliterating Arabic more typically used in English-speaking academia. Because of the official character of French in Morocco, names of relevant Būdshīshi personalities are more often written down following the transliteration of Arabic more commonly followed in the French-speaking world – for example Sīdī Mūrad becomes Sidi Mourad, Qadiri Budshish becomes Kadiri Boutchich, Ahmad

Qustas will be Ahmed Kostas, to mention just a few. For further information on the transliterating system used in this book, refer to the transliteration chart.

30 The *ṭarīqa*'s *silsila* is provided in Appendix 1.

31 One aspect of what literacy means in some parts of Morocco comprises memorizing verses of the Qur'ān without necessarily being able to understand their meaning; the ability to read and write down memorized sections of the book makes you a 'religious person,' in some areas a 'scholar', categories to which a good reputation is attached (Touati, 2013; Eickelman, 1985).

32 There is little information available about this part of the family; some sources claim al-Makkī was the leader of the order prior to 1942, when the first reliable accounts of the *ṭarīqa* occur. For these accounts see Hajji (1992). On the history of the order, see Chapter 2.

33 Apart from the biographical information on the Būdshīshiyya family provided by these authors, unauthored booklets produced by the order (e.g. *Nabadat 'an al-ṭarīqa al-Qādiriyya al-Būdshīshiyya.* n.a. n.d. n.p.) as well as websites such as *saveurs soufies* (available online at www.saveurs-soufies.com/index.php?option=com_content&view=article&id=96:sidi-hamza-qadiri-boutchich&catid=14:la-tariqa-qadiriyya-boutchichiya-voie-vivante&Itemid=35 – (accessed 18 November 2013) or the Moroccan site linked to the municipality of Berkane, available online at http://berkanecity.free.fr/zaouia1.htm – (accessed 18 November 2013), are also rich sources of data.

34 Dates of death are provided for deceased personalities (when available), otherwise those of birth are given (when available).

35 The Būdshīsh family is quite zealous about its privacy, and in terms of their personal life very little is known about them; what follows is, however, the succinct data that is given to the public. In terms of biographical data, it is surprising how scarce the information is that reaches the public about one of the, arguably, most influential families in the kingdom. To my knowledge there are no available written materials, neither digital nor paper-based. A similar picture is obtained by conducting fieldwork among devotees and non-devotees of the order in Morocco and abroad: respondents tend to know very little about members of the Būdshīshiyya family.

36 Available online at www.facebook.com/public/Mourad-El-Kadi (accessed 20 November 2013).

37 The political role the family plays at a regional level has been assessed in Chapter 2.

38 *Qaṣīda* (ar. sing.) and *qasā'id* (pl.) are terms for a form of musicalized classical poetry. It is not uncommon to find these songs posted online – for example, a track with Jamāl singing in Paris is available online at https://soundcloud.com/deenislam4/sidi-jamal-budshishi-qasa-id (accessed 22 November 2013).

39 The central role played by these visits among *fuqarā'* is assessed in Chapter 6.

40 Part of it is rumours about his personal relations, whose veracity is unproven and which generate tremendous controversy within the order; this research is certainly not centred in taking sides in relation to this gossip, but I see it as far more interesting to concentrate on the information the *ṭarīqa*'s leadership provides to the public about him: why this and no other kinds of data, and with what purpose?

41 Available online at www.sufiway.net/ar_Sufism_SidiMounir_ISEG.html (accessed 25 November 2013).

42 Refer to Chapter 2 for further analysis of the doctrinal adaptations the *ṭarīqa* had to undergo in order to be able to expand beyond north-eastern Morocco.

43 There is only a series of Sīdī Hamza 'sayings', quotes written following a classical style of Sufi literature with recurrent reference to Sufi symbolism and metaphors which contrasts with the more direct style of his descendants' writings, made in prose with a clear, less symbolic way of expressing ideas. They are available in various European languages including English at www.tariqa.org/qadiriya/texts/sayings.html (accessed 18 November 2013).

44 For example, *The Importance of Sufism in an Era of Globalisation*, available online at www.sufiway.net/ar_Sufism_SidiMounir_ISEG.html (accessed 21 Novemeber 2013).

45 Some of these presentations are posted online, either transcribed and available online at www.facebook.com/boudchichia/posts/359251997513167 (accessed 21 November 2013); or filmed and available online at www.youtube.com/watch?v=l0hVyReQvCg (accessed 21 November 2013).

46 Available online at http://web.archive.org/web/20030408081844/http://www.sufi-village.org/kostas2.html (accessed 25 November 2013).

47 *Idhn* (ar. sing.) refers to the granting of religious authority by the leadership of the order to an individual, the authorization given by the leadership to a person to lead *dhikr* and initiate disciples.

48 My own translation from French of the original *'écrivain francophone, il se situe entre l'Orient et l'Occident et œuvre pour le dialogue des hommes et des cultures'*.

49 There are a number of academics apart from Skali and Qustas studying Sufism who are Būdshīshiyya devotees. The most famous of those is the once-CNRS-based, Eva de Vitray-Meyerovitch (d.1999), who had written extensively about Sufism (e.g. 1972, 1978, 1984). Others include Ben Driss who published a book (2002) about Hamza based on his PhD, defended in Montreal; and Draper, who at the time of writing his doctoral thesis (2002) on the British Būdshīshiyya was a member of the organization.

50 At its inception during the first Gulf War, the festival was an 'interfaith' endeavour aiming at attracting European and American tourists. It later turned to the Moroccan public that was keen to see in its 'interreligious character' a way of counter-tackling burgeoning trends of religious violence within the country (particularly after the 2003 bombings in Casablanca), although it also maintained its international audiences. For further analysis of the festival, see Kapchan (2008).

51 Escaffit, Jean-Claude. 'Faouzi skali, le sage de fès', interview for the online magazine *La Vie*, 2896, 1 March 2001, available online at www.gfic.net/pub4/DossierTraitement/Article.asp?id=1 (accessed 23 November 2013).

52 Technically speaking, all those above Hamza with authority to lead ritual *dhikr* and initiate devotees are *muqaddimūn*; it is just that Qustas or Skali are almost never referred to that way. The term is more commonly employed to refer to the leaders of single enclaves and not to those in charge of coordinating various enclaves regionally: Qustas in the US, Skali in (urban) Morocco, Munīr in Europe.

53 As these gatherings are gender-divided, people in the Būdshīshiyya mostly meet members of the same sex only. In some groups, male and female members meet outside ritual gatherings and get to know each other. This gender divide is found in all locations; the implications it had for conducting fieldwork have been addressed in Chapter 1.

54 Considered a religious duty, hospitality pervades Moroccan society (Geertz, 1971: 34); its display is believed to increase the social status of the host.

55 Examples of the saintly aura attributed to some women have been, for instance, studied by Kugle (2007), Nurbakhsh (1990), Smith (1977) and Upton (1988), to mention just a few.

56 Narratives on the collective power attributed to practices of remembrance are included in Chapter 6. Fatiha 50 is a particular passage of the book of prayers used during *dhikr* sessions.

57 My own translation from French.

58 This is often referred to as 'excellence of behaviour', a notion that classical Sufism elaborated around the notion of 'spiritual chivalry' and in connection with which subject Skali translated and commented on (1985) a treatise by Abū ʿAbd-al-Raḥmān al-Sulamī (d. 1021).

59 My own translation from the *ṭarīqa*'s booklet in Spanish *El Libro de la Vía* (2006: 11).

60 In some contingents, disciples read and comment together on Sufi texts after the performance of weekly ritual sessions.
61 My own translation from French of the original *'un islamisme agressif, en marge de la société'*.
62 These 'salvation' narratives evince parallels with the narratives of religious conversion that exist, for example, among Pentecostal Christians (e.g. Engelund, 2013).
63 Ibn 'Aṭā 'Allāh's (d.1309) writings, particularly his aphorisms, are popular among some disciples, as these are sold in the central lodge at affordable prices. There are several translations of Ibn 'Aṭā 'Allāh's works into European languages, notably, those into French by Paul Nwyia.
64 The works of the convert Hamza Yusuf present a similar position against religious extremism. See for example Zebiri (2007: 180–1).
65 Available online at http://news.bbc.co.uk/1/hi/world/europe/6670069.stm (accessed 10 November 2013).

References

Bakewell, O., de Haas, H. and Kubal, A. 2011. 'The Evolution of Moroccan Migration to the UK', Scoping Study Report, International Migration Institute. Oxford: University of Oxford, available online at www.imi.ox.ac.uk/pdfs/research-projects-pdfs/themis-pdfs/themis-scoping-study-morroco (accessed 20 August 2012).

Ben Driss, K. 2002. *Sidi Hamza al-Qadiri Boudchich. Le renouveau du Soufisme au Maroc*. Beirut: Albouraq.

Ben Rochd, E. R. 2002. *Le Soufisme. Patrimoine universel méthode d'epanouissement et doctrine d'harmonie*. Casablanca: Dechra.

Bilgili, Ö. and Weyel, S. 2009. *Migration in Morocco: History, Current Trends and Future Prospects. Migration and Development Country Profiles*. Maastricht: University of Maastricht.

Cesari, J. 2004. *When Islam and Democracy Meet: Muslims in Europe and in the United States*. New York: Palgrave Macmillan.

Coffey, A. 1999. *The Ethnographic Self: Fieldwork and the Representation of Identity*. London: Sage.

Dominguez Diaz, M. 2010a. 'Revisiting Moroccan Sufism and Re-Islamisizing Secular Audiences: Female Religious Narratives in the *ṭarīqa Qādiriyya Būdshīshiyya* in Morocco and Western Europe Today', unpublished PhD thesis. London: University of London, School of Oriental and African Studies.

——2010b. 'Performance, Belonging and Identity: Ritual Variations in the British Qādiriyya', *Religion, State & Society* 39(2–3): 229–45. London: Taylor and Francis.

——2011. 'Shifting Fieldsites: An Alternative Approach to Fieldwork in Transnational Sufism', *Fieldwork in Religion* 6(1): 64–82. London: Equinox.

——2013. 'The One or the Many? Transnational Sufism and Locality in the British Būdshīshiyya', in T. Gabriel and R. Geaves (eds) *Sufism in Britain*, 111–36. London: Continuum/Bloomsbury Academic.

——2014. 'The Būdshīshiyya's Tower of Babel: Cultural Diversity in a Transnational Sufi Order', in S. Mukherjee (ed.) *The Politics of Religion and Language*. London: Sage.

Draper, M. 2002. 'Towards a Postmodern Sufism: Eclecticism, Appropriation and Adaptation in a Naqshbandiyya and a Qadiriyya Tariqa in the UK', unpublished PhD thesis. Birmingham: University of Birmingham.

Eickelman, D. F. 1985. *Knowledge and Power in Morocco: The Education of a Twentieth-century Notable*. Princeton, NJ: Princeton University Press.

El Libro de la Via. 2006. Madrid: Universa Terra.

Engelund, S. R. 2013. 'Salvation and Social Work: Conversions and Charity among Pentecostal Christians in Los Angeles', unpublished masters thesis. Oslo: University of Oslo.

Geertz, C. 1971. *Islam Observed: Religious Development in Morocco and Indonesia*. Chicago, IL: University of Chicago Press.

Gilliat-Ray, S. 1999. 'Rediscovering Islam: A Muslim Journey of Faith', in C. Lamb and M. D. Bryant (eds) *Religious Conversion: Contemporary Practices and Controversies*, 315–32. London: Cassell.

Ḥajjī, Muḥammad, et al. 1992. *Ma'lamāt al-Maghrib*, Vol. 5, 1662–7. Salé: Maṭābi' Salā.

Hermansen, M. 1996. 'In the Garden of American Sufi Movements: Hybrids and Perennials', in P. B. Clarke (ed.) *New Trends and Developments in the World of Islam*, 155–78. London: Luzac.

Jonker, G. 2006. 'The Evolution of the Naqshbandi-Mujaddidi: Sulaymancis in Germany', in J. Hinnells and M. Jamal (eds) *Sufism in the West*, 71–85. London: Routledge Curzon.

Kapchan, D. A. 2008. 'The Promise of Sonic Translation: Performing the Festive Sacred in Morocco', *American Anthropologist* 110(4): 467–83. Hoboken, NJ: Wiley.

Karrar, A. S. 1992. *The Sufi Brotherhoods in the Sudan*. London: Hurst.

Kugle, S. A. 2007. *Sufis and Saints' Bodies. Mysticism, Corporeality and Sacred Power in Islam*. Chapel Hill, NC: University of North Carolina Press.

Lewisohn, L. 2006. 'Persian Sufism in the Contemporary West: Reflections on the Ni'matu'llahi Diaspora', in J. Malik and J. Hinnells (eds) *Sufism in the West*, 49–70. London: Routledge Curzon.

McMurray, David A. 2001. *In and out of Morocco: Smuggling and Migration in a Frontier Boomtown*. Minneapolis, MN: University Minnesota Press.

Malik, A. 2004. *Qu'Allah bénisse la France*. Paris: Albin Michel.

Nurbakhsh, J. 1990. *Sufi Women*, trans. L. Lewisohn. London: Khaniqah-Nimatullahi Publications.

Qadiri Boutchichi, M. 2014.'The Importance of Sufism in an Era of Globalisation', *The Sufi Way*, 5 April.

Qustas, A. 2007. *Nibrās al-Mudīr*. Marrakesh: al-Ahmadi.

Sachs Norris, R. 2003. '"Converting to What?" Embodied Culture and the Adoption of New Beliefs', in A. Buckser and S. D. Glazier (eds) *The Anthropology of Religious Conversion*, 171–81. Lanham, MD: Lexington Books.

Skali, F. 1985. *La voie soufie*. Paris: Albin Michel.

——. 1996. *Traces de lumière: Paroles initiatiques soufies*. Paris: Albin Michel.

——. 1999. *Le face à face des coeurs: Le soufisme aujourd'hui*. Gordes: Editions du Relié.

——. 2004. *Jésus dans la tradition soufie*. Paris: Albin Michel.

Smith, M. 1977. Rabi'a the Mystic and Her Fellow Saints in Islam. San Francisco, CA: Rainbow Press.

Touati, S. 2013. *Literacy, Information, and Development in Morocco during the 1990s*. Lanham, MD: University Press of America.

Upton, C. 1988. Doorkeeper of the Heart: Versions of Rabi'a. Putney, VT: Threshold Books (Simon & Schuster).

Vásquez, M. A. 2011. *More than Belief: A Materialist Theory of Religion*. Oxford: Oxford University Press.
Vitray-Meyerovitch, E. 1972. *Mystique et poésie en Islam: Djalâl-ud-Dîn Rûmî et l'ordre des derviches tourneurs*. Bruges: Desclée de Brouwer.
——. 1978. *Anthologie du soufisme*. Paris: Sindbad.
——. 1984. *La mecque: Ville sainte de l'Islam*. Paris: R. Laffont.
Wallis, R. 1984. *The Elementary Forms of the New Religious Life*. London: Routledge & Kegan Paul.
Werbner, P. 2005. *Pilgrims of Love. The Anthropology of a Global Sufi Cult*. Karachi: Oxford University Press.
Zebiri, K. P. 2007. *British Muslim Converts: Choosing Alternative Lives*. Oxford: Oneworld Publications.

4 Būdshīshiyya Online

More than ten years ago, scholars of religion first noticed a remarkable prevalence of religion in cyberspace, a prevalence that keeps expanding today, and that warned of the possible transformation of some of the defining aspects of religion (see, for instance, Brasher, 2001). Religious groups of all kinds, large and small, consolidated and institutionalized online, and the internet turned into a platform for communicating, interacting with and even performing religion in rather new, distinctive ways. These developments have influenced the Qādiriyya Būdshīshiyya, the internet being not only a tool with great potential for enhancing communication among devotees, but also one whose usage could transform the kind of audiences the *ṭarīqa* could reach, with a potential effect on the order's outreach. Information technologies were not only able to transform its proselytizing potential, they also had a prospective impact on the ways devotees could relate to one another and to the leadership of the *ṭarīqa*.

Although it is true that the Būdshīshiyya would not have been what it is today if it had not been for the coming of the digital era, the scale of the digital impact needs to be fairly evaluated. The internet has decisively contributed to transforming this organization and to making it into a transnational phenomenon, but, by exploring the ways in which this has occurred and the implications it has had, this study suggests that, rather than the grandiloquent perspectives one often finds about the capacity of the internet to transform religion, the Būdshīshiyya evidences a more circumspect scenario. Thus, this book argues that the potential that information technologies have by themselves alone in transforming minority religious choices like the Būdshīshiyya is limited. This more cautious perspective is derived from looking at the digital manifestations of the Būdshīshiyya, not on their own, but from a comparison point of view; that is, by contrasting the portrayal of this *ṭarīqa* by its digital appearance with that obtained by conducting fieldwork beyond the virtual arena. This contrast of offline–online data enhances the opportunity to obtain a more nuanced understanding of the digital as well as of the non-cybernated within this Sufi order.

Although to a certain extent the internet has certainly prompted new forms for religious expression, as it allows people to download religious texts, source information and discuss religion, 'visit' religious places and watch ritual gatherings, the prediction made by a first generation of academics who forecasted a dramatic transformation in religious life provoked by the World Wide Web (e.g. Lochhead, 1997; Zaleski, 1997; Wertheim, 1999) does not hold true for the case of this *ṭarīqa*. In this study I contend that, without denying the internet's great potential for social and religious change, we should not overlook its limitations, either. The case of the Būdshīshiyya is one of coexistence of great changes, prompted to a certain extent by the internet, with the persistence of ways of communicating and relating to religion in a pre-digital fashion.

The Būdshīshiyya may have acquired a transnational dimension of its geographical scale, probably thanks to its presence in cyberspace. The urban explosion and middle-class expansion that took place in Morocco during the 1990s and 2000s was associated with increased access to university education for young people (Vermeren, 2001; Sater, 2007). These social components, together with the doctrinal changes introduced in the order discussed in Chapter 2, contributed to the first wave of expansion of this *ṭarīqa* beyond its original *milieu*. These developments coincide in time with the first and abrupt appearance of the internet in Morocco, with initial restricted access which could only be afforded by a small minority of the population, but with a currently rapidly increasing outreach – some estimates point out that internet use in the Middle East and North Africa is growing at a rate higher than any other place in the world.[1]

Transnationalism and the internet

The vast majority of younger followers of this *ṭarīqa* are regular internet users, yet the effect the internet *per se* has had in attracting new devotees among these youngster audiences in the country is not as great as one might initially expect. Most young Moroccan devotees to whom I have talked know the websites of the order, including the substantial amount of videos broadcasting Būdshīshiyya ritual gatherings accessible on YouTube and the many images of Hamza Būdshīsh; but none seems to have had their first encounter with the *ṭarīqa* online, so the extent to which digital technologies alone are responsible for reaching new audiences needs to be taken cautiously. Worth noticing, however, is that when comparing these attitudes with those of older members, a picture emerges that contrasts a younger generation of Būdshīshiyya followers, literate and regular internet users, with an older, mainly Berber generation with significant rates of illiteracy, and no contact with the digital world. These differences seem to be more generational than regional, with the typically dramatic changes introduced by the digital era having also reached the Rif – younger Berber *fuqarā'* are also active participants in this trend of religious digital devotion as they are, in contrast with their parents, habitual *internauts*.

Interestingly, however, none of the digital content posted by the Būdshīshiyya online are in Berber, a fact that can be seen as illustrative of a variety of factors. On the one hand, despite the fact that the mother tongue of the majority of these devotees is Riffian Berber, there is a tendency to associate Islam with Arabic;[2] since these devotees are good *connoisseurs* of Arabic anyway (because they have been schooled in this language), they access the materials of the order posted online in Arabic. On the other hand, and despite efforts to introduce the learning of Berber into the schooling system,[3] most of the young Berbers I have spoken with still seem to think of Berber as an oral language. In most cases they are more fluent writers/readers of *fuṣḥā*[4] than they are of Berber.[5] There is yet another element that seems to matter significantly: the preference for using *fuṣḥā* together with European languages in the digital materials produced by this *ṭarīqa* attests also to the contentious disassociation of the order's identity with those in the country claiming the preservation of Berber identity. Given the public pro-monarchy stance of the *ṭarīqa*, and since *la Berbérité* is a highly contentious political issue in Morocco, there seems to be an intended move by the Būdshīshiyya's leadership not to be seen as associated with it.[6]

In any case, the languages chosen by the leadership of the order to present their materials online are *fuṣḥā* and European languages – most of them are in English, Spanish, French, Italian and Romanian – which can be read as indicative of an attempt to reach wider audiences. The case of the Būdshīshiyya attests that cyberspace is certainly a tool for spreading information more efficiently than by using traditional means, which could in turn be a good catalyst for a transnational spread. One easily becomes aware of that when speaking with devotees: whereas most have read and many are familiar with at least some of the content published by the *ṭarīqa*'s leadership and by fellow *fuqarā'*, significantly lower is the number of devotees who have read a printed book authored by the leadership of the *ṭarīqa* or by a follower of Hamza Būdshīsh.[7]

The internet has brought about the potential of reaching more people; Hamza's texts and the order's worldviews and approaches to Islam have been made available online in various languages, and have been widely accessed by followers and by potential members. At www.saveurs-soufies.com/ one can see the number of visitors currently online, and the cypher can fluctuate, depending on the day, between the one and two hundreds. Internet portals produced by the *ṭarīqa*'s leadership offer the chance of free access to texts akin to the Būdshīshiyya's philosophy, made available to devotees and also to people who are not part of the movement.

This has proven to be a tool for encouraging people's interest in the order with the ultimate potential of their eventually joining the group. In a similar vein, Būdshīshiyya's digital materials have helped to consolidate the presence of the *ṭarīqa* in the West's religious landscape of Sufi groups and New Age religions. European 'spiritual seekers' and followers, as well as those sympathetic to other Sufi orders, have thus come to know this *ṭarīqa* due to its presence online. During the course of this research I have come across people on several occasions for whom the Būdshīshiyya rang a bell due to its online existence – they have never met a member, yet they knew of its existence though the World Wide Web. One can fairly argue that the Būdshīshiyya's web presence has given the order a space in the map of religious choices available online, so the internet of course presents major potential, an opportunity for people with no prior knowledge of this organization to get in contact with them; its digital presence could potentially come to be a springboard to people with no prior knowledge of the Būdshīshiyya to end up joining the *ṭarīqa*.

A minority religious organization and its online appearance

Considering that small religious groups often have problems in making their voices heard, the internet has great potential for them. It allows groups such as the Būdshīshiyya, which can be considered marginal, alternative or, for some, even 'deviant', simply to express themselves. In this sense, 'the Internet is a non-hierarchical environment: all points of view, from the most orthodox to the most atypical or heretical, appear in exact the same manner in the computer screen' (Cesari, 2004: 120–1). In this way, minority religions have found a space to actively participate in the phenomenon of religious revival to the extent that we see today, such that many of these new digital expressions of religious life are produced by members of minority religions. Their participation in the emergence of new, reinvigorated forms of religiosity through the World Wide Web has been stressed by scholars devoted to the study of religious revivalism in Muslim countries as well as in Western Europe.[8]

One effect that the presence of small religious groups online can have is that, due to their active participation, one can get the impression that they are actually much bigger than they really are. This is clear in the case of the *ṭarīqa* this study analyses. The prolific activity of Būdshīshiyya's pages, chats, forums, newsgroups and blogs can easily be taken as evidence of an organization more sizeable than it actually is. It really takes the work of only a small team to build a well-filled website. When looking at most of the websites of the order, one may get the impression that they form the portal of a well-established, widely followed religious organization when, in reality, the *ṭarīqa* outside Morocco may be quite small. What we see online, by contrast, is more frantic activity: the official website in Spanish, for example, www.tariqa.org/espanol/, together with a plethora of websites of communities labelled under the rubric of 'cultural associations', e.g. l'associació cultural Qantara at www.qantara.es/Benvinguda.html (in Catalan); and la asociación cultural Halaqa at http://alhalaqa.org/ (in Spanish), are all designed and run by a very small group of people, fewer than ten. By contrast, each of these sites gives the impression of being run by and representing a much more sizeable following. Choosing to build various sites instead of adding all the materials into one single portal gives the false impression of the existence of a multiplicity of 'organizations', each of them with their own members, suggesting consequently a much more sizeable following overall, when in reality all these various groups with their different names are just one.

Similarly, the order in the UK, with enclaves attended in many cases by fewer than ten people, has, by contrast, an impressive presence in cyberspace. There is what seems to be the official site, www.tariqa.org/qadiriya/index.html, but there are also other very similar sites portraying themselves as being the site of the order in the UK, e.g. www.sufiway.net/, http://thesufiway.co.uk/, and www.deenislam.co.uk/sufinotes/overview.html, among others. These portals do all refer to a small group of followers, yet the variety of sites misleadingly gives the impression that there is a much wider following.

One can perhaps think of this as a 'strategy' for proselytization, as one may also do when the Birmingham group is presented as a 'charity' and in which there is a lack of recognition of any sign of religious allegiance. Their website, called *The Zawiya*, http://thezawiya.co.uk/, defines itself by making no reference to the *ṭarīqa* at all, neither to the religious, nor Islamic, nor Sufi character of the organization:

> Over 20 years ago a group of students and young professionals, from different backgrounds, came together to improve the life chances of young people living in central Birmingham. What began as an informal community association then developed into a registered charity called the Amina Trust. The next priority was to purchase premises to develop and consolidate the activities of the Trust. A derelict community hall was then acquired and renovated over a period of two years. The building is called the 'Zawiya' as this is a word that denotes tranquillity, knowledge and enlightenment. These are values that we endeavour to give expression to across the range of our activities. The Zawiya as well as being the venue for our own community education and development activities also hosts activities and projects linked to a range of public and voluntary sector organizations that share our values and priorities.

The ambiguity in the way the organization presents itself can be read as an attempt to attract Europeans from secularized environments that may tend to think of religion in rather negative terms. Similarly, by depicting an image of a proactive organization that engages in 'activities' with a 'range of organizations' the impression is given of being presented with a bigger group, also one with a participative approach in civil society rather than with a more 'anti-Western', disenfranchised understanding of Muslim social values and mores within European contexts.

The distorted image in terms of the size of the organization could not have been more accurately scaled unless the data were to be contrasted with that obtained by conducting fieldwork in offline settings.[9] I myself fell into this misconception: in searching for the order online prior to my fieldwork, I thought I was looking at a more sizeable *ṭarīqa*. Besides, by surfing the net one comes to think of the Būdshīshiyya as a *ṭarīqa* widely followed by Westerners, or even mainly as a form of 'Western Sufism'. This is because most of its internet output is in French, closely followed by content in English. This picture of a 'European order' becomes debunked once one attends one of the Būdshīshiyya's 'international' gatherings, for example, with estimates of Moroccan visitors in Madāgh being in the scale of the hundreds of thousands, whereas the following from the rest of the world is not more than a thousand. A very similar picture of the proportions of Moroccans and non-Moroccans in this *ṭarīqa* is obtained from the rest of the fieldwork I have conducted among the *fuqarā'* from the various locations.

Thus, Europeans and North Americans account for an, albeit 'digitally', outspoken, numerically negligible minority within the organization. Thence the diverse types of relationship with internet devotees need also to be considered: it is one thing to access materials online, and another to post, discuss and engage with those materials in a more proactive manner. Among European devotees, for example, there seem to be a more substantial number of 'creators' of digital content, whereas among Moroccans there seem to be many more who are only 'consumers'. The more participatory attitude of the European *internauts* contributes to a misleading picture in which they appear over-represented. It needs to be said, nonetheless, that there is also the possibility that some of the content in European languages, especially in French, could have been produced and posted by Moroccans from Morocco. Last but not least, the Berbers, who are by far the most sizeable subgroup in this organization, show less proclivity to online expression and participation, whereas those with the more *intellectualized* forms of religious identity that exist within the *ṭarīqa*, whether from Morocco's urban middle classes or from abroad, tend to be more inclined to use the internet both to read and write about religion.

Reaching new audiences through the World Wide Web?

The more consolidated presence online of the Būdshīshiyya's portals in European languages can be interpreted as if the internet is intentionally used as a tool for proselytization in this Sufi order. From what I have observed, the *ṭarīqa*'s missionary goal seems to be much stronger beyond the Rif region where it originated, which seems to coincide (although it needs to be proved whether these two issues are connected) with the more intense activity of the sites produced in European languages. As seen above with the case of *The Zawiya* website, the narratives of self-representation used in some of the portals may be perceived as 'strategies' for attracting non-Muslims. In some instances the appeal for new members is very evident:

> Today the spiritual master is looking without condition for new disciples, the relationship between the master and the disciple has also been

> transformed, in the past it was the disciple who sought the master, now it is the master who seeks out the disciple.[10]

Yet, having a missionary agenda does not necessarily mean having a successful one, two things often mistaken for each other. So, by taking the opportunity to contrast online data with that obtained by conducting fieldwork, one can analyse the degree of success that using the internet to attract new devotees may have, and the findings were, at least to me, surprising. According to what I could see among the people I have talked to in this study, very few devotees, only one in fifteen, approach the order without knowing anyone related to the organization and then only after consulting information about this *ṭarīqa* online.

However, in most cases the first time devotees heard about the order was through someone they knew and not just by merely surfing the net. So, personal networks still work in a significantly more efficient way than the internet does in leading to the initial call. Many of those who decided to attend a gathering first knew of the existence of the group through a friend, or on exceptional occasions, through a family member. This is then afterwards supported by searching for the group online to get an idea of who they are; as one former *faqīra* put it, '[I checked their website before going to meet them] to get reassurance that they were normal people, not a bunch of crazy people or of Muslim extremists'. In most cases, the internet serves as a support by providing information: people gain a sense of 'security', of a 'reliability' that contributes to consolidating the interest of the person in the *ṭarīqa*. It is actually rare to meet people who knew absolutely no one in the organization, which calls into question the relative success of the internet in attracting new people to the *ṭarīqa*.

Quite clearly, the internet creates opportunities for a greater freedom of religious expression, particularly in relation to minority religions such as the Būdshīshiyya, and propitiates much better conditions and a wider access to their activities. The success of the internet in propitiating conversion and reversion by itself, without serving as a support to more traditionally held ways of proselytizing, has not yet occurred in this Sufi order. This resonates with the results of other research done on proselytizing minority religions, which concludes that the internet has not yet produced any instance of successful mass proselytization (Mayer, 2009).

I would argue that, in fact, the relatively prominent presence of the Būdshīshiyya in cyberspace needs to be related not to *da'wa* alone, as we have seen, but to the increasing need of the order to communicate with a particular type of devotee by using this medium. The internet generates distinctive ways of communication between the leadership and the devotees; it transmits ideas in a clear and organized manner. Despite the emphasis on the 'experiential' and the acknowledged interest in not communicating verbally to its disciples its religious principles, which has been discussed in Chapter 3, the *ṭarīqa* is involved in creating and posting large amounts of materials online that are illustrative of the leadership's opinions, worldviews and religious identity. In a way, those devotees who regularly consume these digital productions have a more *intellectualized* relationship with their leaders than the rest of the followers; these texts speak about who their leaders are and what they think, and, on occasion, seem to answer questions that these (mainly Western) followers consider fundamental to sealing their allegiance to the order. Other devotees, including, but not only, the vast majority of rural followers of Hamza Būdshīsh in north-eastern Morocco, do not give importance to these more intellectual queries and have a relationship to Sufism centred on religious *praxis*. However, such emphasis on religious performance alone is beginning to be challenged by a new generation; the rapid increase of (also digital) literacy rates among younger Moroccans could put an end to the monopoly of the embodied over the word in the Būdshīshiyya's matters of identity, but is yet to be seen if this would actually be the case.

On a worldwide scale the Būdshīshiyya seems to have entered the race to gain wider representation on the net. Aware of the need to be prepared to serve the religious needs of a generation that is likely to rely on the internet as a major source of information, the order has exerted efforts to make available online materials in various languages about the *ṭarīqa* and its leader. Thus, the official web pages of the order in Arabic (www.tariqa.org/ar/index.php), English (www.sufiway.net/), French (www.saveurs-soufies.com/), Spanish (www.tariqa.org/espanol/index.php), and Italian (www.tariqa.org/it/index.php) contain materials in line with the *ethos* of this *ṭarīqa*.[11] In an organization of a transnational nature in which non-Berber followers live thousands of kilometres away from the central lodge, the internet provides an efficient means of providing free information in a way that is easy to access.

The *re-textualization* of Būdshīshiyya's Sufism?

Throughout this book I have defended the need to re-centre the object of study in the analysis of religious phenomena by proposing a move away from the relevance traditionally attributed to religious texts and ideas in favour of the study of the situated, socially and culturally contingent scrutiny of religious embodiment(s). I argue, in line with Vásquez's theories on non-reductive materialism (2011), that religious identity is better understood by looking at the ways in which people manifest it, an argument in favour of prioritizing the scrutiny of embodiment, emplacement, practice, and material culture in the study of religion, at the expense of texts and a more abstract, less dependent-upon-context approach to beliefs and ideas. The focus on situated religious *praxis* and embodiment seems to be particularly adequate when applied to the Būdshīshiyya, as this order in its entirety, from the leadership to the majority of its disciples, places far more importance on the experiential and the sensorial than it does on the textual and the intellectual.

Departing from a rationalistic understanding of Sufism is an explicit command given by Hamza Būdshīsh to his followers, who are urged to minimize their relation to the written and the discursive; *fuqarā'* are prompted to 'experience' Sufism *instead* of 'reading' about Sufism.[12] In the official narratives of the order, the intellectual and the experiential are often portrayed as antithetical approaches to pursuing the spiritual quest, the intellectual being commonly portrayed as an obstacle to the attainment of the Truth, to be reached through the experiential. Accordingly, Hamza Būdshīsh's sayings assert that:

> Understanding is not acquired through books. It would be too easy to lower oneself and collect all the books written about Sufism in order to acquire such understanding. True knowledge comes to you from inside, from your heart, only the heart can truly understand that nothing is outside God.

Besides, a justification of the non-verbal character of the relationship between devotee and *shaykh* is provided:

> He who understands the value of the shaykh knows that his relationship with him does not require exchange of words. You see me. I see you and that is ample and bountiful. […] Verbal teaching is not necessary. It is only the transformation of hearts which is important. Sidi Boumadiane, Sidi Hamza's own master and shaykh, only rarely spoke.[13]

In line with this, Hamza himself opts for a mainly non-discursive style, a leadership framed in terms of physicality and not in relation to speech. Thus, followers are counselled to visit the *shaykh,* to get imbued with his *baraka* by being in the presence of the considered-a-saint's body, be touched by him, and looked at by him. As it is this corporeal dimension that gives him authority and not the addressing of disciples verbally, he is very rarely seen speaking to the public; nor does he give sermons, and nor does he publish books. The quotes presented above are excerpts taken from the only written piece he is said to have authored, a text of fewer than three thousand words containing sayings attributed to him.

Prima facie, one has to wonder what kinds of relationship a religious group with this openly acknowledged 'anti-textualism' can develop with information technologies, considering this is a medium oriented centrally, if not exclusively, to presenting messages in the form of 'texts'. If 'texts' are created and consumed by members of the Būdshīshiyya, it is thence paramount to question what effect the digital direction is having on the experiential approach to religion proposed by the order's leadership – i.e. whether the use of the internet is generating 're-textualizing' trends in this *ṭarīqa.* A first consideration to be looked at is the seeming oxymoron that exists between the leadership's suggestion in favour of 'experiencing' instead of 'reading' about Sufism. In the context of supervising the content of the Būdshīshiyya's websites, the leaders of the order seem to somehow be accepting and bending towards a more text-reliant way of approaching Sufism. Even some in the upper echelon (with the exception of Hamza) nowadays author materials posted on the *ṭarīqa*'s websites – see, for instance, a text entitled *The Importance of Sufism in an Era of Globalisation,* by Hamza's grandson Mūnir,[14] or an interview with Skali conducted *à propos* of a colloquium on 'Sufism in contemporary society'.[15]

One might think that this is an undesired consequence of something the order's leadership simply had to face – namely, the fact that, with the spread of internet use, followers will inevitably turn to cyberspace to express their religious views, inexorably becoming consumers of texts dealing with Sufism. This being an inescapable outcome, the *ṭarīqa*'s *dirigeants* feel impelled, perhaps, to control what it is said in their name by monitoring the content of the sites produced by members of the order. This control, along with the creation of content, could be seen as the leadership's attempt to retain followers in the *ṭarīqa,* with it becoming a major risk that devotees who are consumers of the digital output of other groups end up joining another order. By monitoring and creating online content they do not entirely overcome this challenge, yet they give to Hamza's sympathizers a distinctively Būdshīshi set of texts, a clear identity line on the Sufi-related themes that raise more interest online – e.g. the 'peaceful' character of Sufism, 'Spirituality' in Islam, Sufi music and so forth.[16]

Online imagery and religious charisma

Even though the official line adopted by the Būdshīshiyya often presents 'text' and 'experience' as antithetical – with the motto of 'experiencing' instead of 'reading' about Sufism' – in reality, reading Sufi texts, or at least the digital materials consumed by followers of this order, does not seem to diminish the devotees' interest in 'experiencing' Sufism, i.e. participating in rituals, visiting Hamza and so forth. Despite the potential appeal for *'re-textualising'* Sufism that comes with information technologies, the identity in this *ṭarīqa* still mainly revolves around ritual praxis and the religious charisma corporeally endorsed by the leader. In fact, not only is the internet not contributing to playing down a more physical approach to Sufism, but it often serves as a platform to strengthen it.

The World Wide Web is showing itself to be a powerful tool for strengthening the mechanisms for reinforcing religious charisma and to firming a notion of leadership developed around the physical image of Hamza Būdshīsh. This form of highly personalized, intense, expressive, and emotional charismatic veneration has found a place of reinvigoration on the internet, with images and videos of the saint proliferating successfully on the net. While not all members of the order are regular consumers of online texts or materials posted or related to this *ṭarīqa,* many more seem to be regular watchers of videos and downloaders of images of the *shaykh.* There is, especially among the younger members, a great deal of sharing and exchanging of digital imagery of this kind, perhaps on a more extended scale than there is interest in the texts – type 'Sidi Hamza' into Google images and a noteworthy 26,800 results will come up, and results on YouTube number 994; this is without considering all the related images and videos that appear from typing related terms in different spellings such as 'Boutchichiya', 'Madagh', and so forth.

This iconographic devotion has not come entirely as a result of the use of the internet, but just came about to buttress an already existing pattern: the homes of Būdshīshiyya's devotees are often decorated with pictures of Hamza Būdshīsh, and the success of the shop at the central lodge that sells rosaries and images of the saint and his family also attests to this devotional furore. Hamza's charisma gives him a power undoubtedly based on the attainment of *baraka*, and is thus endowed by the saintly blessings' own qualities and not by rational considerations. At a more practical level, for Būdshīshiyya's devotees images are important; they evoke the personal qualities of the *shaykh* and are central in articulating their religious devotion. For this purpose, the internet has allowed the maintenance of powerful charismatic long-distance relationships in unprecedented ways. In some cases, the internet may be even be fully responsible for creating this devotional relationship, as some of those sharing images and videos have in fact never seen the *shaykh* personally.

Thus, online videos and images of Hamza have made possible the existence of a new type of *shaykh*-disciple relationship. A devotee who stores in her phone many images of the leader, despite having never visited Madāgh, told me she would still accord relevance to personal encounters and suggested that '*baraka* is transmitted with more force face-to-face', but that being able to access these images and videos made her feel closer to him. The case nonetheless highlights the centrality of studying modern technologies to an understanding of modern Sufi sainthood, as the internet frequently contributes to increasing the radius of charismatic influence and to the efficient promotion of charisma on the religious market, as Bilu and Ben-Ari (1992) long ago suggested.

More recently, Campbell (2010) has argued that the marketing of pictures though the internet may increase the charisma of a religious leader. This kind of charismatic relationship sharply contrasts yet coexists with the far less technologically advanced, more geographically restricted influence of Sufi *shaykhs* in relation to their original *milieux*, an online–offline dichotomy also present among Būdshīshiyya devotees. It seems that Berber disciples from north-eastern Morocco are less prone to consuming online imagery than devotees from other places. This evidences the plasticity of the Būdshīshiyya, an interesting case of a modern Sufi order that knows well how to employ long-standing symbolic religious codes in achieving charismatic goals by using new technologies that permit the transposing of charismatic relations in the current globalizing context.

The challenges of a virtual epoch

Information technology has been shown to benefit the Būdshīshiyya in various ways, even if the missionary possibilities attached to it may not have been fully achieved. Yet, as we have seen in the section 'Online imagery and religious charisma', the effect the internet has had in contributing to enhancing the transnational outreach of this organization does not come without a price: the challenges faced by the very presence of the order online are also to be weighted as part of the broader picture.

The first aspect to be noticed is related to the monitoring of digital content. The materials contained in the official sites of the *ṭarīqa* are highly regulated by the leadership; simple devotees, for example, cannot post their messages freely. Instead, those interested in contributing need to send their texts to regional leaders, who will then make decisions on whether to post them or not. More casual exchanges, such as issues discussed on forums, are open to the public for readership, but participation is restricted and has to be approved by the *muqaddimāt*. Despite this, a rich diversity of unregulated content on the Būdshīshiyya mushrooms online day by day, and the organization can certainly do nothing to diminish the visibility of more critical views on this *ṭarīqa.*

It is not only a question of critics: a challenge is also posed by the vast amount of material on Sufism posted by other religious organizations, which underlines the fact that, while the internet might have facilitated the transmission of religious knowledge to small and geographically scattered religious contingents within a given organization, it has also imposed the necessity of dealing with a greater pressure as it increases or at least makes more visible the rivalry between the various religious groups existing in a given 'religious market'. The internet makes available information on a wide variety of other Sufi groups and makes devotees more aware of the market of religious choices in which the Būdshīshiyya exists. Minority religions exist in competitive contexts along with a variety of other religious options and the internet makes devotees fully aware of that competition.

Nowadays, and largely because of the internet, it becomes more difficult to regulate what followers come to know about the order and about other religious groups. During the course of this study I came across various ex-devotees who say they abandoned the group due to information they discovered on the internet about the order[17] – one even declared the internet to be responsible for her leaving the organization as well as becoming affiliated to another *ṭarīqa*, the Naqshbandiyya. The rather intermittent nature of people's commitment to the order can be further exacerbated by the challenge that, in this sense, the internet poses to the organization. On the other hand, disaffiliation as a result of accessing information online is something relatively common among members of minority religions (Mayer, 2000).

These dynamics evidence the somehow more democratic character of the internet, a *milieu* in which opinions of all types can in principle be openly expressed. In relation to the Būdshīshiyya, the democratic character of cyberspace is particularly crucial in reference to Morocco, a country in which freedom of speech and press is sometimes still a struggle. The public profile the *ṭarīqa* has acquired in the country, because of its more recent political involvement, has caused it to gain fervent supporters as well as furious enemies, a heated ideological battle that, although it is more openly manifested online than in other media, is restricted as well in many of its digital appearances.

There has been a sustained practice by the Moroccan Government of blocking access to sites whose content has been deemed to be anti-royalist or supportive of the Western Sahara cause, or taking any form that could be considered 'religious extremism'. It is thus expected that more criticisms would have been voiced if those restrictions had not been in place. Nonetheless, and despite censorship, a lot of the more critical online material on the order does come from Moroccans. In this sense, it is interesting to see that the tension with other Sufi organizations – a subject of more concern to European audiences – is almost imperceptible online; the number of critical voices online that do come from European devotees of other Sufi groups is minimal compared to criticisms raised by Moroccans, who criticize either what they see as cultic characteristics of this *ṭarīqa*, or its role in national politics. It may well be that some of the sites are accessible from Europe but blocked in Morocco.

The internet and the reality of migration have both provided platforms able to effectively surpass the limits of traditional censorship, whether this limit on expression is latent in the media and imposed by the government, or is more informally endorsed by cultural codes of social correction. During the course of my fieldwork, although some of the people with whom I talked in Morocco openly expressed their views without hesitation, others were reluctant to discuss their ideas with a stranger. For example, in the region surrounding the central lodge, some of those who were more critical of the Būdshīshiyya expressed their views in a rather secretive manner; they often did not want to talk about these things in the street and invited me to their homes, away from the scrutiny of neighbours. This cautious attitude contrasts with what one finds when speaking to Moroccans living in Europe, as well as with some of the views that are presented online but possibly only accessible from outside the country.

The increased relevance of minority religious choices in cyberspace could somehow contribute to building a distorted image of these groups; whatever the case, this highlights the need for qualifying research findings on religious groups on the net with data obtained 'in the field'. The combination of both gives us a more accurate and realistic picture of the size of religious organizations. A comparative perspective of the online and offline appearance of this *ṭarīqa* suggests that the portrayal of the order online can somehow be misleading. However, such biases are suggestive of aspects of which further scrutiny, I contend, is relevant in contextualizing our study, the internet being, thus, one more locus that needs to be considered within the multidimensional geography of the order. The Būdshīshiyya online seems to be a larger organization than it actually is; this is particularly the case in reference to the materials posted in European languages, of which there is a prolific output if compared with the size of the organization in the West.

These efforts to consolidate a strong presence in cyberspace can be viewed, however, as less successful missionary attempts, with most members having met the order via offline social networks. The internet has seemingly not had in itself a central role in attracting new people to the organization; on the contrary, it may have prompted instances of disaffiliation by opening up an easy-to-access window for the criticisms directed towards the group. When judged by its online presence, the order seems also to have a larger proportion of Europeans than it actually does, with Berber identity being largely under-represented on the World Wide Web, which provides glimpses of how *la Berbérité* is negotiated in the Moroccan social, religious and political landscape. Besides, it seems clear that the order's over-representation in European languages serves a function in terms of consolidating the *ṭarīqa*'s presence in the West's landscape of Sufi groups. It also helps to meet the leadership's need to communicate a clearly defined religious identity to some of their followers outside Morocco. The upper hierarchy's participation in cyberspace may be indicative of an incipient introduction of a more *textualized* approach to religion prompted by the digital era, although the 'experiential' understanding of religion not only prevails but seems also to have been further reinforced by the arrival of information technologies, with, for example, the new phenomenon of promoting online charisma opening up fascinating new fields for scholarly inquiry into the interplay of religion and the internet.

Notes

1 Internet World Statistics, 'Middle East Internet Usage and Marketing Report' available online at www.Internetworldstats.com/me/Reports.htm (accessed 21 April 2012). Access to the internet in the Mediterranean Muslim area is limited and unevenly distributed. The expectation is that, over the next decade, access will grow dramatically as Robertson (2003: 15) once predicted. The internet market shows strong trends of growth; in 2001, internet users in Morocco accounted for 1.4% of the population, whereas in 2008 they accounted for 32.98% – 10,300,000 people (CIA World Factbook). Despite the encouraging evolution of recent years it should be noted that most users still live in urban areas.

2 It is not only scholarship but also religious matters, more broadly, that are generally dealt with in *fuṣḥā* throughout the Arab world, whereas spoken versions of Arabic and of other Middle Eastern languages are left for communicating about subjects socially considered of less importance. The sociolinguistic dimensions of this functional diglossia have been analysed by Albirini (2011).

3 In 2003, the Berber language was for the first time introduced as a subject for all students in public primary schools in Morocco. This language policy has been assessed by El Aissati, Karsmakers and Kurvers (2011).

4 *Fuṣḥā* is the formal and standardized written version of Arabic. It substantially differs from the spoken versions of Arabic that exist throughout the Arab world. The regional oral varieties are often learnt at home and form Arabs' native language, while the formal language is subsequently learnt in school.

5 Berber has predominantly been maintained throughout the years and transmitted orally with a weak and heterogeneous process of standardization of its dialects' writing system. The original alphabet in which Berber was written is known as the *Tifinagh* writing system. In 2003 a modernized version of this alphabet, used by

Berbers before the switch first into Arabic script and later Latin characters, was made official in Morocco. Nevertheless, and despite attempts to promote it, its usage is still quite limited, with the result that Berber languages are still largely oral, and, when written, use of Latin characters seems still to be the overriding trend.

6 However, further analysis would be needed to clarify the causes and consequences of this seemingly intentional dissociation. For an analysis of the actual state of affairs between the Berber movement and the state, see Maddy-Weitzman (2013).

7 For further information on the Būdshīshiyya's literary output, see Chapter 3.

8 One of the first studies, yet still one of the most complete produced so far, on the impact of the internet on Islam is Bunt (2000). A good collection of essays on the revival of religions thanks to the World Wide Web is by Dawson and Cowan (2004).

9 Even by contrasting digital appearance with fieldwork data, the fluid membership of the order makes accurately estimating the size of this *ṭarīqa* a very difficult enterprise; for further analysis, please refer to Chapters 1 and 3.

10 Available online at www.yanabi.com/index.php?/topic/253430-sayyid-shaykh-sidi-hamza-al-qadiri-boudshishi/ (accessed 13 January 2014).

11 The teachings of certain Sufi orders (e.g. Naqshbandiyya, the Sufi order International of Inayat Khan) are considered 'deviant' by the Būdshīshiyya's authorities and members are recommended to distance themselves from people from these other organizations. Most of these 'deviant' groups are seen as eclectic and thus un-Islamic; many are transnational orders with a stronger presence in Europe than the Būdshīshiyya. However, others, equally transnational and as big as the Būdshīshiyya in size, but with a similar cultural background, and with a religious ethos similar to that of the Būdshīshiyya (e.g. 'Alāwiyya), are seen as friendly orders. Būdshīshiyya's followers are encouraged to read 'Alāwī texts (e.g. Lings, 1971) and to befriend 'Alāwī devotees, though it is not permitted to attend their religious gatherings.

12 However, several are the contingents that hold collective reading sessions in which Sufi texts are discussed. On these, see also Chapter 3.

13 Quotes available online at www.sufiway.net/sec2=edcu=TQsaying811326.html#sid (accessed 21 June 2013).

14 Available online at www.sufiway.net/ar_Sufism_SidiMounir_ISEG.html (accessed 12 July 2013).

15 Available online at www.tariqa.org/rp/entretien1.php (accessed 12 July 2013).

16 An example of this can be seen in the headings by which the website of *Saveurs Soufies* is organized: *'Islam, religion de paix'*; *'Soufisme, voix d'amour et de beauté'*; *'La spiritualité coeur de l'Islam'*; *'sama'* and so on. Available online at http://saveurs-soufies.com/islam-&-soufisme/ (accessed 12 July 2013).

17 From newspaper articles (e.g. www.mafhoum.com/press10/298S28.htm [accessed 21 December 2009]) to forums contrasting Sufi *vs* Salafi positions (e.g. www.yabiladi.com/forum/read-2-748654-page=2.html [accessed 21 December 2009]).

References

Albirini, A. 2011. 'The Sociolinguistic Functions of Codeswitching between Standard Arabic and Dialectical Arabic', *Language in Society* 40(5): 537–62. London: Cambridge University Press.

Bilu, Y. and Ben-Ari, E. 1992. 'The Making of Modern Saints: Manufactured Charisma and the Abu-Hatseiras of Israel', *American Ethnologist* 19(4): 672–87. Arlington, VA: American Anthropological Association.

Brasher, B. E. 2001. *Give Me that Online Religion*. San Francisco, CA: Jossey-Bass.

Bunt, G. R. 2000. *Virtually Islamic: Computer-mediated Communication and Cyber Islamic Environments*. Cardiff: University of Wales Press.

Campbell, H. A. 2010. 'Religious Authority and the Blogosphere', *Journal of Computer-Mediated Communication* 15(2): 251–76. Oxford: Blackwell.

Cesari, J. 2004. *When Islam and Democracy Meet: Muslims in Europe and in the United States*. New York: Palgrave Macmillan.

Dawson, L. L. and Cowan, D. E. 2004. *Religion Online: Finding Faith on the Internet*. New York: Routledge.

El Aissati, A., Karsmakers, S. and Kurvers, J. 2011. '"We Are All Beginners": Amazigh in Language Policy and Educational Practice in Morocco', *Compare: A Journal of Comparative and International Education* 41(2): 211–27. Chicago, IL: Comparative and International Education Society.

Lings, M. 1971. *A Sufi Saint of the Twentieth Century: Shaik Ahmad al-Alawī: His Spiritual Heritage and Legacy*. London: Allen and Unwin.

Lochhead, D. 1997. *Shifting Realities: Information Technology and the Church*. Geneva: World Council of Churches (WCC).

Maddy-Weitzman, B. 2013. 'The Amazigh Factor: State–Movement Relations under Mohammed VI', in B. Maddy-Weitzman and D. Zisenwine (eds) *Contemporary Morocco: State, Politics and Society under Mohammed VI*, 109–19. London: Routledge.

Mayer, J-F. 2000. 'Religious Movements and the Internet. The New Frontier of Cult Controversies', in D. E.Cowan and J. K. Hadden (eds) *Religion on the Internet: Research Prospects and Promises*, 249–76. New York: JAI Press.

——2009. 'Religion and the Internet. The Global Marketplace', in E. Barker, J. A. Beckford and J. T. Richardson. 2003. *Challenging Religion: Essays in Honour of Eileen Barker*, 32–41. London: Routledge.

Robertson, R. T. 2003. *The Three Waves of Globalization: A History of a Developing Global Consciousness*. Halifax, NS: Fernwood Publications.

Sater, J. N. 2007. *Civil Society and Political Change in Morocco*. London: Routledge.

Vásquez, Manuel A. 2011. *More than Belief: A Materialist Theory of Religion*. Oxford: Oxford University Press.

Vermeren, P. 2001. *Le Maroc en transition*. Paris: Découverte.

Wertheim, M. 1999. *The Pearly Gates of Cyberspace: A History of Space from Dante to the Internet*. New York: W.W. Norton.

Zaleski, J. P. 1997. *The Soul of Cyberspace: How New Technology is Changing our Spiritual Lives*. San Francisco, CA: Harper Edge.

5 *Ziyāra*[1]

Veneration of *awliyā' 'Allāh*[2] and tomb worshipping are very widespread practices in Islam. Enacted throughout the Muslim World, from South to West Asia, from North to South Africa, these devotional acts are performed in concomitance with a particular form of Muslim pilgrimage (*ziyāra*). Literally meaning 'visit', *ziyāra* is a ritual journey undertaken to sites marked with saintly aura. *Baraka* is conveyed to the territorial landmarks by either living or dead saints; in fact, when alive, the actual body of the saint constitutes in itself one of these markers. These locales are *ziyāra*'s final destination, and, around them, festivals attracting thousands that last up to several days are organized. Sufis attach great importance to *ziyāra*; within the Būdshīshiyya, *ziyāra* constitutes one of the most important performative acts in the lives of *fuqarā'* – to the extent that even some devotees do not seem to ever go on *ḥajj*, thus *de facto* 'replacing' it as one of the canonical duties. *Ziyāra* is pivotal in the construction of a sense of group identity among Hamza's followers. It embodies the social structure that sustains internal relationships within the *ṭarīqa* and fully displays the meanings attached to the world of Sufi ritual.

This chapter explores religious journeying among the female members of the Būdshīshiyya. By looking at a compelling example of modern *ziyāra*, I discuss a variety of aspects of the annual visit of followers of Hamza to the central lodge in Madāgh, in north-eastern Morocco; particular attention is paid to the variety of meanings given by different female devotees to *ziyāra*. The festival is said to bring different peoples together; a journalist that reported on the event said about the visitors:

> They arrive, they are all there, the murids [*sic*], the *fuqarā'*, the ones aspiring to become, those full of hope, the desperate, men and women from everywhere in Morocco and from beyond the seas, of all ages, all colours, of all kinds. It is brutal, this little silent corner of l'Oriental is transformed into a mini-Benares (the Mecca of Indians) as a foreign *faqīr* called it.[3]

A central idea invoked both by attendees at the festival and by scholars on religion (e.g. Turner and Turner, 1978) is that pilgrimages make the impossible come true by bringing disparate peoples together and creating a sense of communal solidarity unique to the pilgrimage context – one, it is claimed, that has the power to mitigate economic, social and cultural differences. Part of the chapter is devoted to analysing these portraits from a critical angle, as well as *vis-à-vis* fieldwork material.

In today's Būdshīshiyya, *ziyāra* are held to celebrate the *Mawlid an-Nabī*. More commonly referred to simply as *Mawlid*, this is one of the major events in the calendar of *fuqarā'*, consisting of an entire week of celebrations at the central lodge in Madāgh. Held during the third month of the Islamic calendar *(rabi' al-awwal)*, it commemorates the birthday of the prophet Muḥammad. The *Mawlid* is an increasingly popular festival. It is reported that 5,000 people gathered in Madāgh for the event in 2006, but figures rose to 12,000 in 2007, and to 70,000 in 2008. In 2013 it attracted around 100,000 people, although the optimistic estimates made by some of Hamza's followers suggest the number is too cautious. Whatever the precise figure, when looking at the crowds participating in it, one can only think of Sufism, not as the religiosity threatened with extinction that the earlier scholarship of the 1960s predicted, but one, on the contrary, with an immense vitality, as almost two decades ago Hoffman had already noted (1995: 18).

In Madāgh, visitors begin to arrive many days before the celebration; people from all over Morocco, not necessarily devotees of Hamza, but participants of a widespread culture of *ziyāra*, come with their families prepared to spend several days at the lodge. They bring thick blankets for the cold nights, and presents for the *shaykh*. In the car are left snacks, nuts and fruits for the lost hours between rituals, but inside the lodge there is only what one shares with fellow pilgrims, with nothing to be kept for oneself. There is a hard-working atmosphere: an old woman changing her shoes and putting on clean socks, another organizing food and the terracotta pottery they will use for cooking it. When we arrived, there were people who had been there days before the actual start of the celebrations; they are willing to help with the organization of an event, to cook, to get the sleeping quarters clean and ready. Voluntary work is a central aspect of the pilgrim's experience, and, for rural Moroccans, who are the bulk of those who volunteer this form of service, it is alloyed with social prestige. They will cook couscous with vegetables, the ingredients for which are brought from home; some will even sacrifice a sheep and offer it to other visitors. These offerings are imbued with religious significance and give status to the volunteer within the community. From outside Morocco, formal adherents to the order arrive in small contingents – a few with family members, most with people from their enclave with whom they meet weekly to perform *waẓīfāt*. They are a minority: most of the attendees are Moroccans who often think of these Europeans not as devotees of Hamza but as 'tourists'.[4]

The event gathers many people to a relatively small house, a labyrinthine architecture of corridors that connects small spaces and, overall, with relatively little infrastructure considering the number of people it has to host.

Only four toilets for all the women and children, no drinkable running water; those who come by car often park outside the village and sleep inside their vehicles, or just on the fields near the house. Some years ago, there was relatively little planning to ensure the safety of the event; back in 2008, there was only an ambulance and the discreet deployment of the local police. An outdated metal detector at the main entrances was only set up on days with more visitors; males and females had separate 'security' gates through which they had to pass and at which they could be randomly frisked.

The system was rather rudimentary but, as the Būdshīshiyya gains public notoriety in the political field, the event is becoming both larger and increasingly securitized. For previous attendees, the increased police presence and their more proactive attitude of 'frisking' – almost everybody had to go through bodily searches – was shocking. When a *faqīra* from Europe asked why there were so many police, nobody wanted to answer; those in the crowd tried to play it down, and when I directly asked a group of women to comment on the safety issues they thought I was a journalist, but equally said I should not be worried because we were under the protection of Sīdī.

A *moussem* in Madāgh

Although the Būdshīshī *ziyāra* has some peculiarities due to its international nature, much of it is not dissimilar to saint visitation in other Moroccan lodges and in other parts of the Muslim World. For Hamza's followers, visiting the saint's lodge is held to be one of the most important spiritual duties, yet not all of them seem to understand it in the same way. For rural Moroccans this is a *moussem* (pl. *mouassīm*), an occasion to reinforce the bond of the (Berber) community to the spiritual realm. It marks, as other *mouassīm* do, an important hallmark of the agricultural calendar. The community here means the kin group of the family, or of the village, not the entire body of Būdshīshiyya's disciplehood. The visit is understood to be a material demonstration of Berber identity: 'Here in Madāgh lives our *Agourram* [Berber word for *walī*]', a woman told me, and she said that since Hamza is Berber it is even more important for them to come. The event is widely attended by Berbers from southern Morocco and the High Atlas, and less so by locals from the immediate surrounds of the *Zāwiya*; most of the locals attend the shops in the market outside[5] (a very significant source of income for many families from the area), but few seem to participate in the religious gatherings held at the lodge.

Instead of a proof of allegiance to this specific Sufi organization, the celebration is, in the narratives of those Berbers I encountered, often presented as part of a network of *mouassīm* dispersed throughout the territory. When explaining aspects of their *ziyāra* to Madāgh, they often make reference to the celebration of similar events in sites devoted to other *marabouts* not necessarily related to Hamza: they mention the *mouassīm* of Tafraout and of Salé, someone speaks about the Ben Aïssa *moussem* held in Meknès, and someone else says that the largest of all is that of the Tuaregs in Tan-Tan; but some consider this last one has lost its religious dimension. The *Mawlid* at Madāgh is one of those *mouassīm* that attracts Berbers from different tribes and regions, and constitutes to some extent a demonstration of Berber pride. A walk through the car park is sufficient to see how it serves to celebrate Berber diversity: many of the cars are waving colourful flags representing the various groups of the 'Berber nation', while two cars waving the same flag salute each other by tooting their horns. Similarly, some, especially among the older women, wear traditional dresses characteristic of the tribe to which they belong. The *Mawlid* congregates urban and rural Berbers, people from Agadir, Taroundant and Oarzazate and the (often poorer) peasants of the High and Middle Atlas.

A trip to the 'extraordinary'

Ziyāra is an important religious event in the Sufi universe; just as the one who prays a lot or performs *dhikr* a lot is regarded as a better and more pious *faqīra*, so the one regularly undertaking *ziyāra* also gains greater respectability.[6] The *ziyāra* to Madāgh constitutes a break from routine for people and, despite being considered a religious obligation by the upper echelons of the *ṭarīqa*, is often not felt to be a burden, but experienced with a thrill by most of the attendants.

One of the visitors, whom I will call Nada (not her real name), said she was being a tourist and going to Sufi sites like this; she said she does it for fun and compared it to 'going to a rock concert'. I was slightly shocked by the comparison: other attendants definitely look at coming here as a life-changing experience, certainly nothing to be compared to the insubstantiality of a concert. By contrast, Abdar Rahman Eatwell, a boy raised in the order who is close to the upper and middle echelons of the organization, declares 'I realized that these trips to the Zawiya [*sic*] have been the most amazing times of my life. They have been the foundations for my life, both spiritual and otherwise'.[7] But even Nada, who sees it in a less mystifying fashion, considers the *ziyāra* to be something exceptional. She would usually attend several *mouassīm* at various times a year, always with her friend who also attended. Nada explained she particularly liked sitting close to the groups of women scattered everywhere within the premises of the lodge reading the Qur'ān together; she liked the sound, the rhythm of the recitation, enjoyed 'being there'. She said she also likes the fact that people at the *Zāwiya* treated each other warmly 'as if they were family'; she acknowledged that going there reminded her of her childhood.

Unlike Nada, peasants seem to have fewer chances to enjoy occasions of this kind; the *Mawlid*, one lady explains, is a big occasion, one of the very rare instances of 'vacation'. It means going away from home for a few days and not having to work in the fields; however, the home is not left unattended, there is always someone left at home. She explains that this year it was her son who could not come as he had to stay to take care of animals, but next year someone else will stay and her son will come to visit Hamza. People come well prepared to camp out, bringing snacks, toys for their children, comfortable clothes for 'hanging around' and other clothes to dress up in for special gatherings. Some teach children religious songs or how to perfect their Qur'ānic reciting techniques. Although the celebratory nature of the event, expressed in all its joviality, is clear, not everything about it is a joyful pastime; I met peasants who came to ask both Hamza and his dead relatives to intercede for the recovery of a sick infant, the eradication of disease for a chronically ill man, the finding of a job for a young son, and prosperity to those who left for Europe. So, central to the visit are the demands for intercession at the cemetery and at the outer shrine,[8] and several attendees speak about being in Hamza's presence and about 'touching' him.

Many seem to share a sense of bewilderment as to what they are witnessing. Eatwell describes in his blog feeling 'a wave of butterflies' and confessing amazement at how the 'centre of the universe could be situated in such an unlikely place'. For one woman thinking about converting to Islam, for example, going to Madāgh gave her the chance to get 'a real taste of Sufism', she said. Most of the converts and reverts I met thought about the first time they came to the lodge in terms of 'before and after', a moment of profound spiritual realization. They typically presented it as a sort of rite of passage, a new beginning for them, an experience that made them 'realize' the need to follow the Būdshīshiyya's path and Hamza's teachings. A French woman in her mid-fifties told me that going back to her normal routines as a nurse at a local hospital after her first visit to the *Mawlid* felt unreal, as if everything had been a dream because the experience had been so amazing.

This sense of bewilderment resonates with the 'ground-breaking experience' the Turners described in their core work on Christian pilgrimages: '[I]t is true that the pilgrim returns to his former mundane existence, but it is commonly believed that he has made a spiritual step forward' (Turner and Turner, 1978: 15). Similar instances have been described for Islam, whether for *ziyāra* or *ḥajj* (e.g. Eickelman and Piscatori, 1990). Indeed, the non-observant Muslim anthropologist Abdellah Hammoudi (2006) acknowledged being spurred on to reconsider his own ideas about faith and rationality after going on *ḥajj* (an experience written in a critical spirit that constitutes one of the best accounts of Muslim pilgrimage written so far).

Securing affiliation?

Ziyāra to Madāgh is assumed to hold such a transformative power that several of those European *faqīrāt* I met had declared their decision to join the order after attending the *Mawlid*. Sara (a pseudonym) felt slightly pressurized to undertake a more formal commitment after having attended weekly gatherings for some time, but thought going to the *Mawlid* would help her decide. She thought of 'going to Madāgh [as being] less about making formal commitments and [...] more about allowing the heart to speak and to feel God'. She converted to Islam and joined the organization while still in Madāgh. Of course, most formal members see in *ziyāra* a potency that always tilts people in favour of joining, and many of these narratives of 'amazement' when circulated among the indecisive can also be seen as tools of *da'wa*; but there are also some who, after visiting Madāgh, decide not to join. The success of conversion may after all be relative; most of the *faqīrāt* I interviewed who had come from Europe were there for the first time (and the few who had been there before, attained, as a result, a remarkable reputation).

A Muslim who, before going to the *Zāwiya*, was dubious about the righteousness of the Būdshīshiyya was disappointed on seeing the relationship the *marabout* and his disciples had; it contained what she defined as 'a servility' that was, in her view, not what Islam teaches. Similarly, I conversed with devotees who claimed they became aware that the Būdshīshiyya is a 'cult' after seeing all these women wanting to kiss the hands and feet of the leader and not even looking at his face. Similarly, another one-time aspirant declared herself still interested in Islam but not in joining 'a sect' (also, in this case, her own words).

When a potential member travels to Madāgh, it is widely understood, his/her interest is firmer than a temporary curiosity, so even for those who do not undertake *bay'a* immediately after coming back, the trip to Morocco is often perceived as entailing a stronger commitment, even if (still) not a formal one. Generally speaking, interested but not formal devotees describe being treated more empathically as if they 'already belonged' to the community after visiting Madāgh. The experience of *ziyāra*, thus, is a symbolic way of acknowledging engagement to the group, in most but not in all cases followed by *bay'a*. This applies both to revert Muslims in Morocco and abroad as well as to converts in Europe.

One of the aspects deemed extraordinary in conducting *ziyāra* is the feeling of amity developed out of the experience of journeying and in being together at the pilgrimage centre. This rhetoric, recurrent among *faqīrāt* who have completed the pilgrimage, is in itself a quite effective proselytizing mechanism. Beyond any spiritual considerations, it is this feeling of comradeship and of community, which a devotee referred to as 'a community that supports you and is made of people like you', that seems to exert appeal. Indeed, various disciples report having had a sense of solitude and disorientation before entering the *ṭarīqa* that goes away when befriending other *faqīrāt*.[9]

An instance of how the appeal of amity works around people interested in joining the Būdshīshiyya is evident in *The Retreat*, a BBC2 reality show in which six British 'contestants' (Muslim and non-Muslim) volunteer to spend a month in La Alqueria de los Rosales,[10] an 'Islamic spiritual retreat' run by the Būdshīshiyya in Southern Spain, 'involving themselves in a course of spiritual self-development, the Islamic way'.[11] The documentary evidences the profound impact that the experience of communalism attached to being in a 'retreat' and the regime of 'spiritual routines' (from praying to cooking) has on some of the attendees, some of whom actually revert/convert to join the order after the experience.

Iḥsān and factionalism

The *ziyāra* to Madāgh compels us to revisit Turner and Turner's' (1978) notion of *communitas* (the idea that those social divisions that normally occur disappear or become attenuated among pilgrims in the course of pilgrimage). Whereas pilgrimages, in this view, open up a space for the development of a unique form of social amity, one imbued with an ethos of equality capable of transcending divisions of class and ethnicity (e.g. Eickelman and Piscatori, 1990; Coleman and Eade, 2004), I contend that what goes on in Madāgh partially corresponds with what Turner called 'normative' *communitas* in which, 'whilst the pilgrimage situation does not eliminate structural divisions, it attenuates them, removes their sting' (1974: 207).

I am interested in exploring the mechanisms through which 'normative' *communitas* takes place, by which solidarity is appealed to while distances between factions and social groups are subtly preserved. In Sufism, overcoming factionalism with 'companionship' has traditionally been understood to be a religious obligation (Trimingham, 1971: 5) – not exclusive to the pilgrim – and as such it is recurrently exerted in the written materials of the Būdshīshiyya.[12] It is certainly taken seriously by Hamza's disciples, often highlighted by those who had approached the order and not necessarily developed rapport with devotees. It is the extreme kindness and consideration (which they call excellence of behaviour: *iḥsān*) with which one is treated by members of this *ṭarīqa*, with no regard to one's religious intention or affiliation, that many people, even outsiders, remember after meeting them. For example, a French observer told me he remembered them being 'radically nice'.

Whereas scholars have often noted an increased strength in networks of camaraderie when *ṭuruq* exist in diaspora conditions (e.g. Werbner, 2009), in the Būdshīshiyya amity is common throughout all the enclaves, to everybody and from everybody. At the lodge, an atmosphere of *compagnonnage* was enjoyed most of the time by everybody. On these relations, Eatwell (n.d.) comments:

> [P]erhaps the best aspect of it [the *ziyāra*] for me is the hundreds of friends that I make with every visit. These are not the type of friends that one finds elsewhere. This is partly due to the Moroccan culture but also due to the relationship that is forged from the heart when one does something that is not for worldly or material gain […] These friendships are not dissimilar to those found within close families.[13]

Other devotees have defined what feels good in being on pilgrimage in Madāgh as a combination of 'service' to the community and the development of ties of trust with peers. Some devotees openly acknowledged making efforts when back home to mirror practices of *iḥsān* they see in Madāgh: '[I will] become a good Muslima by imitating [other women at the lodge]'. *Ziyāra* brings to European followers of Hamza the opportunity to experience this religiosity in its original setting. Probably because of that, devotees often try to reproduce what they see in Madāgh by adopting attitudes understood to be more 'authentic' back home. Several disciples consider that it is this special feeling of amity that makes them want to go back.

By undertaking *ziyāra* together, pilgrims reinforce the bond based on kind-heartedness and trust. It is not only what they experience at the lodge (central to developing these relationships is gathering in bigger, louder ritual sessions, something discussed in Chapter 6), it is also the experience of intense communalism derived from travelling together which creates long-lasting bonds that endure beyond *ziyāra*. In the words of a British *faqīra*, 'by journeying together we become friends forever'. A young Moroccan from Casablanca made a friend on her first trip to the *Zāwiya*, with whom she has remained close ever since.

Most in Morocco come by car or bus; many from abroad prefer to take this journey in the most traditional way possible. They consider the whole trip to be important, a woman from Spain said, because it gradually transforms you inwardly. Even those who prefer to travel by plane will spend part of their trip on the road, as the nearest major airports are Melilla (170 km away), Fes (340 km) and Casablanca (600 km). For some of the younger Moroccans coming from the cities, these are the only trips they have undertaken alone, without relatives; they are awaited with anxiety. For those coming from France, Spain, the UK, it seems, there are several who have hardly ever visited any country outside Europe, which adds to the exceptional character attached to the trip. The leadership of the order is fully aware of how journeying induces trust and confidence and helps to build imperishable bonds – an asset in favour of sealing commitment to the organization – so it persistently encourages members to organize national and international meetings, visit each other and do it in groups.

As paradoxical as it might sound, the pyramidal hierarchy presided over by Hamza is used to promote egalitarianism among disciples. Submission to the hierarchy of the *ṭarīqa* is supposed to minimize social and economic differences, in that before the *walī* everybody is a simple *faqīr/faqīra*; theoretically, at least, no differences are marked between rich and poor, Berber and Arab, peasant and urbanite.

Food is perceived to be the central element in this symbolic realm; free meals are provided by the lodge for everybody during the entire week and in the *Zāwiya* everybody eats the same food. Coexistence is also part of the egalitarian ethos, as devotees will be spending the days together and sleeping under the same roof. A closer look at relations between devotees, however, brings about a less romantic picture. Thence, *communitas* may be understood better as 'aspiration' than as 'realization'. On the one hand, scattered disputes occur as a result of the continued interaction; on the other, the invoked amity does not dilute parochialism within the organization, as divisions of class, ethnicity and nationality stay firmly in place: the woman who becomes angry as her belongings have been moved to make room for another group of devotees that need to be allocated a place to sleep; another who is suspicious her camera may be stolen if left in its bag unattended; or the affluent Arab *faqīra* talking pejoratively about 'superstitious' peasants.

In reality, whereas *faqīrāt* develop strong in-group ties with people from the same enclave, or from similar contingents, there are symbolic barriers on display between different groups of followers, and these borders hinder interaction between devotees from the different 'factions' (religious orientations, economic background and geographical origins). Whereas mixing is in theory encouraged, factionalism is expressed in the (lack of) communication between the groups and the ways in which the space is organized.

Thus, when food, for example, is served in big Moroccan-style dishes, devotees will eat, together with those from the same enclave, from the same plate, strengthening thus communalism, and next to other groups from similar 'factions'; but will rarely come into contact with dissimilar disciples. When sleeping, devotees will be placed in the same lodging-rooms with those from the same or similar contingents. The areas that accommodate foreigners and people from the Moroccan elites are far more luxurious than those destined to lodge the peasantry, which are colder at night and uncarpeted. Space is organized in such a way that commingling of people in Madāgh still preserves clear patterns of the social structure that underpins social relations in the outside world. As a result, the overriding egalitarian ethos is actually 'compartmentalized': the peasant does not meet the urbanites; Europeans rarely relate to non-Europeans; Moroccans living abroad mostly stay with Moroccans – and do not interact with European devotees.[14] In ritual gatherings people congregate together, although they sit alongside those of their enclave, and visits to Hamza also occur in 'groups' of like-minded *faqīrāt*.

The contrast between the ideology of egalitarianism among devotees promoted by the order and the factionalized way in which the leadership relates to *fuqarā'* is often met with criticism, both from European and Moroccan disciples. Hishām (not his real name), a convert, is representative of these views; he decided to leave the *ṭarīqa* after seeing the preferential treatment given to Europeans in Madāgh, which, he thought, was because Europeans may donate more money than peasants, and which felt to him 'utterly un-spiritual'. Nonetheless, even critics such as Hishām like to join 'the spirit of egalitarianism' while in the lodge, and although divisions and competitions are also part of the experience of pilgrimage, people overlook these and keep glorifying what they see as an equitable *milieu*. After all, if, compared to what goes on outside the pilgrimage site, what the *Zāwiya* creates is a space where the antagonisms that occur in the outside world are turned down – expressed in most cases with less vehemence, or temporarily postponed – then, as Eickelman puts it when referring to the 'artificial' environment of *ziyāra*, 'there is a suspension of overt hostilities' (Eickelman, 1976: 173).[15] Overall, the equalizing ethos they experience with those of their contingent is presented as a camaraderie *inter pares* that applies to everyone, as it seems the pilgrim 'wants to believe' in *communitas* and seems rather uninterested in critically assaying those aspects of the social interaction between pilgrims that are less idyllic.

A gendered community

Sacred space is characterized by a clear separation between the sexes. From ritual praxis to the voluntary work undertaken by devotees, everything is allotted according to gender: women mainly cook food, clean the site and prepare tea for the whole community, whereas men carry out electrical work and put carpets in the various gathering rooms. When rooms for women's gatherings are being prepared by male *fuqarā',* the work is done in advance of the arrival of guests in order to avoid men and women seeing each other during the celebration. The lodge is a big building with a labyrinthine structure. It is designed with two different 'routes', one for men and one for women. In this way, when following corridors designated for women only, one comes across rooms for gathering, places to rest and spaces to eat that will only be occupied by women and children. The only mixed space is a big patio outside the *Zāwiya* – although even there men and women are not supposed to interact in excess. Since the model itself generates the need for someone to mediate between the two gendered communities, women from Hamza's family bring the food cooked by women to the men, accompany the women who clean male spaces and discuss with the men issues of an organizational kind.

In this understanding of space, women hold the privilege of being allowed to watch men, an 'advantage' they certainly are not shy to exploit, particularly the youngsters. The roof of the building and the upper terraces are reserved for women; the place holds a series of tiny windows through which one can see the men's gathering area. Windows are crowded with young girls looking at and gossiping about the boys below.[16] What happens inside the spatially gendered *Zāwiya* happens here on its roof terraces, too; from these terraces women can see men in the street, but the men in the street will in principle not see them.

The gendered distribution of the sacred space in the lodge of Madāgh resembles the organization of 'lay' space in (at least the most conservative sections of) Moroccan society; but because of the lodge's sacred nature, the boundaries demarcating gender are less fluid than those in lay spaces. Some, mainly second-generation revert Muslims, who are familiar with but often critical of Moroccan culture, have difficulty in accepting the gender divide. The *ṭarīqa* shows a certain level of understanding towards them in Madāgh, and women from Hamza's family do sometimes in the end arrange meetings in private spaces where male and female members from Europe can meet altogether. These encounters go unnoticed by the rest of people in the lodge and last less than half an hour; they are extremely sporadic and might occur only once during the entire week. In the opinion of Ẓahīra (not her real name), '[the gender divide] is a feature of Moroccan culture, not of Sufism, one that we do not need to follow, it has nothing to do with spirituality'. She thinks these meetings help to dissipate complaints related to gender issues.[17]

Thus, despite their universalizing claims, this case points out that transnational forms of Sufism such as the Būdshīshiyya remain more often than not rooted in local religious cultures. The case illustrates the extent to which religious practice and ethos are perpetuated beyond the *loci* that originally produce it, although the incorporation does not always occur without contestation. Arguably, Sufism epitomizes this combination of a particularistic orientation, directed towards the veneration of one (local) saint, with a universalistic one, towards God; a seeming contradiction latent at the discursive level of modern *ṭuruq* (Werbner, 2007: 199). In most cases, the pattern of gender division is accepted, to the extent that it permeates the attitudes within the order beyond the ritual setting.

In Europe, the gender divide prevails in devotees' homes when they are visited by other Būdshīshī devotees. For example, *faqīrāt* in Paris receive visits from other parts of the continent when international European meetings are held in the city, and they ensure that female visitors do not encounter any men during their stay in private homes or when visiting the local *Zāwiya*. This means that sometimes very small flats (50 m^2) are gender-divided on these international occasions. One underlying aim of these visits is to show excellent behaviour to other members of the *ṭarīqa*, and another is to present oneself as a devoted member – perhaps, then, we should regard the gender divide at home as an attempt to reproduce religious codes that are considered to be 'authentic' because they have been seen operating in Madāgh.

The observance of this behaviour would seem to indicate that, despite the universalizing appeal of its religious discourses, the Būdshīshiyya in Western Europe may, in some respects at least, be a local religious culture exported to new lands. On balance, gender attitudes among European members of the order overtly contradict the image of adaptability to new environments often associated with Sufi orders in the West (Hermansen, 2004: 62). As Geaves et al. have suggested, in highly centralized orders the place of origin has an aura of 'authenticity' (2009: 5). The above example demonstrates that *ziyārāt* can provide opportunities to learn behaviours which can be reproduced and developed abroad, behaviours which devotees come to expect of each other.

The dividing line between what should prevail because it is part of the religion and what should be discarded because it is part of the culture is often not clear. Many visitors seem to find in Madāgh an inspirational behavioural pattern. Accordingly, they adopt a certain behavioural etiquette, a social code that is converted into a religious norm. Nowhere are the dynamics of 'glocalization' – in which local cultures find themselves intertwined with outside elements due to the effects of globalization – more evident than among transnational forms of 'hybrid' Sufism (Geaves et al., 2009: 4). Today's

Būdshīshiyya is an example of how 'hybrid' *ṭuruq*, while promoting a religiosity grounded in local values, 'use forms of globality to their own purposes' (Beckford, 2004: 258).

A somewhat humorous example of how these various worlds meet is that *ziyāra* in Madāgh sometimes serves as a platform to arrange marriages between attendants.[18] I have met girls of the *ṭarīqa* in Europe who visit Madāgh with the intention of 'meeting someone'.[19] The local Būdshīshī network[20] may be sufficient in most cases to meet that other half, though Madāgh is always a good place to seek transnational engagements.[21] Moroccans may sometimes think enormous economic benefits result from marrying a European; at the lodge one finds Moroccan women attending who have the clear intention of acquiring partners for their sons – carrying with them pictures, and even cvs.[22] Although a pilgrimage centre somehow creates an atmosphere of exceptionality where the social dynamics of the outer world can be temporarily suspended, it also integrates some of the economic and social tensions in which the followers are immersed in their daily lives. Of these concerns, the struggle to get into Europe figures prominently among the peasants I talked to, so the *ṭarīqa* is also a manifestation of the disparity apparent in the 'lay' relations between the northern and southern shores of the Mediterranean.

Whereas most peasants travel with their (gender-mixed) families, the journey to Madāgh is made in gender-segregated groups by the rest of the contingents, with groups of men and women from the same location generally arriving at the lodge separately and often even on different days. The belief in *communitas* also results in a sharper differentiation between the world of the *Zāwiya* and the outside world. Some in these female delegations travelling from Europe have never been in a Muslim country before and have a mixture of feelings about gender segregation, both in the organization and in Moroccan society.

This is Fatima's (a pseudonym) first visit to the Muslim World; she dislikes the segregation she has seen in Morocco but says she feels more comfortable at the *Zāwiya* being surrounded only by women rather than by a mixed crowd. Other *faqīrāt* report finding it difficult to travel alone, and they accuse young Moroccan men of harassing them, but in most cases a separation is built between the *ṭarīqa* and the outer world. One says men in Morocco are like this because of the very limited interaction they have with women, but conversely she also thought segregation within the order was beneficial; she thought it was easier to make friends because of what she described as the relaxed atmosphere generated when one is among women alone.

A distinction in categorization is also made between insiders and outsiders: 'You can differentiate from miles away a Moroccan who follows Sayyid from those who do not; their attitudes towards women, particularly if they see that you are European, are totally different'. The leadership seeks to reinforce the boundaries between insiders and outsiders of the *ṭarīqa,* by, for example, coordinating taxis (often *fuqarā'*) to pick up contingents of *faqīrāt* at the border or airport upon arrival in Morocco – good for the drivers who earn extra cash during the *Mawlid* celebrations, and for the women who do not need to negotiate prices and who avoid being scammed as tourists. Visits to nearby towns during their stay and mixing with the local populations of the villages that surround the lodge in Madāgh are equally strongly discouraged by the leadership. The market outside the lodge is one of the few places where insiders and outsiders have the opportunity to interact. There I have heard disrespectful comments by foreigners towards the local vendors, saying that Moroccans treat women like whores, that one has to be careful, and that this is the worst thing about going to Madāgh; some complain of having to cover up: 'even if you come in summer you have to cover up so much'. Disregard for Moroccan culture, something not completely uncommon among European devotees, is sometimes framed along the lines of gender discrimination rhetoric.

These comments, often not a reaction to offensive behaviour, are contradictorily toppled with romanticized ideas of Morocco as a pre-modern country in which the truthful values of life and community have not yet been eroded. The endurance of an approach heavily dependent on the paradigms of Orientalism is evidence that the post-9/11 dynamics between 'the West' and 'the Muslim world' also permeate the order. Whereas Moroccans do not seem to have an interest in (beyond trying to make use of) Europeans, the latter often lack a genuine interest in the culture of the *walī* to which they are devoted. For example, with the exception of a few members that have ever lived in the country, most Europeans have not visited Morocco.[23] With a tendency to oversimplify the complexities of social life with recurrent bold generalizations of the form 'Muslims are ... Muslims are not', and no interest in political, economic or social aspects, they nonetheless typically develop a taste for iconic aspects of so-called Moroccan culture (food, dress, music).

A moral economy?

Modern Sufi orders, particularly those whose scope is trans-regional or even transnational, generate flows of cash and goods that need to be understood as pivotal in the logistics of Sufi sanctity, for they symbolize a sacred exchange in which the devotee who gives money or goods receives in exchange spiritual guidance. The economic dimension is also central to understanding the wealth of *ṭuruq*, wealth that enables these religious organizations to expand beyond their regional *milieux*. As Werbner has noticed,

> these flows of tribute [...] characteristic of Sufi cults [...] underpin the organization of the regional cult in and across space, and have enabled the building and expansion of its central lodges [...] the saint is conceived to be the great nurturer, the source of infinite generosity.
>
> (2005: 27)

Such donations not only help to build up Sufi networks beyond the original locality, but they are crucial in improving conditions in the original enclave (Soares, 2005); in the case of Madāgh, the exponential growth of the *ṭarīqa* in recent years has permitted the improvement of the premises and the building of an annex that serves as a 'university' on religious subjects, offering summer courses and short stays.

Disciples of Hamza recognize in the saint an extra-mundane generosity that needs to be recompensed by regularly sending donations to the central lodge. This is a way of showing their gratitude to the saint. For peasants, Hamza's wealth is a physical manifestation of the magnificence of his extra-mundane power,[24] and although Europeans do not seem, overall, to share this understanding that connects wealth to *baraka*, they still contribute and probably make the biggest donations. Generally, when disciples from a contingent visit Madāgh (not necessarily during the *Mawlid*), they bring the cash collected among *fuqarā'*, contributions which are not compulsory but which help increase the reputation of the devotee within the group and enhance their spiritual standing; it is often believed that these donations make you a better person.[25]

A *faqīr* contrasts these donations with giving money to a charity by saying that, whereas many people give lots of money to charities to try to make a better world, if they continue to focus on its material side this world will always be a materialistic place full of egoistic people. He sees their contributions as seeking the spiritual betterment of society, and considers that donating makes them better human beings by helping to create a more peaceful world. An important aspect of making a donation is the symbolic nature of the act of offering. In Madāgh, after hours of queuing (and sometimes forming an avalanche of people), groups of *faqīrāt* enter the room where Hamza is in bed. They sit on the floor – there has recently been placed a cordon separating him from the devotees – because some years ago people use to rush to his bed to hug him in adoration, which could nowadays be problematic because of his age.

Some women feel disappointed they cannot 'touch him' (an expectation many have prior to encountering the *marabout*). Once seated, the *muqaddim*/*muqaddima* of the group hands over an envelope containing the money, while people sit in silence in front of the saint until he orders them to leave. Those who cannot go to Madāgh send their donations with their *muqaddim*. Evers Rosander has pointed out that the donations of those who cannot visit the saint symbolize the presence of the absentee: 'corporeal absence is compensated by the physical co-presence of money, which increases their social capital and is converted into moral capital' (2004: 70). However, in the case of the Būdshīshiyya these contributions tend to be depersonalized: devotees from one enclave put their donations together in one envelope in such a way that the *shaykh* does not know how much money is donated by each individual.[26]

Donations can be made in cash or goods, and whereas a combination of both is typical among peasants, urban members, whether from Europe or

Morocco, tend to opt for cash. I was told that material offerings have changed over the years, with more 'traditional' products such as handmade pottery, carpets, part of the crop, or even goats or sheep being progressively replaced by cash and imported goods. Donations of cash are more common; a Moroccan told me that these envelopes (collected between various donors) never contain less than 1,000 dirhams [around 90 euro], but an estimate of overall quantities is rather difficult to provide. Some of the groups organize activities to collect money – concerts, small parties, events – and the leadership of the order has more recently been trying to encourage these kinds of activities. The viability of the organization rests after all on these donations, so it is not surprising that devotees are encouraged to donate. I have heard accounts of people who felt slightly pressurized to donate. Those more critical of donations tend to be those who have recently entered the organization. Doctrinally, part of the success in expanding the *ṭarīqa* lies in the idea that *fuqarā'* should have jobs and working is portrayed as a moral duty:

> Work is paramount in this world because Divine Law requires that one has to provide for one's family, spouse and children. One also has to remain well focused on working for the Path. One therefore has to reconcile these three areas which constitute the hallmarks of one's life.[27]

By visiting the lodge, people gain a more real sense of the organization to which they belong, and that translates into the occurrence that some of those previously reluctant to contribute monetarily turn out to be happier to contribute once they visit the saint in Madāgh.

Notes

1 *Ziyāra;* pl. *ziyārāt* (Ar.): Sufi pious visitation, pilgrimage to a holy place, generally a *Zāwiya,* or tomb or shrine. In Morocco it is also commonly called *moussem* (pl. *mouassīm*).

2 *Walī 'Allāh*; pl. *awliyā' 'Allāh* (Ar.): *walī* can be translated as manager, guardian, protector, and also intimate or, most commonly, friend. *Walī 'Allāh*, generally translated as 'friend of God', is the term used to designate a Muslim 'saint', one who intercedes for others as God's deputy or vice-regent on earth. It is (especially in North Africa) also commonly rendered as *marabout* (a French adaptation of *murābiṭ*, the one at the *ribāṭ*, the lodge or retreat); Berbers often use the Amazigh term *agourram* (masc.), *tagourramt* (fem.).

3 My own translation from French; the article is in the magazine *Tel quell*, available online at the blog: http://jnoun735.skyrock.com/2591037367-Cheikh-Hamza-vient-de-designer-a-84-ans-son-fils-aine-Sidi-Jamal-comme.html (accessed 13 November 2013).

4 Foreigners are almost always assumed to be tourists, perhaps with the exception of a few Spaniards who work across the border. The *Zāwiya* is presented as a place with potential for attracting 'religious tourists' in a report seeking to convey directives to develop tourism in the region, the least touristic region in the country. See online at www.ccis-oujda.ma/documents/Le%20Tourisme%20dans%20la%20r%C3%A9gion%20orientale.pdf (accessed 18 November 2013).

5 Every time a *moussem* is held in Morocco, a 'lay' market is set up in its immediate surrounds; there only are two 'shops' in the 'sacred' premises of the lodge: one sells Būdshīshiyya's rosaries (*subḥāt*), imagery and literature, while the other offers products of 'first necessity' for foreigners (toilet paper and bottled water). These markets have often been considered 'lay' despite being referred to by the same word that denotes the religious ritual, to the extent that many people when speaking about a *moussem* are referring to the market, not to the pilgrims' celebration. Certainly, the relationship between the commercial and the ritual part of *moassīm* is so tight that one does not exist without the other, and their meanings are mutually reinforced. Whereas transactions in the market have a religious value (people for example consider that the products of these markets are better than those in a regular *sūq* because they have been blessed), rituals are understood as transactions in which material goods are exchanged by the immaterial favours that result from saintly intercession. Simenel (2010) thinks, consequently, that the way in which *baraka* is understood in classical scholarship should be revised to incorporate this 'mercantile' dimension.

6 Similar findings have been reported among the followers of other contemporary Sufi orders (e.g. Evers Rosander, 1991; 2004).

7 Available online at www.sufiway.net/ar_Sufism_cornerstone-zawiya.html (accessed 10 December 2013).

8 The guardian of the tombs' complex is a healer whose role and relationship to disciples is assessed in Chapter 7.

9 Similar circumstances were encountered by Köse (1996: 150) in his study of British conversion to Islam, especially in relation to Sufism.

10 The 'retreat' holds regular courses on religious education for 'Western Muslims'; see for example http://vod.alqueriacampus.com/ (accessed 17 December 2013).

11 The programme is made available online at www.youtube.com/watch?v=2kYyTOJ-mqI (accessed 17 December 2013).

12 See, for instance, the order's booklet *El libro de la Via* (2006: 8).

13 Available online at http://www.sufiway.net/ar_Sufism_cornerstone-zawiya.html (accessed 10 December 2013).

14 For some Moroccans living abroad, being members of the Būdshīshiyya is a way of maintaining contact with their home country. It has been argued that pilgrimages create small social worlds that are periodically reconstituted with those who otherwise live in geographically dispersed locations (Urry, 2002: 264).

15 Eickelman (1976) has studied the Moroccan pilgrimage centre of Boujad and has similarly found that the *Zāwiya* is a place where different social groups meet but generally do not interact. His analysis of the differences between the two types of Islamic pilgrimage (*ḥajj* and *ziyāra*) is insightful.

16 This particular way of dividing the space resembles the way in which large Moroccan homes are built: the whole structure is constructed around a patio where visitors are received. A series of floors above the patio contain the bedrooms for unmarried women and couples, whereas the chambers of unmarried men have their windows on the building's *façade*, facing the street. The top floors and the flat roof are spaces for women to gather. These terraces on top of the building constitute a public space where women from different families meet.

17 In some of the *ṭuruq* that have settled in the West, the gender divide typical of the original *milieu* has tended to blur (Lewisohn, 2006), whereas in others gender equality and mixing is almost non-existent. It should be noted that these two qualities (gender equality and mixing) do not necessarily go hand in hand; in the case of the European Būdshīshiyya, we find female participation in the local structures of decision making (which does not occur in most Moroccan enclaves), although gender separation, even beyond ritual practice, remains almost complete.

18 Cases of arranged marriages within Sufi orders where one partner is a convert have been documented in the West. See for instance Hermansen (2006: 257).

19 Thus, the common assumption, already questioned by some scholars (Badran, 2006: 203), that converts embrace Islam encouraged by their Muslim partners is clearly not the case within the Būdshīshiyya, where most members enter the *ṭarīqa* either alone or already married, but not to a Muslim. For a European woman to convert to Islam and join the order after getting married to a Moroccan would be quite exceptional: such women are few in number, and they generally stay in the *ṭarīqa* for only a short period of time.

20 *Dhikr* sessions and Sufi-related activities tend to be seen as good occasions for socializing and are at the basis of building up new social relations – including meeting potential partners – within orders. Similar instances can be found in *ṭuruq* around the globe. See for example the cases of Jakarta (Howell, 2007: 234), Cairo (Chih, 2007) and Birmingham (Werbner, 2007).

21 This is what two devotees told me, although I had no way of confirming that such arrangements are planned by the leadership.

22 If people from lower social strata see in Madāgh a gate to Europe and economic improvement, those from a more privileged background (Moroccan urbanites) often use *ziyāra* as a way of promoting their businesses. I met a woman from Rabat looking for clients to buy property – Morocco is one of the fastest-growing markets for Europeans purchasing second homes, and this quite bizarrely also found expression at the lodge.

23 Interestingly, though, many *fuqarā'* visit Andalusia – a place idealized as symbolizing the most glorious and open-minded expression of Islamic civilization and the mixture of 'East' and 'West.'

24 A similar link between wealth and spiritual power has been found among Khalwatī devotees in Upper Egypt: 'in the eyes of his followers, he [the shaykh] is rich because he is pious; this manna is the fruit of his *baraka*, the sign of God's beneficence towards him' (Chih, 2007: 32). In Senegal this is a well-extended conception though it has also encountered fierce critics. Rich *shaykhs* eager to display their wealth are sometimes derogatorily called 'Marabout Cadillac'.

25 In the same way, Villalón (2007) notes a similar understanding of offerings perceived as opportunities for spiritual and ethical growth among the *mouride* community in the diaspora.

26 Some studies have underlined forms of financial exploitation perpetrated by living *awliyā' 'Allāh* on devotees (e.g. Ojanunga, 1990; Sherani, 1991). Although the present research shows how the lodge benefits from the donations of supplicants, the attitude adopted by the Būdshīshiyya seems far less exploitative than the cases presented by Sherani and Ojanunga.

27 Hamza's sayings translated into English by a British member of the order are available online at www.tariqa.org/qadiriya/texts/sayings.html (accessed 2 July 2009).

References

Badran, M. 2006. 'Feminism and Conversion: Comparing British, Dutch, and South African Life Stories', in K. van Nieuwkerk (ed.) *Women Embracing Islam: Gender and Conversion in the West*, 192–232. Austin, TX: University of Texas Press.

Beckford, J. A. 2004. 'New Religious Movements and Globalization', in P. C. Lucas and T. Robbins (eds) *New Religious Movements in the Twenty-first Century: Legal, Political and Social Challenges in Global Perspective*, 206–14. London: Routledge.

Chih, R. 2007. 'What is a Sufi Order? Revisiting the Concept through a Case Study of the Khalwatiyya in Contemporary Egypt', in J. Day Howell and M. Bruinessen (eds) *Sufism and the 'Modern' in Islam*, 21–38. London: Tauris.

Coleman, S. and Eade, J. 2004. 'Introduction: Reframing Pilgrimage', in S. Coleman and J. Eade (eds) *Reframing Pilgrimage: Cultures in Motion*, 1–26. London: Routledge.

Eatwell, A. R. n.d. 'Cornerstone, zawiya'. Available online at www.sufiway.net/ar_Sufism_cornerstone-zawiya.html (accessed 10 December 2013).

Eickelman, D. F. 1976. *Moroccan Islam: Tradition and Society in a Pilgrimage Center*. Austin, TX; London: University of Texas Press.

Eickelman, D. F. and Piscatori, J. P. 1990. *Muslim Travellers: Pilgrimage, Migration, and the Religious Imagination*. London: Routledge.

El Libro de la Via. 2006. Madrid: Universa Terra.

Evers Rosander, E. 1991. *Women in a Borderland: Managing Muslim Identity where Morocco Meets Spain*. Stockholm: University of Stockholm Department of Social Anthropology.

Evers Rosander, E. 2004. 'Going and not Going to Porokhane. Mourid Women and Pilgrimage in Senegal and Spain', in S. Coleman and J. Eade (eds) *Reframing Pilgrimage: Cultures in Motion*, 71–92. London: Routledge.

Geaves, R., Dressler, M. and Klinkhammer, G. 2009. 'Introduction', in R. Geaves, M. Dressler and G. Klinkhammer (eds) *Sufis in Western Societies. Global Networking and Locality*, 1–12. London; New York: Routledge.

Hammoudi, A. 2006. *A Season in Mecca: Narrative of a Pilgrimage*. Cambridge: Polity Press.

Hermansen, M. 2004. 'What is American about American Sufi Movements?', in D. Westerlund (ed.) *Sufism in Europe and North America*, 36–63. London: Routledge Curzon.

Hermansen, M. 2006. 'Literary Productions of Western Sufi Movements', in J. Malik and J. Hinnells (eds) *Sufism in the West*, 28–48. London: Routledge Curzon.

Hoffman, V. J. 1995. *Sufism, Mystics and Saints in Modern Egypt*. Columbia, SC: University of South Carolina Press.

Howell, D. J. 2007. 'Modernity and Islamic Spirituality in Indonesia's New Sufi Networks', in M. Bruinessen and D. J. Howell (eds) *Sufism and the 'Modern' in Islam*, 217–40. London: Tauris.

Köse, A. 1996. *Conversion to Islam: A Study of Native British Converts*. London: Kegan Paul International.

Lewisohn, L. 2006. 'Persian Sufism in the Contemporary West: Reflections on the Ni'matu'llahi Diaspora', in J. Malik and J. Hinnells (eds) *Sufism in the West*, 49–70. London: Routledge Curzon.

Ojanunga, D. N. 1990. 'Kaduna Beggar Children: A Study of Child Abuse and Neglect in Northern Nigeria', *Child Welfare* 69(4): 371–80, Washington, DC: US National Library of Medicine.

Sherani, S. R. 1991. 'Ulema and Pir in the Politics of Pakistan', in H. Donnan and P. Werbner (eds) *Economy and Culture in Pakistan. Migrants and Cities in a Muslim Society*, 224–6. London: Macmillan.

Simenel, R. 2010. 'Le Grand Commerce de la Baraka. Les Moussem du Sud Marocain', in F. Mermier and M. Peraldi (eds), *Mondes et places du marché en méditerranée formes sociales et spatiales de l'échange*, 215–26. Paris: Karthala.

Soares, B. F. 2005. *Islam and the Prayer Economy: History and Authority in a Malian Town*. Edinburgh: Edinburgh University Press for the International African Institute.

Trimingham, J. S. 1971. *The Sufi Orders in Islam*. Oxford: Oxford University Press.
Turner, V. W. 1974. *Dramas, Fields, and Metaphors; Symbolic Action in Human Society*. Ithaca, NY: Cornell University Press.
Turner, V. W. and Turner, E. L. B. 1978. *Image and Pilgrimage in Christian Culture: Anthropological Perspectives*. Oxford: Blackwell.
Urry, J. 2002. *Consuming Places*. London; New York: Routledge.
Villalón, L. A. 2007. 'Sufi Modernities in Contemporary Senegal. Religious Dynamics between the Local and the Global', in M. Bruinessen and D. J. Howell (eds) *Sufism and the 'Modern' in Islam*, 172–92. London: Tauris.
Werbner, P. 2005. *Pilgrims of Love. The Anthropology of a Global Sufi Cult*. Karachi: Oxford University Press.
Werbner, P. 2007. 'Intimate Disciples in the Modern World: The Creation of Translocal Amity among South Asian Sufis in Britain ', in M. Bruinessen and D. J. Howell (eds) *Sufism and the 'Modern' in Islam*, 195–216. London: Tauris.
Werbner, P. 2009. 'Playing with Numbers. Sufi Calculations of a Perfect Divine Universe in Manchester', in R. Geaves, M. Dressler and G. Klinkhammer (eds) *Sufis in Western Societies. Global Networking and Locality*, 113–29. London; New York: Routledge.

6 Ritual

Sufism has historically been understood as a behavioural guide to human psychology that is accompanied by a series of ritual exercises, aimed at bringing about the inner transformation of the seeker. Sufism is said to be, above all, a 'practice', one that aims to 'denude the heart' (Ben Rochd, 2002: 26)[1] in order to bring the seeker to God by lowering the *nafs*. This cornerstone notion of Sufi doctrine is often translated as 'inner self', soul or ego. The Qur'ān presents it in three different phases: in its initial phase, it is considered an unrefined state of being, as it represents the animal side of humans, the instinctive aspect of us that leads to evil behaviour (Schimmel, 1975: 112–14). Individuals are supposed to awaken their conscience, in a second phase, and to accuse themselves, repent and ask for forgiveness, in order to reach the final stage, one in which the *nafs*, purified, rests at peace and the seeker unites with God. Sufism can be defined as the set of techniques the devotee develops to perfect the *nafs*, and, far from it being required to embark on major philosophical quests, the metamorphosis is to be attained by the regular performance of certain religious rites. Hamza explains in his sayings:

> Regularly practiced invocation [*dhikr*] will progressively make desires and impure thoughts disappear. Likewise, if hunters go every morning to the forest and shoot their guns, all the animals, in fear, will flee when they hear the shots. They will return a little later in the day, but if the hunters come back every day, the animals will change location.

Instead of seeking answers to major existential questions, Hamza has advised his disciples: 'There is no need to ask why, just let yourself be guided';[2] 'Within the Path […] remain firmly anchored to one's practices'; and 'Do not seek the Truth; first try to purify yourself'.[3] Such purification is attained by embodying *iḥsān* (adequate moral behaviour) as well as through ritual performance: 'The two royal gates that give access to God are invocations (*dhikr*) and generosity'.

The importance given to practice supersedes the need for *a priori* religious knowledge, an 'experiential' approach in which 'authenticity' is often equated with 'performance' rather than with doctrine, something that has historically given and continues to give Sufism its characteristic adaptability and success in reaching new audiences.[4] The Būdshīshiyya welcomes those with scant knowledge of Islam and allows them to fully participate in the activities of the group, and Būdshīshī authorities do not ask members to learn anything about Islam; nor do they ask devotees to read particular books or to embark on a particular religious training. Aspirants are only asked to attend congregational ritual sessions in an organization that is confident about the positive effects of performing them, as follows: 'Progressively, with the practice of *dhikr*, one shall develop the intuition of what is a proper action to take in every situation' (Hamza in Draper, 2002: 180).[5]

Because ritual holds such a central position in the Būdshīshiyya's understanding of Islam, studying it throws light on the diverse enactments of religious life within this *ṭarīqa*.[6] *Dhikr* (the Sufi ritual *par excellence*) is performed worldwide, but precise accounts demonstrate that *dhikr* is actually manifested in manifold variances (Gellner, 1969; Zubaida, 1995). Moreover, since rituals are articulative of the identity of their performers (Mauss, 1973), introducing the reader to the rich universe of Būdshīshiyya ritual practices will aid better understanding of religious identities within this order.

Remembering

Differing from other forms of prayer, *dhikr*, literally meaning 'remembrance', is not obligatory but voluntary. It consists of reciting a series of litanies[7] with the aim of achieving a state of being in God's presence. The majority of these litanies contains Qur'ānic verses, so *dhikr* can be seen partly as a particular form of Qur'ānic recitation (*tajwīd*). In the Qur'ān human beings are asked to remember God: 'Remember me, I will remember you' (2: 152). While it serves as a reminder to the disciple of God, it is also used as a way of interiorizing the Qur'ānic message (Ernst and Lawrence, 2002: 27). There are two types of *dhikr*: *dhikr djali* refers to the performed ritual when the formula is uttered aloud, whereas *dhikr khāfi* refers to the one practised either in silence or in a low voice. Both modalities can be performed either individually or collectively.[8] Each *ṭarīqa* has its own way of performing *dhikr*, the style being determined by variances in rhythm, volume, body movements, breathing pace and facial expressions and hand gestures. Although there are subtle variations[9] between contingents of the Būdshīshiyya, style is fairly consistent throughout the order.

Among the varied Būdshīshiyya rituals, the key one is undoubtedly the collective weekly *dhikr* performance known as *waẓīfa*. Although, technically speaking, *waẓīfa* only refers to the part of this ritual dedicated to the invocation of *'Allāh*'s qualities, most of the members use the term to refer to *dhikr* sessions performed in groups.[10] They are often performed in a space devoted to that purpose in one of the *zawāya* or in one of the devotees' homes (in those groups that are not in close proximity to one of the lodges). The home in question needs to have certain features and be approved for that use by the authorities of the order. It must be a room clear of furniture in the centre, and be clean and quiet. Sometimes a picture of the *shaykh* presides over the space but that is not compulsory. Moroccan groups sometimes also have pictures of Morocco's king (illustrating how the religious nature of his title is identified with the 'sacredness' of certain spaces devoted to ritual performance) and of other members of the Būdshīshiyya's *silsila*. These images are placed to the side and none of the ritual praxis is oriented towards them. Whereas in some enclaves the sessions are always celebrated in the house of the same devotee, in other cases it rotates. The room and the house at the time of the gathering become 'sacred' space, thence gender-segregated (if men are at the house they will leave when the *faqīrāt* arrive).

Privacy is what partly gives *dhikr* sessions their distinctive atmosphere: telephones are switched off, bags left at the back of the room; in most cases there are no late arrivals or early departures, and the room is closed for the entire duration of the event, something that differentiates this kind of ritual from others held at 'public' spaces such as mosques or prayer rooms. The event is met with solemnity, and awaited with anxiety: several attendees have declared that they wait the entire week for the *waẓīfa* to come. It is an occasion to reunite and rejoice with God, *Sayyid* and the rest of the *faqīrāt*.

In Morocco there seem to be no obstacles in organizing such gatherings, but some difficulties have occurred in European locations. In a post-9/11 world, meetings in flats where attendees pray and sing repeatedly and invoke *'Allāh* over several hours have been met with animosity by neighbours, who more than once have called the police. Various devotees have expressed not wanting to hold meetings in their houses as they fear deteriorating relations with neighbours. One of the groups reached a situation in which they had no place to hold their gatherings; an ISKCON (International Society for Krishna Consciousness) centre offered them a space to use and they began to hold sessions there, presumably authorized by the *ṭarīqa*'s leadership. Some devotees said they felt disgusted at performing *dhikr* next to a statue of Vishnu – the paradox of multi-religious Europe, where a human-shaped Hindu figure was present at a gathering of an aniconic religion! The initiative, however, it seems, did not last long, and sessions at a devotee's home were soon resumed.

The duration of the *waẓīfa* varies from group to group, as does the volume of the chanting during the ceremony. In general terms, these sessions last between two and five hours, although the order suggests it is 'better to keep [*dhikr*] recitation short while having the wish to see God's face, than to do it for a long period while remaining attached to the wishes of the ego' (Ben Rochd, 2002: 26).[11] In some groups it is performed fairly quietly, while others are more expressive. The longer the *waẓīfa* is and the more numerous the crowd of performers, the more likely it is that attendees will enter ecstatic states (*aḥwāl*, sing. *ḥāl*).[12] The entire session consists of the recitation of litanies, mainly Qur'ānic passages, with *faqīrāt* sitting cross-legged and barefoot in a circle on the floor, with their backs straight and their eyes, for the most part, closed. Women dress modestly – since modest dress is required and considered a sign of one's intention (*niyya*)[13] to 'lower' the *nafs*: some of them wear *jilāba* or long skirts and all wear *ḥijāb* for the occasion.

The crowd is mixed, with a varying degree of commitment to the organization. Whereas some are initiated, others are more loosely affiliated to the *ṭarīqa* (although the order's leadership considers that in *dhikr* sessions words lose their regular meaning and adopt an esoteric[14] meaning which only those who are initiated will be able to grasp). Moroccans critical of the Būdshīshiyya condemn the fact that non-Muslims could be allowed at a *dhikr* session, something also typical of certain *dhikr* congregations elsewhere (e.g. Shannon, 2006: 123).[15] Other orders allow Muslim and non-Muslim 'observers' (e.g. Raudvere, 2002: 189), but proactive participation of 'people just trying it out' (as they are often termed in Būdshīshiyya's circles in Europe) is also quite frequent in other transnational *ṭuruq*, albeit rarer among less proselytizing groups. Among Būdshīshiyya contingents, 'observers' are infrequent; in most cases only 'participants' attend.

The vast majority of *faqīrāt* appears to have learnt the techniques of *dhikr* performance (Būdshīshiyya's style), not while growing up, but by training through imitation when taking part in the event. The transmission of this kind of knowledge is rather informal: newly initiated people just tend to follow those that are more experienced in *waẓīfa* performance. The *formulae* recited – that is, the verses and phrases, the number of times they are repeated and the order in which they are chanted – change from time to time. These *formulae* tend to be periodically 'renovated', in the light, it is believed, of the changing needs of the community of performers, with every specific formula designed to address the particularities of a specific *milieu* at a particular time. The *formulae*, contained in booklets (outside Morocco, in transliterated Arabic), are carefully kept by the *muqaddima*. Devotees believe that the litanies' sequence, the 'order' in which they are recited, gives the *waẓīfa* a sacred character, hence its being monitored by Madāgh and hence its confidential character.[16]

I contend that these renovations and their confidentiality contribute to providing legitimacy to the religious authorities, since one of the most significant roles of Hamza as a leader is to design the new *formulae* in accordance with the requirements of each *époque* and community. This is something, devotees argue, only he in his position as 'living' *shaykh* can do, in contrast to orders that follow masters who are not alive; this is the way, it is believed, in which he guides the disciples in their ascendant Path towards God. A *faqīrā* used the metaphor of Hamza as her doctor, with the *formulae* being the medical prescription which will cure her 'spiritual sickness'. Another disciple told me she believed Hamza knows each of them 'at a spiritual level', although he may not be able to recognize them in person, and she attributed this to the 'special' and 'immaterial' character of the disciple/master bond.[17]

Nowadays, despite yearly changes, some of the basic components in these litanies remain the same. The session is always opened by reciting the first *sūra* of the Qur'ān – called the Opening – and repeating it ten times. There are verses that are entirely recited: *sūrāt* 56, 36, 110, 111 and 112; and there are others from which only some parts are taken. There are parts of verses that are repeated at different stages of the recitation (e.g. 37: 180–2), whereas others are just recited once (e.g. 6: 103; 6: 63–4; 40: 65). There are stages of the *waẓīfa* in which a particular phrase is repeated several times – the number of times may vary from 100 to 1,000 times, but the phrase is always the same. The counting is done by the person leading the ritual, either intuitively or by using a *subḥa*.[18]

Most of the performance and expression of emotions occur in a relatively predictable, patterned way, which, I suggest, supports Katz's (1978: 26–7) repudiation of the unmediated nature of mystical experiences based on the argument that participants are being conditioned by the cultural and religious background of the mystical tradition in question. In the Būdshīshiyya's case, some parts of the *waẓīfa* are accompanied by a subtle rhythmical body-bouncing, and others provoke a much stronger effect in the performer. For instance, after they have pronounced *'Allāh* or *yā latīf* several times it is common to see some of the attendants entering what in the Būdshīshiyya's parlance is often called 'having a *ḥāl*'; such states are less frequent when other phrases are recited. In bigger gatherings, when in ecstasy, it is typical to see women hitting their chests, sweating, crying, shouting and sometimes falling on the floor and convulsing bodily. Peer attendees tend to let them remain in trance for a while but try to gradually contain them by calming them down and comforting them. Of the different women I have seen in this state, it was particularly shocking to me to witness the trance of a pregnant woman. Entering these states is neither discouraged nor promoted by the order's leadership. Finally, every *waẓīfa* finishes by pronouncing what is called *ad-du'ā'* prayer, normally translated as *recueillement*,[19] a set of phrases that conclude once again with some of the verses in *sūra* 37, which marks the end of the ritual ceremony.

There are certain ritual prescriptions that need to be observed in order to perform a *waẓīfa* session. First, there must be at least four people; second, the *waẓīfa* should be led by an authorized member of the *ṭarīqa* – this is generally the *muqaddim/a* of each group; third, the group should meet in an appropriate space, one that is clean and quiet, and the location must be authorized by the leadership in Madāgh; fourth, groups should consist of members of the same sex. Mixed *waẓīfa* sessions are unauthorized and are believed to bring utterly negative consequences to individuals' health, 'because of the mixing of energies'; a disciple explained to me that men and women are believed to be biologically different and, consequently, to have distinctive and complementary but antagonistic bodily forces.[20] Participants are also expected to undertake ritual ablutions prior to the commencement of the session.[21]

Although *waẓīfāt* are always felt to be deeply moving and transformative, the *waẓīfa par excellence*, the one held to be the most powerful of all, is that which takes place during the *Mawlid* celebrations in Madāgh. It is a unique, intense experience, due to the twofold effect of *baraka*. The physical space of the lodge is consecrated by the permanent effect of saintly blessings upon it: the ritual act in itself is believed to have a sacralizing effect – *faqīrāt* say that some of Hamza's *baraka* is made present every time a *waẓīfa* is performed in any part of the world. But when it is performed at the central lodge the magical vibe is believed to be expressed more powerfully. Also, *waẓīfāt* performed in the central lodge are viewed as unparalleled because they are generally led by a member of Hamza's family, and this is seen as increasing the effects of *baraka* in ways it is impossible for lower authorities within the *ṭarīqa* to achieve.

At these gatherings at the central lodge women are crowded together and the congregation can involve up to a few hundred devotees. The collective chants, the rhythmic movements, the stifling heat (the venue is on most occasions poorly ventilated), the crying and groaning: the effect can be stunning.[22] For most of those who attend a collective *waẓīfa* of this size for the first time, the experience is not only shocking but sometimes psychologically unsettling. A member of the order from France commented to me that after her first *waẓīfa*, she felt morally disturbed, a very strong feeling difficult to put into words. Only after a few sessions did she begin to feel more relaxed and enjoy it. I myself had felt dizzy observing these sessions on various occasions. Some people who participate in these sessions speak of profound experiences, of the strongest *aḥwāl* coming about only in large gatherings of this kind, something that may be linked to the size of the congregation or to the deeper feelings arising in the course of pilgrimage; under these circumstances, people may discover a more direct way of experiencing the divine (Turner and Turner, 1978: 3).

Beyond the actual moment in which the event takes place, these gatherings have proven to have long-lasting effects in many of their attendees. Often, the characteristic feeling of companionship among *faqīrāt* does not develop through shared intellectual concerns, but rather through participating together in these strongly charged emotional experiences – and in light of the effectiveness of journeying to Madāgh in peer bonding it is not surprising that the order encourages devotees to visit the lodge regularly: it helps to seal the commitment of the disciple to the organization, as discussed in Chapter 5. Collective *waẓīfāt* in Madāgh generate even stronger feelings of *compagnonnage* between people than those performed 'back home'. *Waẓīfāt* everywhere, though, are major occasions for socializing and are the place where most of the intra-*ṭarīqa* relations and mingling occur, bonding being a very important aspect of these events, which has also been noted in the study of other *ṭuruq* (e.g. Werbner, 2005).

In the Būdshīshiyya, local contingents organize weekly *dhikr* sessions, and in most but not all instances, the session finishes with a collective meal prepared by the person who hosts the event, something categorized as impinging on religious merit (*ajr*). These meals are special moments, illustrative of how emotional peer support manifests within the organization. These are occasions for talking about families, jobs and daily life in general and commingling with 'friends who are like family' (quoting the words of a *faqīrā*). Whereas *waẓīfāt* can decisively help people to become friends, the opposite, it seems, may also hold truth. The leadership encourages the organizing of meetings of this kind with people with whom one feels like-minded, not with people with whom one does not identify (e.g. with different religious inclinations, views on ethics and religious law, and even political worldviews).

This results in groups being somehow more or less socially homogeneous; for instance, Europeans (whether reverts or converts) often do not attend sessions with Moroccan migrants, and in Morocco wealthy people tend not to gather with members of lower economic strata. The *ṭarīqa's* religious authority is aware that different followers have diverse approaches, and that disputes often emerge when they meet one another. For that reason, they encourage people to gather with those who are like-minded, in order to avoid internal conflicts. This has been stated to different groups by the leadership at international gatherings[23] and in multiple email communications. In consonance with the close relationship between bonding and ritual performance, one may think of the fact that male members of the *ṭarīqa* perform *waẓīfāt* separately as conducive to the general lack of relations between most *faqīrāt* and *fuqarā'*. The resulting sense of solidarity is often understood as an authenticating proof, as bearing witness to the truth of Hamza's message and guidance. Rituals thus play a central role in the enhancement of community belonging.[24]

Individual *dhikr*

Individual *dhikr* is less common among contingents of this order than its collective forms: 'a little bit of *dhikr* with companions is better than a lot of dhikr without them' (Ben Rochd, 2002: 26).[25] When it is performed, however, it has to be performed silently.[26] It is believed among followers of Hamza that the power of vocalized invocation is so strong that it can turn negative if performed individually and without the support of the group. It is said that one woman invoked *'Allāh* out loud more than a hundred times when alone, which caused her to start seeing monster-like faces when looking at people she knew. Only by visiting Madāgh and following the ritual prescriptions recommended by Hamza was she helped to recover from seeing scary faces everywhere. Similar stories are told about people who could not stop trembling or became seriously ill after performing *dhikr* out loud when alone. These cases can be viewed as warnings to those who want to practise Sufism without entering the order, bypassing Hamza's authority. Similarly, the case of another woman who saw scary faces as a result of her adherence to an order led by a 'false *shaykh*' is used to illustrate what might happen to those who follow more than one – or just the 'wrong' – Sufi path.[27]

Silent individual performance is only recommended to some and in very particular circumstances in which *dhikr* is part of the devotee's training; it seems it is designed according to the needs of each individual, as it is believed that the pace of spiritual progress varies from one person to another. Sometimes, when devotees are going through a period of psychological unease, they may ask the *muqqaddim/a* to 'prescribe' individual *dhikr*, if it could be of help. The case of Ḥamīda, not her real name, who had been previously diagnosed with a mental disorder and was currently under medication, is relevant here. She went to ask for a formula of individual *dhikr* that might help her to get rid of the voices she always heard. However, in cases like hers it is believed that the effect of *dhikr* can be too strong and therefore detrimental. Instead, she was recommended to read some Sufi tales, and the writings of the medieval Sufi master Ibn 'Aṭā 'Allāh.[28]

In another case a woman who told me she was depressed was asked to perform individual *dhikr;* she strongly believed it would have beneficial health effects, and, after being authorized and spending some time performing individual sessions, she reported feeling much better, which led her to be reassured of the truth of Hamza's message. The role of the *muqaddim/a* in this is certainly important, as it is s/he who acts as a broker between Hamza and the *faqīr/a*. S/he leads the local contingent, and, accordingly, it is s/he who transfers the *formulae* that Madāgh decides to grant in those exceptional cases in which devotees also perform *dhikr* individually. To this extent Hamza is meant to act as a mediator between the devotee and the exemplary figure of the Prophet (not with God since the relationship between the believer and *'Allāh* is in Islam conceived as unmediated); and the *muqaddim/a*, it can be argued, is therefore 'the mediator's mediator'. As this is considered the proper spiritual training, and a central reason to join the *ṭarīqa*, no instructions for individual performance are ever given to those who have not been initiated.

Usually, individual *dhikr* is only prescribed in very specific situations and it seems that many members only perform *dhikr* in the group situation; all they are asked to perform when alone are the five daily *ṣalāt*. It is interesting, however, to notice that although collective performance is much commoner than individual performance, the relationship of *walī*/devotee is thought to be individual.[29] Each disciple understands she has a personal relation to Hamza and that progression along the Path occurs on an individual basis: 'a spiritual discipline is more than anything else a personal and interior practice' (Ben Rochd, 2002: 22).[30]

Other prayers

There are other forms of prayers practised by devotees of this order. Some Moroccan devotees congregate with friends or family members with assiduity to recite Jazūlī's (d.1465) *Dalā'il al-Khayrāt*, the famous book of prayers devoted to the Prophet of Islam widely recited around the Muslim World. In addition, members of this *ṭarīqa* also perform *ṣalāt*, in exactly the same way as would be mandatory for any Muslim. Although most consider it a ritual obligation there seems to be variance in the degree of observance of this practice, for it seems more widely practised in Morocco than in Europe[31] (or it is perhaps that public acknowledgement of skipping it is more often considered taboo in Morocco), but in any case, the vast majority of my informants said they pray five times a day.

Some exceptions were found among those who can be categorized as New Age followers, both in Morocco and in Europe, and among some of the revert Muslims in continental Europe. Similarly, some of the converts have expressed finding it difficult to stick to the discipline of *ṣalāt.*[32] Not all variance in adhering to this discipline, however, stems from individual choice; the context also seems to exert a certain degree of influence, with adherents in Britain, it seems, being more inclined to fully observe *ṣalāt* than people in other European Budshīshī locations, such as Spain and France. Atypical variances may also occur: I have encountered, for example, a devotee who concentrated the five prayers in two longer sessions, one early in the morning and one at night; she, a convert, found it difficult to stick to the discipline, hence the twice-a-day regime seemed to offer an acceptable if provisional middle ground to her, an example, that attests once again to the malleability, adaptability and resulting hybridity of the Būdshīshiyya in adjusting to different *milieux* and variegated lifestyles.

Another two *faqīrāt* explained to me that being able to keep their new religious identity a private matter facilitated their process of conversion to Islam, since it gave them the freedom to tell only those whom they felt 'would understand'. If prayer had to be performed five times a day they would inevitably have had to be publicly identified as Muslims. It is interesting to observe that it is only in the UK that members of this *ṭarīqa* want to publicly express their religiosity when they become members of the order (either through conversion or reversion to Islam). Some British *fuqarā'* seem to ask for time to pray in their workplaces, or are regular users of praying rooms provided in public spaces such as universities, airports, etc. Interestingly, members in different *milieux* seem to have adopted ways of expressing their religious identity which are suitably adapted to the predominant discourse of the society in which they live. In multicultural Britain devotees seem more relaxed about publicly admitting their adherence to Islam, whereas French and (by osmosis) Spanish and Belgian *laïcité* means that members of this *ṭarīqa* prefer to keep their religiosity a private matter.[33]

Fasting and food

The subject of food can provide a valuable key to understanding the ritual world of Sufis, although this area has often been neglected in academic studies of Islamic spirituality. Scholars such as Werbner (2005: 127–8) have pointed out the need for a better understanding of the meanings given to food by *fuqarā'* and *faqīrāt* in order to elucidate the religious world of Sufi orders. No case could be more suitable for such an approach than the Būdshīshiyya *ṭarīqa*, as the order apparently owes its very name to a meal. There is a story that widely circulates among devotees about Sīdī Alī al-Qadirī, who was the first *Qadirī* of the line of the Būdshīshiyya. According to this narrative, he arrived in Morocco in the seventeenth century and founded a Būdshīshī lodge in the town of Taghjirt (in the region of the tribe of the Béni Snassen).[34] From his story all subsequent people in the *silsila* derive their names.[35] According to this tale the name Būdshīshī is derived from Abū Shish (Bu-shish), because Sīdī Ali al-Qadirī is reputed to have fed the poor in his *Zāwiya* with *shisha* (traditional Moroccan soup made with ground wheat, *blé concassé*) in times of famine (Ben Driss, 2002: 13).

Other versions tell us that he not only fed the poor but also influential politicians who came to visit him at the lodge, denoting his even treatment to everybody regardless of wealth or social status. Both stories highlight the important symbolic meaning attached to food in the *ṭarīqa*: the infinite benevolence of the *walī 'Allāh* is represented by the act of feeding others. The Būdshīshiyya identifies *baraka* with providing nourishment to such an extent that the very act of feeding others is considered a hallmark of Sīdī Ali al-Qadirī's generosity, rooted in saintliness.

In the agricultural context in which the Būdshīshiyya first emerged, the *walī 'Allāh* was he who was adored for protecting the crops from inclement weather and for overseeing the harvest. It is only on the occasion of the *Mawlid*[36] (as explained in Chapter 5) that those dedicated to agriculture leave their lands to visit the *Zāwiya*, with Hamza, and the Būdshīshiyya's *awliyā' 'Allāh* before him, being invested with a vital role in the correct completion of the agricultural cycle. The *walī* helps people to improve their harvest; they in exchange thank him for his saintly intervention with their donations; and the *walī* finally feeds them in Madāgh in an act that symbolically seals his belonging to a saintly domain. In addition, the generosity exhibited by the provision of these meals is seen by *fuqarā'* as an example to be followed.[37] So the excellent behaviour towards others that the order demands from followers is here exemplified by Hamza's action. Almost every *waẓīfa* performed by adherents to the *ṭarīqa*, every meeting of people of this organization and many of its public activities, culminates in a communal meal. In many cases they cook Moroccan food and eat it in the 'Moroccan way', using only a spoon and sharing one big plate with four or five other people.

Central to the overview of the ritual lifecycle is the month of fasting, *Ramaḍān*. *Ramaḍān*, like the other ritual practices, is differently endorsed and understood by different members of the order in different locations. Whereas Moroccans tend to think of it as an event that connects them to the *Umma* worldwide – in accordance with what Buitelaar (1993), for example, has found among Moroccans who are not part of the organization, some

European devotees see it as a connection not to Muslims worldwide (the idea of the *Umma* being often less interiorized than among Moroccans) but to the Būdshīshiyya *corpus* of believers. In Morocco, *Ramaḍān* is a constituent of a calendar, one in which each time of the year is endorsed with a distinctive identity (for example, the months before and after fasting hold different meanings); most of the European devotees I have met are unaware of such insights, and, even if they still respect these calendar hallmarks, they are approached as 'conventions,' thus detached from the meaning often transferred to these occasions in Morocco. For example, it is common in the month preceding *Ramaḍān* to increase the frequency of programming *ħīlāt,* long sessions of ritual performance typical of North African Sufism,[38] that combine recitation, music and dance in which *mluk* (sing. *mlek*) (a particular type of 'spirit,' *jinn*)[39] are believed to be made present to come to terms with or pacify the relationship between the performer and the entity. They are common in the month before *Ramaḍān* as the practice of fasting is often believed to help to clear them out, after being pacified during the *ħīlā*. Although with lesser frequency, *ħīlāt* are also scheduled among European contingents, but most people seem uninformed about the 'spiritist' role the ritual is commonly associated with in North African Islam.

In general terms, the practice of *Ramaḍān* is observed by the majority.[40] The associated festivities celebrated at the end of fasting (*'aīd al-fiṭr*) are equally observed. Among new Muslims, the personal characteristics of each individual are a factor; some people will find it easier than others, with occasionally *faqīrāt* seeing fasting as a problem as it makes it difficult to keep their Muslim identity private, as happened with prayers. Besides, I have noticed that, as happens with other rituals, the size of the group seems to contribute to determining the degree of success in observing fasting, bigger groups often being more committed. By contrast, those cases I met of people who fast intermittently, ending it early or even avoiding it on certain occasions, belong to smaller enclaves. As happens with prayers there are also cases of ritual adaptation: I met a devotee who lives in the mountains who did not fast at all during the 2007 autumn *Ramaḍān*; he regretted this afterwards and fasted some months later so as 'to catch up'.[41]

Samā'[42]

Differing from what is typical in other North African orders (in which dance and instrumental music facilitate the achievement of trance during *dhikr* sessions),[43] the Būdshīshiyya, as a sub-branch of the Qādiriyya, forbids the use of musical instruments in its *waẓīfāt*, and chanting style during rituals is 'sober' so that, it is argued, these enactments are not misunderstood as aesthetic manifestations departing thus from their truly religious character, rather than being understood as the form of prayer they really are.[44]

Music, however, plays a very significant role within this *ṭarīqa,* with a plethora of bands, interpreters and instrumentalists who happen to be Hamza's disciples. In fact two of the highest personalities within the order, Skali and Qustas, are the head organizers of the most famous festival of religious music worldwide, the Fes Festival of Sacred Music. Held annually since 1994 in Fes, the festival was originally intended as an interfaith endeavour with 'Western' audiences in mind. As it grew in popularity both abroad and in Morocco, and after 9/11 and the 2003 bombings in Casablanca, it gradually became used to elaborate on a rhetoric that could relate religion to democratic ideals and human rights, and 'Moroccans began to think of the festival as an event that would counter its own domestic extremism' (Curtis, 2007: vii).

It has become very popular: in 2001, it was selected by the United Nations as one of the world's twelve events that most contribute to civilizational dialogue. It remains unclear whether Hamza supports the endeavour; Curtis, who did develop a close relation to Skali during her fieldwork, suggests that the leader of the Būdshīshiyya 'does not whole-heartedly approve of the festival, but at the same time he has not outright condemned it' (Curtis, 2007: 18). A number of other music initiatives have taken place in the order, and it seems that these enterprises have been followed closely from Madāgh. Thus, a number of bands performing *samā'* have appeared in several locations, whose name and *repertoire* are closely monitored by the *ṭarīqa*'s authorities, evidencing the debated nature of the use of music in relation to Islam.[45]

One group had to change its name because it was deemed inappropriate by the leadership of the organization. The group was called Rāb'ia, whose name honours the famous medieval Sufi woman Rāb'ia al-'Adawiyya (d.891), commonly seen as passionate and not particularly religiously 'sober'. Madāgh asked Rāb'ia to change its name to *ṣafā'*, which simply means purity. The performance style also is supervised, so that chants of these bands will always be performed following a particular Moroccan style (more *Arabicized*, less *Berberized*, and eliminating any of the sub-Saharan influences that Moroccan *samā'* music frequently displays).

Samā' groups have been helpful in publicizing the order outside religious circles, portraying a positive image of a popular genre to wealthier audiences and influential foreigners. For example, the concerts in which members of the *ṭarīqa* perform at Rabat's Palais Tazi have become evening events that attract, among others, the bourgeoisie, the political elites and foreign representatives of diplomatic bodies. Outside Morocco, *samā'* concerts also serve to publicize the order[46] and attract new members to the *ṭarīqa*.[47] For example, this popularity of *samā'* is manifested by the project of the *fuqarā'* of Birmingham to create a *samā'* radio station to broadcast the performances of diverse Būdshīshī groups.[48]

The introduction of *samā'* as a means to try to recruit new members is backed by several stories that circulate among disciples of this *ṭarīqa*. Although these stories are varied they share certain characteristics. Usually there is a disoriented youngster, often a Western European man, who has been through a period of emotional suffering and subsequently embarks on a spiritual search. He has an interest in performing music, professional or amateur. He is interested in styles understood to be 'modern' by those who narrate the story (e.g. rap, rock, heavy metal). Typically, he encounters in his search several 'false religiosities' (e.g. often other Islamic groups, other Sufi orders, New Age spiritualities). The young man at some point gets to know the Būdshīshiyya, commonly by reading de Vitray-Meyerovitch's or Skali's books or by travelling to Madāgh (either accidentally – he found Madāgh as he was travelling around Morocco, which somehow seems improbable – or else he accompanies a friend there). He takes the *ba'ya* and becomes a *faqīr* of the Būdshīshiyya. As a result of the emerging love he feels for his master, he begins to compose music that speaks about his spiritual awakening. In some versions, he abandons his passion for 'modern-style' music and starts a new *samā'* group. In others, he is a professional musician who begins to write lyrics with Sufi content, but sticks to his own musical style.

I will present here two stories which illustrate this pattern. The first is that of the *samā'* group al-Jīlānī (which takes its name from the founder of the Qādiriyya). The group is composed of three men, members of a former French heavy metal band, who were, apparently, interested in 'spiritual teachings', which is the reason why, after being invited to other religious groups (different people relate the story in different ways: for some they were members of a neo-Hindu group,[49] others say they were interested in Hare Krishna), they ended up in Madāgh. Nobody seems to know who or what brought them there, but the fact is that their presence generated great controversy among the people of the village. Some in Madāgh apparently commented the fact that, while they should not be allowed to visit Hamza with their heavy metal look of long hair, tattoos and black clothes, Sayyid did in fact decide to receive them, confirming his non-judgmental attitude and infinite love for humankind. The story goes that Hamza said that if he was to be their real master they would realize themselves how and why they should change their external aspect, without the need for him to impose any rules on them.

This facet of the story illustrates the modern Būdshīshiyya *ethos* which makes the *faqīr/a* himself/herself the decision maker in matters of discipline rather than obedience to rulings merely being imposed from above. As might be expected, it is reported that the three musicians did indeed suffer a profound transformation when they saw Hamza, and immediately decided to become his disciples. It was while still there in Madāgh that they took the *ba'ya*, cut their hair and transformed their heavy metal band into a *samā'* group; today, their third album is on its way.

The second story is similar in certain respects, but it has its own distinctive touches. It concerns Abd al Malik, a singer with the rap band NAP (New African Poets), whose biographical account has been assessed in Chapter 3. The musicians of al-Jīlānī were tempted by New Age spiritualities, whereas with Malik it is the 'religious market' available for Muslim youths in the *banlieues* that is presented as being 'on offer'. As stated in his biography, after being tempted to follow 'an aggressive Islamism at the margins of society'[50] (Malik, 2004: cover) as invoked by various preachers and organizations, he decided to enter the *ṭarīqa* Būdshīshiyya. Since then, Malik's musical career has experienced a shift, with his more recent albums containing some songs about Sufism, which tell of the love for his *shaykh* Sīdī Hamza, and speak out against the politicized Islam of the ghettos.[51]

We can indeed discern this 'fixed structure of signs' within our two stories of the band al-Jīlānī and of Malik, both of which can be perceived as complementing the official discourse of the order. The ultimate point in developing and spreading them, I contend, is precisely because they are voiced by *ṭarīqa* members and not by its authorities (though approved by them). And the fact that these are the stories of *fuqarā'* imbues them with symbolic value, making them more convincing to many, particularly to those who do not entirely support the hierarchical structure of the organization. Those who do feel called by a spiritual interest, but are not quite sure about all the notions that aim to legitimize the power structure within the Būdshī shiyya, will definitely find more credible the words of Malik or the tale of the heavy metal band than any of the messages contained in Skali's books or in the booklets produced in Madāgh. One might conclude that the most powerful element in these stories is that they are perceived to be 'the voice of the common people' – 'common' in the sense of the position they occupy in the *ṭarīqa*'s hierarchy.

Rituals are a means of ordering and understanding the world. They are also the evidence that religious meta-narratives are adapted and negotiated by individuals and their particular circumstances. Within the Būdshīshiyya, rituals seem to reveal the specificities of the order. Thus, rituals have a central role in intra-*ṭarīqa* bonding among peers, and are central to the perpetuity of the order transnationally. When reformulated,[52] rituals evidence the adaptability of Sufism to new social *milieux*; when performed similarly across groups, rituals manifest the extent to which there is cohesiveness in terms of religious identity within the organization. Besides, since the Būdshīshiyya's leadership seems to believe that there are fundamental differences between men and women, rich and poor, they explicitly promote the performance of collective rituals which adhere to boundaries of class and gender.

The role of music in the order is significant, although instrumental music, central to the publicizing of the *ṭarīqa*, is vetoed in the 'sober' ritual style of the organization. As *samā'* groups proliferate, the *ṭarīqa* seems to increase its control over any activity related to music, aware of the fact that it can be a source of religious controversy. In the end, rituals represent a complex dynamic of signs and meanings that are not external to religion but constitutive of its central core: they add subtle transformations to daily experience, and contribute towards shaping the universal claims of religious thought. As Douglas once put it, 'rituals […] create unity in positive contributions to atonement' (2004: 2).

Notes

1 My own translation from French of the original '*dépouillement du cœur*'.
2 My own translation from Spanish text emailed to the followers of the order in Spain, entitled *El estado del discípulo* (The disciple's state).
3 In Hamza's sayings, available online at www.sidihamza.us/SidiHamzaSayings.swf (accessed 3 January 2014).
4 In western newly emerging religiosities, for example, the authority of sacred texts often appears to be de-emphasized, while the belief in bodily experiences as containers of godly messages gains ground (Geaves et al., 2009: 5); a *milieu* with conditions that would facilitate the Būdshīshiyya and other orders to successfully take root. A similar emphasis on physicality can be found in other modern *ṭuruq* such as the Pakistani Chishtī Sabīrī (Rozehnal, 2007a: 174). I have met devotees who see *dhikr* sessions as 'spiritual exercises' and equate them with techniques drawn from other traditions (e.g. yoga). It is this kind of case that permits us to situate certain religiosities within the Būdshīshiyya alongside religiosities catalogued as New Age. There are devotees with this approach both in Europe and in Morocco, evidencing bi-directional flows of cultural influences: while Sufism has influenced certain religiosities developed in Western Europe and North America (Geaves, 2004), certain Sufi religiosities in the Muslim World have been influenced by New Age trends (e.g. Howell, 2007). On the experiential and 'anti-textualist' approach of this organization, see Chapter 4. Although traditionally in Sufism informal disciples of a given order (i.e. the bulk of people who attended Sufi gatherings without being initiated, hence Sufism's missionary success) were never required to become literate on religious matters, religious knowledge has often been a requisite for initiation (Schimmel, 1975). In the Būdshīshiyya, changes introduced in the initiatory process have been discussed by Haenni and Voix (2007) and in Chapter 2 of this book.
5 The emphasis that the *ṭarīqa* puts on practice and the de-prioritization of the textual 'tradition' in Islam – the notion is used here in the 'Asadian' (Asad, 1986) sense of the term – as a prerequisite to enter the Path means that a substantial proportion of disciples are not really inclined to engage with precise matters of dogma or with the intricacies of religious scholarship; they prefer to leave these matters to their *muqaddimāt*. This is a feature that means it makes even more sense to centre this study on the embodiment and emplacement of religious praxis rather than on doctrines and religious texts in line with the materialist approach proposed by Vásquez (2011). The order, however, is inclined to transfer at least the basics of religious knowledge to its discipleship so, often, after *dhikr* sessions, short 'lectures' led by those better versed in the sciences of Islam are imparted. In these sessions medieval Sufi texts are read as a way of introducing devotees into basic Sufi terminology.
6 The relevance of ritual in Sufism contrasts with the relatively scarce attention it has received in scholarly literature, which ironically enough has tended to concentrate on more theosophical, historical or literary aspects. Perhaps the most comprehensive study conducted on ritual so far is that of Netton (2000), who discusses the meanings attached to rituals in the Ni'matullahi and the Naqshbandi *ṭuruq*, although he uses mainly texts with occasional reference to ethnographic accounts. Thick descriptions of ritual within particular *ṭuruq* are still scarce (e.g. McPherson, 1941; Padwick, 1961; Gilsenan, 1973; Ernst, 1997: 92–8; Raudvere, 2002).
7 I use the term 'litany' as it refers to the reiterative character of the phrases pronounced. Raudvere, however, has objections on the suitability of the (originally Christian) term (2002: 207).
8 Schimmel has pointed out (1975: 167) that a literal reading of the Qur'ān might lead us to think that both practices are equally condemned: 'Be not loud-voiced in

thy worship, nor yet silent therein, but follow a way between' (17: 110). This 'quiet' style is followed in the Būdshīshiyya and only challenged in the biggest gatherings such as those sessions held at the lodges in Madāgh and Argenteuil.

9 I have discussed some of these variations in a comparative perspective on various European branches: see Dominguez Diaz (2011).

10 This study tries to use terminology in the same way as it is used by members of the order; this is done in order to provide a more accurate picture of members' understanding and to facilitate reference to specific aspects of their religiosities. Therefore, although aware of the inaccuracy involved, we will, as Būdshīshī *fuqarā'* do, use the terms 'collective *dhikr*' and '*waẓīfa*' interchangeably.

11 My own translation from the original in French, *'peu de dhikr avec souhait de voir la Face de Dieu vaut mieux que beaucoup de dhikr avec attachement aux differents désirs de l'ego'*.

12 *Ḥāl*; pl. *aḥwāl* (Ar.): generally translated as 'condition' or 'state'. In medieval Sufism it meant the state of realization of an encounter with the Divine, a moment described as acquaintance of perfect balance of the soul due to the acceptance of this encounter. Today the term is used to refer to states of ecstasy attained during *dhikr* sessions. They are neither encouraged nor condemned by the leadership of the order, although the disciple is directed towards having other 'spiritual goals': 'do not seek spiritual states, ecstasies, proposals or visions! Seek only the knowledge of God. Desires and visions may shield us from this knowledge. Internal advancement must spring out and impact external behavior' (Hamza in Draper, 2002: 181). An interesting array of cases on trance in Moroccan Sufism can be found in a volume edited by Chlyeh (2000). The most widely studied case of ecstatic experiences in Moroccan Sufism is that of the *ṭarīqa* of the Gnawa, recently analysed by Kapchan (2007), although probably more interesting are the insights given by Claisse (2003) and Chlyeh (1998).

13 *Niyyā* (Ar.): often translated as intention. It refers to the will of a person to do something for the sake of *'Allāh*. It is, among others, a prerequisite to the performance of *dhikr*.

14 Some disciples are interested in the Sufi tradition of the esoteric reading of the Qur'ān, something in which upper echelons of the order are also engaged.

15 In Aleppo before the war, *dhikr* groups used to allow 'visitors' (typically non-Muslim foreign researchers) who were interested in the musical or performance aspects of the ritual, but were uninterested in becoming part of the religious circle (e.g. Shannon, 2006: 123).

16 Although I had occasional access to the *formulae* I will not reveal their content here for ethical reasons. However, what I will do is highlight some of the common characteristics of these recitations. Draper, the only researcher who has dealt with the Būdshīshiyya so far – a member of the organization himself – published in his PhD thesis (Draper, 2002) the detailed content of the 2001 litanies, causing an avalanche of criticism, which was presumably what led him to leave the *ṭarīqa*.

17 The doctrinal reforms undertaken by the order (addressed in Chapter 2) meant that the original, personalized way of transmitting knowledge was replaced by a new concept of 'religious instruction' in which 'spiritual love' (perceived as the tool for knowledge acquisition) takes the place that personal training with the master once had. This approach, otherwise uncommon in Moroccan Sufism, is common in other areas of the Muslim World, with, for example, Sufi organizations led by a 'directing' *shaykh* with similar functions to Hamza having been well documented in South Asian Sufism (e.g. Buehler, 1998; Rozehnal, 2007a), whereas these formations were previously led by a 'teaching' *shaykh*, a *walī* in charge of leading both *dhikr* sessions and the daily routines of the initiated (who usually lived with him). When the role of the *walī* ceases to be of a 'teaching' nature and becomes a 'directing' function, he keeps being the 'teaching' *shaykh* of a close group of the

initiated, but he also directs a less attached circle of sympathizers who come to visit him sporadically, and ask for his intercession on mainly mundane concerns (Buehler, 1998: 12). Generally speaking, this move seems to be either the origin or the consequence of the expansion of Sufi orders beyond their original *milieu,* as 'directing' *shaykhs* seem to be quite common when *ṭuruq* become transnational; see for instance the case of *mouridisme,* analysed by van Hoven (2003). The case of the Būdshīshiyya exemplifies a third stage of transformation of this pattern, one in which the 'teaching' role is completely removed in favour of a 'guiding' role – Hamza is meant to instruct disciples by exclusively 'guiding' their ritual performances, a guidance, it is believed, that is not conducted face to face.

18 *Subḥa* is a rosary generally used to perform silent *dhikr* in order to count the repetitions in reciting particular phases. Every *ṭarīqa* has its distinctive *subḥa*, and in some the object is given to the aspirant when he enters the order. In others such as the Būdshīshiyya, *subḥāt* are available for purchase at the central lodge in Madāgh.

19 The means to reunite or gather oneself together in a spiritual sense; it seems to have no English equivalent. It can be translated as meditation or contemplation, but by using these terms we probably lose some of the original meaning.

20 However, I have been told a story, which I could not verify, of a couple living in an area with no Būdshīshiyya contingents. It is said that Hamza allowed this wife and husband to perform weekly *waẓīfāt* together, even though the general rule indicates that the ritual shall observe strict gender segregation. This, if true, is rather exceptional. In contrast with other Sufi religiosities which soften their approach to gender issues when they are exported to the West (Geaves et al., 2009: 4), gender segregation in the Būdshīshiyya is not being questioned at all.

21 There are no substantial differences between the prescriptions relating to ritual cleanliness in the *ṭarīqa* Būdshīshiyya and the general rules displayed in the Islamic tradition; *faqīrāt* perform their ritual ablutions before starting *waẓīfa* sessions and some also do so before prayers – according to some interpretations, ablutions performed for the first prayer of the day suffice unless there has been an intervening event polluting bodily function (Lowry, 2008). Various devotees keep a jar of water and a plate by the nightstand to perform their ablutions before night prayers. For some, the carrying out of ablutions is tedious; a devotee substituted the canonical *wuḍū* with an alternative dispensation. In Islam, travellers can perform *wuḍū* with dust when water is unavailable, but a *faqīra* carried around a stone (as a substitute for dust) that she used for purification purposes, even when water was easily obtainable, because she thought it served the same purpose and it was easier for her. She thought Hamza would approve the alternative practice – because the method (*tayammum*) is grounded in Islam. It is worth noticing that although the whole symbolic system associated with purity is not immediately adopted by people when they enter the *ṭarīqa* Būdshīshiyya, it is nevertheless surprising to see how some elements are often incorporated almost immediately after taking the *ba'ya*. Purity, as applied to spaces, is a case in point. Some European members, for example, who may otherwise be described as quite lax in their ritual observances, do keep their houses very clean; this is seen as important in their religiosities. In the homes I have visited you take your shoes off upon entering, a custom characteristic of Muslim homes; those homes used for performing weekly *waẓīfa* sessions are kept particularly tidy. A similar scrupulousness is often observed in matters related to bodily hygiene. New devotees who were not previously familiar with any Muslim tradition have to interiorize a whole symbolic system; some adopt the new practices quicker than others. Peer devotees as well as texts (e.g. Lings, 1971) explaining the symbolic meaning of rituals are of support to some new members in the adoption of these practices (again, an interesting paradox of the anti-textualist approach analysed in Chapter 4). The transmission of religious norms and values

from parents to children is an important factor in ensuring the perpetuity of religious traditions worldwide, but the children of Būdshīshiyya do not automatically become members of the *ṭarīqa* – they take the pact when they are considered adult enough to understand the meaning and implications of what they are doing, but in any case never under the age of 16. The information I could obtain on rites marking birth, circumcision and death was too limited to be able to draw general conclusions.

22 Images of the *Zāwiya* and of one of the rooms where the collective *waẓīfa* sessions are performed can be found online at www.sufiway.net/sec2=edcu=teaTQ811326.html (accessed 10 December 2013). An interesting description of these collective rituals as performed by members of the Tijāniyya in Northern Nigeria can be found in Hutson (2006).

23 This has been stated to different groups by the leadership at international gatherings and in multiple email communications.

24 The importance of friendship within this order extends to the fact that some devotees have even acknowledged that it is these feelings between *faqīrāt* that have kept them attending gatherings every week. In other modern Sufi organizations with a marked missionary character (e.g. the Naqshbandī Mujaddīdī in Germany), the growth in popularity of these feelings of *camaraderie* seems to undermine the devotees' support for the hierarchical structure. In other words, the engagement of members in a closely knit community tends to replace the hierarchical approach to spirituality (Jonker, 2006: 79), although the Būdshīshiyya, at least, has not yet gone this far.

25 My own translation from French for the original *'peu de dhikr avec compagnonnage vaut mieux que beaucoup de dhikr sans compagnonnage'*.

26 Many orders do not see any problem in the performance of loud *dhikr* in isolation. It seems to be a common practice among the followers of the Naqshbandī Zindapir regional cult both in Britain and in Pakistan (Werbner, 2005: 138). The Naqshbandī Mujaddidī seem to have a similar attitude but Shaykh Farooqui has recently incorporated the teaching of silent *dhikr* to be performed in isolation in his UK-based group. This case has recently been pinpointed by Werbner (2007: 209) but the reasons for Sufi orders in western countries progressively incorporating this type of ritual practice are still under-researched.

27 Interestingly, the so-called 'false *shaykh*' was the shaykh of the *ṭarīqa* Naqshbandiyya, one with which the European Būdshīshiyya regularly competes to gain the attention of potential followers.

28 Although it is not very common in the Būdshīshiyya for Sufi literature to be recommended, Ibn 'Aṭā 'Allāh is one of the texts most used in the order, to the extent that it is sold in the central lodge at affordable prices. There are several translations of his works into European languages, notably those into French by Paul Nwyia.

29 The *ṭarīqa* shows, in this regard, similarities with New Religious Movements of the 'world-accommodating' type in which typically most rituals are performed collectively, although its performance is presented as being of individual benefit to the adherents (Wallis, 1984: 36).

30 My own translation from French, *'une discipline spirituelle est avant tout une practique intérieure et personelle'*.

31 It has been roughly estimated that around 48% of Muslims in America regularly perform their prayers, with born Muslims being more likely to do it (50%) than converts (37%). For further information on these statistics see Section 2 of the report, 'Muslim Americans, no signs of Growth in alienation or support for extremism', by the Pew Center (2011), available online at www.people-press.org/files/legacy-pdf/Muslim%20American%20Report%2010-02-12%20fix.pdf (accessed 2 January 2014).

32 Other studies on conversion to Islam in Western Europe and North America have discovered people encountering similar difficulties in performing the five daily prayers. A convert woman explained to Anway: 'The five daily prayers are probably the most difficult, since our American lifestyle often doesn't allow for them to be performed at their proper times' (2007: 68). Similar cases in which converts have found difficulties in adapting to the five daily prayers have been reported by Zebiri (2007: 115).
33 The Būdshīshiyya, though, is not an isolated case. Followers of other *ṭuruq* in Europe, like the German Burhāniyya, also prefer to avoid outward manifestations of their religious identity (Lassen, 2009: 153).
34 For further information on the historical development of the order, see Chapter 2.
35 Būdshīshiyya's *silsila* is available in Appendix 1.
36 Festivity to celebrate the birth of the Prophet. See Glossary and Chapter 5 for further information.
37 The relation between saint visitation and agriculture in Morocco is discussed by Eickelman (1976) in his exploration of the pilgrimage centre of Boujad. Further discussion of this point can be found in Chapter 5.
38 It is a practice not exclusive to, but made quite famous by, the Gnawa; for further analysis on the ritual as performed by the Gnawa, see Kapchan (2007) and Sum (2011).
39 *Jinn;* pl. *junūn* (Ar.): literally meaning 'invisible', hence supernatural. In Islam *junūn* are immaterial creatures thought to be the offspring of demons. *Mluk* is a term derived from *mālik* (owner) *and malaka* (to possess), and it refers to those spirits that may possess humans. For a more detailed account, see Maarouf (2007).
40 There are very few studies on religious fasting, despite its centrality in Islam. A major contribution has been that of Buitelaar (1993), a fieldwork-based study partly undertaken in Berkane, an important Būdshīshiyya node.
41 It is noteworthy that in Europe some adherents keep celebrating what are considered Christian festivities after joining the order. For example, some continue to celebrate Christmas with their families, or even with peer Būdshīshiyya devotees, and have argued in favour of those celebrations along Guenonian lines (i.e. these are all expressions of the Divine). On Guenonianism, see Dominguez Diaz (2013) and Sedgwick (2004). Roald (2006: 64) found that most converts either skip the Christmas celebration or transform it into a new kind of festivity within an Islamic framework. She suggests that the few who celebrate do so because they feel pressure from their non-Muslim families. In the European Būdshīshiyya, degrees of adherence to the Christian calendar are diverse.
42 *Samā'* (Ar.) literally refers to the act of hearing; it more precisely denotes 'that which is heard'. In Sufism, *samā'* is often used to refer to the hearing of music, the spiritual concert, in a more or less ritualized form (During and Sellheim, 2009). More information is provided in the Glossary. An interesting article which discusses the use of music in the ritual sessions of the Chistī Sabīrī is that of Rozehnal (2007b).
43 The most famous case in Morocco is probably that of the Gnawa. See Chlyeh (1998); Claisse (2003); Kapchan (2007).
44 Something similar has been found among *dhikr* circles in Istanbul; see studies by Raudvere (2002: 192).
45 For further discussion on the debate about music in Islam, see Halstead (1994). Further, Frishkopf (2009) has shown how second- and third-generation Canadian Muslims' assumptions on the illicit nature of the use of music in Islam have been confronted by the widespread use of music with religious purposes in Muslim majority countries.
46 For instance, the aforementioned group is French but was interviewed by the Spanish newspaper *La Vanguardia*, on 11 June 2008.

47 This is also a common attitude in other Sufi orders in Europe. See for instance the case of the Haqqaniyya in Britain, analysed by Draper et al. (2006: 106).

48 The radio broadcasts internet concerts of *samā'* music which follow ritual prescriptions of the Būdshīshiyya. See radiosama.com.

49 The term 'neo-Hindu' is often used to describe different movements which have little in common, hence further clarification would be needed for one to use the term in a meaningful way. However, I am not judging here whether the devotee's characterization of a particular phenomenon as 'neo-Hindu' is correct. I am simply reproducing the devotees' use of the term.

50 My own translation from French of the original '*un islamisme agressif, en marge de la société*'.

51 As this research shows, discourses tend to differ from social praxis. Ideologies may be rigid sets of notions, but they usually acquire a more nuanced, sophisticated nature when articulated through human experience. Personal narratives are never just a matter of black and white: they are more fluid than that because they involve complementary dialectics with reality (Ricoeur, 1992). Within narratives words need to be calibrated in order to make sense of reality. To this extent, one can argue that identity, although presented as if it were a sort of personal account, actually constitutes ideology, discourse. For this reason, as Pratt Ewing suggests, the subject tends to hide and obliterate details in their story, to make it appear more harmonic and consistent (Pratt Ewing, 1997: 103). If, for example, Malik had found something appealing in the speeches of the *banlieue* preachers, or if the men of al-Jīlānī had found the New Age religiosities at all interesting, this would have detracted from the clarity of the message that these stories want to transmit. Therefore particular aspects of the story have to be omitted; otherwise the whole meaning attached to the reasons for conversion to the Būdshīshiyya could be questioned, interrogated and put in doubt by those who read the story. By contrast, fieldwork material reveals that these narratives are actually dominated by greys, not by true and false, black and white. When the spoken word is used, personal narratives that are sincere and genuine stories of how people experience their own processes are always seeded with a seemingly contradictory mixture of doubt, disenchantment, commitment and drive. This contrast in relation to Islamic narratives and texts was previously suggested by van Nieuwkerk (2006). In the stories referred to above, all the elements fit together, each being a link in a seemingly perfect chain of logic. It is precisely this unquestioning neatness that converts these tales (whether real or not) into ideologies and tools for proselytization. More than personal accounts, they are indeed particular ways of looking at the world. These are definitely not narratives in the sense of being reports of one's own sometimes contradictory trajectory. These stories are identity, since 'identity constituted through the invariant ideological gaze […] stands in tension with a narrative self, a "self of stories". Ideology constitutes an identity as sameness within a fixed structure of signs' (Pratt Ewing, 1997: 103).

52 These variances within the Būdshīshiyya seem also to be characteristic of Sufi orders that, after being exported to western lands, maintain links with the original enclave (e.g. Haqqaniyya, Jerrahiyya). Among these groups, there is often compliance with *sharī'a* and Muslim identity – at least, more so than among other Sufi groups in Europe (e.g. Inayat Khan). However, even among the *sharī'a*-compliant orders a drift towards a more eclectic understanding of Sufism that incorporates New Age elements can already be discerned. As Hermansen has observed, many of these movements have ended up in schisms, the resulting sub-branches being composed on one side of migrants only, and on the other of converts only (2009: 37). Yet it seems difficult to predict whether the Būdshīshiyya will follow this pattern; although in Europe it combines both Islamic and eclectic trends, the fact that young revert Muslims of Moroccan background gather with

their European counterparts and not with the groups of Moroccan migrants leads us to think that there may be a different future – one without schisms – for the order.

References

Anway, C. L. 2007. *Daughters of Another Path. Experiences of American Women Choosing Islam*. Lee's Summit, MO: Yawna Publications.

Asad, T. 1986. *The Idea of an Anthropology of Islam*. Washington, DC: Georgetown University, Center for Contemporary Arab Studies.

Ben Driss, K. 2002. *Sidi Hamza al-Qadiri Boudchich. Le renouveau du soufisme au Maroc*. Beirut: Albouraq.

Ben Rochd, E. R. 2002. *Le soufre rouge*. Casablanca: Dechra.

Buehler, A. F. 1998. *Sufi Heirs of the Prophet: The Indian Naqshbandiyya and the Rise of the Mediating Sufi Shaykh*. Columbia, SC: University of South Carolina Press.

Buitelaar, M. 1993. *Fasting and Feasting in Morocco: Women's Participation in Ramadan*. Oxford: Berg.

Chlyeh, A. 1998. *Les gnaoua du Maroc: Itinéraires initiatiques, transe et possession*. Rabat: Editions la pensée sauvage.

——2000. *Le transe*. Rabat: Marsam.

Claisse, P. A. 2003. *Les gnawa marocains de tradition loyaliste*. Paris: L'Harmattan.

Curtis, M. F. 2007. 'Sound Faith, Nostalgia, Global Spirituality and the Making of the Fes Festival of World Sacred Music', unpublished Masters thesis. Austin, TX: University of Texas.

Dominguez Diaz, M. 2011. 'Performance, Belonging and Identity: Ritual Variations in the British Qadiriyya', *Religion, State and Society* 39(2–3): 229–45. London: Routledge.

——2013. 'Traditionalism', in *Encyclopedia of Psychology and Religion* (2nd ed.), 912–13. New York: Springer.

Douglas, M. 2004. 'The Two Bodies', in M. G. Fraser and M. Greco (ed.) *The Body: A Reader*, 78–81. London: Routledge.

Draper, M. 2002. 'Towards a Postmodern Sufism: Eclecticism, Appropriation and Adaptation in a Naqshbandiyya and a Qadiriyya Tariqa in the UK', unpublished PhD thesis. Birmingham: University of Birmingham.

Draper, M., Nielsen, J. and Yemelianova, G. 2006. 'Transnational Sufism. The Haqqaniyya', in J. Hinnells and J. Malik (eds) *Sufism in the West*, 103–14. London: Routledge Curzon.

During, J. and Sellheim, R. 2009. 'Samā'', in P. Bearman, Th. Bianquis, C. E. Bosworth, E. van Donzel and W. P. Heinrichs (eds) *Encyclopaedia of Islam*, 2nd ed. Brill online: School of Oriental and African Studies (SOAS), available online at www.brillonline.nl/subscriber/entry?entry=islam_COM-0992 (accessed 1 April 2009).

Eickelman, D. F. 1976. *Moroccan Islam: Tradition and Society in a Pilgrimage Center*. Austin, TX; London: University of Texas Press.

Ernst, C. 1997. *The Shambhala Guide to Sufism*. Boston, MA: Shambhala.

Ernst, C. and Lawrence, B. 2002. *Sufi Martyrs of Love: The Chishti Order in South Asia and beyond*. New York: Palgrave Macmillan.

Frishkopf, M. 2009. 'Globalizing the Soundworld. Islam and Sufi Music in the West', in R. Geaves, M Dressler and G. Klinkhammer (eds), *Sufis in Western Societies. Global Networking and Locality*, 46–76. London; New York: Routledge.

Geaves, R. 2004. 'Contemporary Sufism', in C. Partridge (ed.) *Encyclopedia of New Religions: New Religious Movements, Sects and Alternative Spiritualities,* 135–6. Oxford: Lion Publishers.

Geaves, R., Dressler, M. and Klinkhammer, G. 2009. 'Introduction', in R. Geaves, M. Dressler and G. Klinkhammer (eds), *Sufis in Western Societies. Global Networking and Locality,* 1–12. London; New York: Routledge.

Gellner, E. 1969. *Saints of the Atlas.* London: Weidenfeld & Nicholson.

Gilsenan, M. 1973. *Saint and Sufi in Modern Egypt: An Essay in the Sociology of Religion.* Oxford: Clarendon Press.

Haenni, P. and Voix, R. 2007. 'God by All Means ... Eclectic Faith and Sufi Resurgence among the Moroccan Bourgeoisie', in M. Bruinessen and J. Day Howell (eds) *Sufism and the 'Modern' in Islam,* 241–56. London: Tauris.

Halstead, J. M. 1994. 'Some Reflections on the Debate about Music in Islam', *Muslim Education Quarterly* 12(i): 51. Cambridge: Islamic Academy.

Hermansen, M. 2009. 'Global Sufism. "Theirs and Ours"', in R. Geaves, M. Dressler and G. Klinkhammer (eds) *Sufis in Western Societies. Global Networking and Locality,* 26–45. London; New York: Routledge.

Howell, D. J. 2007. 'Modernity and Islamic Spirituality in Indonesia's New Sufi Networks', in M. Bruinessen and D. J. Howell (eds) *Sufism and the 'Modern' in Islam,* 217–40. London: Tauris.

Hutson, A. S. 2006. 'African Sufi Women and Ritual Change', in P. J. Stewart and A. Strathern (eds) *Contesting Rituals: Islam and Practices of Identity-Making,* 145–65. Durham, NC: Carolina Academic Press.

Jonker, G. 2006. 'The Evolution of the Naqshbandi-Mujaddidi: Sulaymancis in Germany', in J. Hinnells and M. Jamal (eds) *Sufism in the West,* 71–85. London: Routledge Curzon.

Kapchan, D. A. 2007. *Traveling Spirit Masters: Moroccan Gnawa Trance and Music in the Global Marketplace.* Middletown, CT: Wesleyan University Press.

Katz, S. T. 1978. 'Language, Epistemology and Mysticism', in S. T. Katz (ed.) *Mysticism and Philosophical Analysis,* 22–74. Oxford: Oxford University Press.

Lassen, S. C. 2009. 'Growing Up as a Sufi. Generational Change in the Burhaniya Sufi Order', in R. Geaves, M. Dressler and G. Klinkhammer (eds) *Sufis in Western Society. Global Networking and Locality,* 148–61. London; New York: Routledge.

Lings, M. 1971. *A Sufi Saint of the Twentieth Century: Shaik Ahmad al-Alawī: His Spiritual Heritage and Legacy.* London: Allen and Unwin.

Lowry, J. E. 2008. 'Ritual Purity', in Jane Dammen McAuliffe (ed.) *Encyclopaedia of the Qur'ān.* Brill online. School of Oriental and African Studies (SOAS), available online at www.brillonline.nl/subscriber/entry?entry=q3_COM-00178 (accessed 9 May 2008).

Maarouf, M. 2007. *Jinn Eviction as a Discourse of Power: A Multidisciplinary Approach to Moroccan Magical Beliefs and Practices.* Leiden: Brill.

McPherson, J. W. 1941. *The Moulids of Egypt.* Cairo: N. M. Press.

Malik, A. 2004. *Qu'Allah bénisse la France.* Paris: Albin Michel.

Mauss, M. 1973. 'Techniques of the Body', *Economy and Society* 2(1): 70–88. London: Routledge.

Netton, I. R. 2000. *Sufi Ritual: The Parallel Universe.* Richmond: Curzon Press.

Nielsen, J. S., Draper, M. and Yemelianova, G. 2006. 'Transnational Sufism: The Haqqaniyya', in J. Malik and J. Hinnells (eds) *Sufism in the West,* 103–14. London: Routledge Curzon.

Padwick, C. E. 1961. *Muslim Devotions; A Study of Prayer-Manuals in Common Use.* London: SPCK.
Pratt Ewing, K. 1997. *Arguing Sainthood: Modernity, Psychoanalysis, and Islam.* Durham, NC: Duke University Press.
Raudvere, C. 2002. *The Book and the Roses: Sufi Women, Visibility and Zikir in Contemporary Istanbul.* Istanbul: Swedish Research Institute in Istanbul.
Ricoeur, P. 1992. *Oneself as Another.* Chicago, IL; London: University of Chicago Press.
Roald, A. S. 2006. 'The Shaping of a Scandinavian "Islam": Converts and Gender Equal Opportunity', in K. van Nieuwkerk (ed.) *Women Embracing Islam: Gender and Conversion in the West*, 48–70. Austin, TX: University of Texas Press.
Rozehnal, R. T. 2007a. *Islamic Sufism Unbound: Politics and Piety in Twenty First Century Pakistan.* New York: Palgrave Macmillan.
——2007b. 'A "Proving Ground" for Spiritual Mastery: The Chishti Sabiri Musical Assembly', *Muslim World: A Journal devoted to the Study of Islam and Christian-Muslim Relations* 98(iv): 657–77. Hartford, CT: Wiley Blackwell.
Schimmel, A. 1975. *Mystical Dimensions of Islam.* Chapel Hill, NC: University of North Carolina Press.
Sedgwick, M. J. 2004. *Against the Modern World: Traditionalism and the Secret Intellectual History of the Twentieth Century.* Oxford; New York: Oxford University Press.
Shannon, J. H. 2006. *Among the Jasmine Trees, Music and Modernity in Contemporary Syria.* Middletown, CT: Wesleyan University Press.
Sum, M. 2011. 'Staging the Sacred: Musical Structure and Processes of the Gnawa Lila in Morocco', *Ethnomusicology* 55(1): 77–111. Champaign, IL: Illinois University Press.
Turner, V. W. and Turner, E. L. B. 1978. *Image and Pilgrimage in Christian Culture: Anthropological Perspectives.* Oxford: Blackwell.
van Hoven, E. 2003. 'Saint Mediation in the Era of Transnationalism: The Da'ira of the Jakhanke Marabouts', *Africa: Journal of the International African Institute* 73(2): 290–308. Edinburgh: Edinburgh University Press for International African Institute.
van Nieuwkerk, K. 2006. 'Gender, Conversion and Islam. A Comparison of Online and Offline Conversion Narratives', in K. van Nieuwkerk (ed.) *Women Embracing Islam: Gender and Conversion in the West*, 1–18. Austin, TX: University of Texas Press.
Vásquez, Manuel A. 2011. *More Than Belief: A Materialist Theory of Religion.* Oxford: Oxford University Press.
Wallis, R. 1984. *The Elementary Forms of the New Religious Life.* London: Routledge.
Werbner, P. 2005. *Pilgrims of Love. The Anthropology of a Global Sufi Cult.* Karachi: Oxford University Press.
——2007. 'Intimate Disciples in the Modern World: The Creation of Translocal Amity among South Asian Sufis in Britain', in M. Bruinessen and D. J. Howell (eds) *Sufism and the 'Modern' in Islam*, 195–216. London: Tauris.
Zebiri, K. P. 2007. *British Muslim Converts: Choosing Alternative Lives.* Oxford: Oneworld Publications.
Zubaida, S. 1995. 'Is There a Muslim Society? Ernest Gellner's Sociology of Islam', *Economy and Society* 24(2): 151–88. London: Routledge.

7 Healing

Sufism at large has traditionally been associated with healing (*shifā'*), evidence of which is key in testing the veracity of claims to supernatural powers which are made by most potential *awliyā'* (Werbner, 2005: 213). Litanies were recited in the past by Sufi *shaykhs* with the aim of curing diseases,[1] and healing attributions are still in vogue today.[2] In this chapter I explore healing-related issues because of the importance that ideas of health and disease have in moral systems, and thus in religiosities. Practices related to healing are frequently performed in Madāgh, to the extent that a significant dimension of the *ṭarīqa*'s saintly legitimacy is (at least for some among those who follow Hamza) related to the healing powers of the *baraka* attained by him, the members of his family and the shrine complex. Health issues have come to play a major role during the course of the fieldwork on which this book is based.[3]

Qādiris: A healer's tradition

A widely held belief among Sufis is that the founder of the Qādiriyya order,[4] the Baghdadi 'Abd al-Qādir al-Jīlānī (d.1166), is second only to Jesus[5] in the scale of those with divine powers to cure. Among the miracles attributed to al-Jīlānī, those to do with healing are the ones that have most contributed to his saintly reputation; he is said to have brought the dead back to life (Kugle, 2007: 71), or cured the deafness of a girl by whispering the call to prayer in her ear (Schimmel, 1975: 208). The Qādirī tradition of healing has survived into our own times;[6] today there are still Qādirī groups throughout the Muslim world that whisper the ritual *fātiḥa*[7] in the presence of the sick person in order to induce his/her recovery (Schimmel, 1975: 208).

Al-Jīlānī marks the beginning of a tradition that associates Qādirī descendants with healing powers, a tradition that has found in Morocco a favourable ground to flourish and persist until today. Fes has been a remarkable example of Qādirī healing for centuries, where the Qādiriyya brotherhood that first arrived in the Maghreb from the Iberian Peninsula in 1492 settled (Draper, 2002: 172) and where they began a distinctive tradition of niche carving and decoration, through which they gained a reputation for saintliness.

Progressively, a Qādirī community was built around the first tomb of the complex, that of the surgeon and Qādirī 'Alī Ibn Abu Ghālib (d.1399),[8] who, it is said, miraculously healed the sick both during his lifetime and after death. Hagiographical accounts speak of his shrine being a famous centre for healing-related pilgrimage throughout the region; followers travelled from distant places to drink the water of a nearby fountain and to take in their hands the earth of his tomb for healing. To celebrate Abū Ghālib's famous gift for healing, it is said that on the anniversary of his death local political powers provided free circumcision to children whose families could not afford to pay for the ritual surgery (Kugle, 2007: 70). Successive Qādiris who settled in Fes continued to promote his fame as a healer; the place where his tomb is said to have been is today's Abū al-Quṭūt lodge, a place still commonly visited for *ziyāra* purposes.

Healing practices today

Visitation to shrines for purposes related to *shifā'* is widely practised in Morocco, a practice in which the Būdshīshiyya also participates. Other healing practices, however, are related to this brotherhood in its character of an order being led by a *maître vivant*, which gives this *ṭarīqa* its distinctive fame. The belief in the saint's curative powers is constantly nourished by oral transmission; stories of people being cured of strange diseases are common among the followers of Hamza. During my fieldwork, however, I never saw anything which might be perceived as a miracle, and I noticed that stories of miraculous cures were always presented in the third person. It was never the person who told the story who had actually experienced the cure; it was always someone else within the narrator's social circle. These narratives, I suggest, work as 'somatic images' (Csordas, 1990), stories that reproduce and transmit 'knowledge'. These tales inculcate *techniques du corps,* detailing the precise ways in which healing has to occur, by predetermining how healing is embodied and emplaced, and subsequent cases are framed in culturally similar ways. In this way the religious identity of the performers is reproduced and maintained (Csordas, 1990: 20).

Some of the most widespread 'somatic images' circulated within the order refer to the curing attributes obtained by 'touching Hamza', perhaps the most widespread practice with regard to healing as it concerns the Būdshīshiyya. It is based on the notion that the *baraka* believed to be emanated by Hamza's body can be transmitted by physical contact. Many of the visitors the *walī* receives intend to actually 'touch him' with the view of obtaining some of his saintly blessings; like many other *awliyā',* Hamza is commonly believed to possess the gift of modifying body conditions (e.g. curing the sick, helping to conceive) by 'interceding'.

But things have begun to change. Various women have reported disappointment at the recent measure that vetoes physically touching Hamza, allegedly instilled due to the increasing number of people who visit him and his advanced age. The *Zāwiya* in Madāgh, despite the banning, still receives a large number of visits both from the uninformed and the hopeful, all seeking divine healing-related assistance. The practice of *baraka* transmission by 'touching Hamza' is neither endorsed nor condemned by the *ṭarīqa*'s leadership. Instead both leaders and disciples tend to speak of the *walī*'s relationship with healing in an unclear, metaphorical way, which can be interpreted as a mechanism presumably intended to avoid criticism – seeking *baraka* has been a source of controversy throughout the Islamic world, because its critics consider it a form of idolatry for supplicants, who, they argue, may look towards the *walī* instead of towards God.

Also recurrent is the belief that Hamza's ability to heal does not necessarily depend upon physical contact, but can even be acquired in the (non-corporeal) spiritual exchange that occurs between master and disciple as a result of being part of this organization. Among Hamza's followers, narratives that depict the disciple's soul as 'being sick' prior to 'knowing' Sayyid (i.e. not necessarily meeting him face to face but entering the order), and having been cured as a result of receiving the *walī*'s love, are commonplace. The proselytizing tone of these 'narratives of recovery' has been eloquently assessed by one of the few academics critical of this organization to have emerged so far. Bouasria states that:

> In fact, the whole discourse of the Boutchichi [sic] order revolves around the fact that we are all, as human beings with shortcomings, 'sick' and our doctor is the spiritual master. According to this logic, one is doomed to feel a void, emptiness, and a yearning for a 'perfect man' and it is this hole that is the structure of *jouissance* [used here in the Lacanian sense].[9] […] When one joins the order, s/he remembers his/her previous 'life' as one of sickness and always repeats the words of the Guru Sidi [sic] Hamza: 'we are all sick and our hospital is the order.' Using *pathos* as a mode of recruitment has a double function: claiming a special cure that is found nowhere else, and discrediting all competing claims.
>
> (2011: 426)

Such 'narratives of recovery' depict healing in most cases as derived from the master–disciple relationship and thus occurring through the actual practice of Sufism, mainly based on a long-term sustained practice of ritual performance. Other forms of healing based on an intercession less extended over time do not involve Hamza himself and perhaps for this reason receive less publicity, yet they are also frequent practices within the world of the Būdshīshiyya. Miraculous healing in Islam is related to a sophisticated eschatological conceptualization of this world and the hereafter, thus we find dead and living healers acting simultaneously. However, the performance of healing miracles by living and dead saints differs in that the dead *walī* needs the assistance of a broker to transmit the curative powers from the hereafter to this world.

Although some claim that anybody in a state of ritual purity can undertake such a mediatory role, a *faqīrā* told me that it needs to be someone familiar with the 'two worlds' and in permanent relation with the two spheres of reality. In the Būdshīshiyya, the person who fulfils this role is the guardian and caretaker of the shrine complex, commonly referred to as Sīdī Bābā (literally meaning 'beloved father'), a man in his late sixties who lives permanently in the *Zāwiya*, and who cleans and watches over the shrine and the neighbouring cemetery.[10] A tree[11] serves as the landmark around which the complex has been built; under its shade, Bābā often sits surrounded by groups of women. Some women come with pictures, most with bottles of mineral water. They are seeking intercession to cure a person; in some cases the sick person is also under allopathic treatment, while in others conventional medicine has failed. Fatḥiyya (not her real name) shows me a picture of her son, a young man who is being treated at a hospital in Agadir for a rare condition. She tells me of her visit to various doctors, and that they cannot afford to pay for treatment in Europe. Bābā interrogates her at length, asking for her son's name, occupation and civil status and the symptoms he evidences.

Another woman told me that, on certain occasions, the sick person may be brought to the healer, so that s/he can be examined. Some disorders are believed to be the result of spirit (*jīnn*)[12] possession and people think it is safer that the healer contacts the *junūn* to try to pacify them, rather than regular people, who are more likely to upset them and generate undesired outcomes. The healer's intercession is not the cause of recovery – it is blessed water, whose purifying qualities are believed to extirpate the *jīnn* from the sick body. Bābā's job, thus, is to recite a series of Qur'ānic litanies while touching the mineral water[13] brought by the supplicant, water that will then be administered in small regular doses to the sick person. Another woman told me the water is not always swallowed but may in some cases be boiled and inhaled or be used to bathe the sick. Often the treatment is accompanied by long sessions of healing prayers performed by the supplicant, both at the Būdshīshiyya shrine complex, and when back home, sitting next to the sick person.

Healing prayers are not only common among those who refer to Bābā for intercession: it is a widespread practice among other adherents of this order who have never been in touch with the tombs' guardian; the practice is encouraged by the *ṭarīqa*'s leadership as well. For example, a British disciple explains that rituals of prayer such as the *Haḍra*, a form of *dhikr* invocation that is often performed standing, have curative effects needed for 'modern malaises':

> the Hadra [sic] […] is so needed for the sick heart in this modern day, our hearts are being plagued with dunya-worldly [sic][14] sickness, pains and trials from people, desires and our egos are overriding and destroying our spiritual heart to breathe, taste and live.[15]

Some other healing outcomes have been attributed by disciples to the collective gathering for reading the *Book of the Healing of the Sickness and Pains* by the Moroccan theologian Muḥammad ibn Ja'afar al-Kattānī (d.1927), and saying *Ya Laṭīf* prayers, 'practices which expiate prior and later wrong actions'.[16] Baṣīra (a pseudonym) explained to me that she recited the *fātiḥa* near her grandmother's ear when she was severely sick,[17] whereas Fāṭima (not her real name) told me how she spent a night reciting litanies and thinking of Hamza in a hospital ward while a member of her family was having an operation. In December 2008, the eldest of Hamza's sons, Jamāl, travelled to Paris to have an operation; collective emails were sent to all *fuqarā'* asking them to pray and perform ritual invocations that would help him to recover: 'Sīdī Jamāl asks you to pray with him in mind in all your invocations, so he gets rapidly well'.[18,19]

Healing-seekers and religious legitimacy

Although rituals that seek to bring health improvements to the sick, such as those done by Bābā, are performed both for men and women, the majority of people who ask for them are women, meaning that in many cases the person asking for healing is not the sick but someone on the sick's behalf. All the healing-seeking supplicants I met in this fieldwork were women, and informants confirmed it is in most cases women who seek these services; a study on healers also suggests that within the Rif region religious healers are always men, whereas their clients tend to be women (Mateo Dieste, 2013: 13). The proportion of peasants among those women that sought Bābā's assistance during the *Mawlid* celebrations was significant, something that could be easily attributed to the poor access to hygiene and allopathic facilities of these communities and a resulting higher incidence of disease, which, as argued by earlier scholarship (e.g. Capranzano, 1973) is higher in rural areas of the country.[20]

In Morocco, some forms of faith healing are, despite their popularity, positioned at the margins of religious legitimacy and therefore, with regard to the Būdshīshiyya at least, a close look reveals that the middle classes and the better educated do not altogether reject healing practices of this kind. These healing techniques have often been criticized as backward superstitions and charlatanism (*sha'wada*),[21] whose grounding in Islam is contested, especially but not only within reformed-minded Muslim circles.[22] The counter-hegemonic status the healing practices of the Sufis have acquired in Morocco is explained to me by a woman from Oujda, who tells me about who visits shrine-based healers like Bābā; she says that, whereas in the past people went to seek these services during major gatherings at Sufi lodges such as the *Mawlid*, they are increasingly going at times with fewer people around, as 'they do not want to be seen'. This is because they think they are asking for something that it is increasingly believed to be religiously forbidden and thus socially unacceptable, and/or because they sometimes ask for intercession on 'malaises' which are nonetheless considered taboo – quite typically, these are interventions for psychological ailments or infertility.

However, not all practices related to faith healing are deemed as sorcery; healing usages given in the Qur'ān, for example, are often considered normative, by both reformist and non-reformist audiences. In particular, healing prayers, and drinking water over which Qur'ānic recitations have been pronounced or which has pieces of paper bearing verses dissolved in it are widely used practices, which are likely to find less opposition in terms of religious normativity (although are often deemed as more acceptable when they are not performed by a Sufi). In the case of prayers and of blessed water, the distinction between what is and is not permitted is generally determined by agency: whereas healing *per se* is often not condemned, the attribution of healing to anyone or anything other than God is what is proscribed. In that sense, a lot of arguing, at least in Morocco, revolves around the ways in which supplicant and healer frame what they do, stating that a *jinn* or a healer or a particular substance or talisman has been what has healed the sick is often deemed as *ḥarām* (forbidden), whereas understanding these agents as channels though which God exerts his/her/its will is viewed as *ḥalāl* (permissible).

In practical terms, this translates into the existence of a variety of healers, whose methods and provenance respond differently and negotiate diversely their discursive detours to demonstrate attachment to the norm. On the one hand, there is the *fuqahā'*,[23] 'Qur'ānic' healers: their activities and narratives used to legitimize their techniques are generally considered (when they are not Sufis) to operate within the grounds of 'orthopraxis'.[24] Faith healing of this kind is often referred to as *ruqiyya* or as *ṭibb al-nabawī* (prophetic medicine). There are, on the other hand, the practices traditionally performed by the Sufis, usually considered as witchcraft and sorcery, and often understood to be prohibited by Islam. In reality, nonetheless, Qur'ānic and Sufi healers represent contrasting discursive spheres of the hegemonic/counter-hegemonic. These are ideal models that more often manifest in dialogue, with most healers adopting partially or selectively these stances according to a variety of circumstances.

Clients, as well, selectively use discourses and practices of each of these healing traditions, according to the needs, social conditions and family pressures they experience. This demonstrates the need to look at the interplay between these types of healing as part of the dialogue that occurs *quotidiennement* between Sufism and Reformism; without diminishing their antagonistic claims, Sufism and Reformism in practice often blur their theoretically very sharp boundaries, inadvertently borrowing from each other.[25] In the same way that it is easy to identify patterns of the maraboutic system within reform-minded and arguably anti-Sufi groups (see Chapter 2 for an example of this), the case of the Būdshīshiyya evidences the striving of 'sober' Sufis to be accepted as part of an increasingly hegemonic religious discourse that stands against the belief in the power of miracle performance traditionally attached to *awliyā'*.

This is not only the result of Sufism's interaction with Reformism, but of pressures to force Sufism to conform to changing ideals of 'religious normativity' which predate the birth of Islamic Reform. Historically speaking, in Morocco, at certain moments, the *ulamā'* have rejected the doctrines of Sufism and publicly denied the power attributed to Sufi saints. If these *awliyā' 'Allāh* were to gain the support of religious scholars, and in doing so to situate themselves closer to the spheres of religious and political power, they need to conform to the traditions of *uṣūl ad-dīn* and *uṣūl al-fiqh* and to show their pious adherence to the Sunna of the Prophet. This meant that the doctrinal basis of Moroccan Sufism could never lie too far from a more normative understanding of Islam. As Cornell points out: 'Even miracles had to conform to juridical ideals' (1998: 275).

Accordingly, a system was established in order to differentiate between unacceptable and acceptable *karāmāt.* Certain types of miracle were deemed to be unacceptable – including, for example, curing the sick and enriching the poor. By contrast, miracles that expressed extraordinary aptitudes for, and/or knowledge of, religion were to be tolerated, e.g. learning the Qur'ān by heart at a very early age (Cornell, 1998: 275). Ever since, Moroccan sainthood has been characterized by a certain gravity of behaviour among the *awliyā'*; Islamic scholarship would be willing to recognize miracles only if they were grounded in textual scholarship and the *awliyā'* demonstrated a vast knowledge of Islam, whereas those miracles based on acting upon the physical world (e.g. curing the body, increasing wealth, etc.) would not be acknowledged. A large gap developed as a result, between, on the one hand, the self-portrayed image of the *awliyā'* as guarantors of sober forms of Sufism,[26] and on the other, the fervour for more exalted religiosities still popular today.

The sobriety that characterizes Hamza's approach when it comes to his position on *karāmāt* represents the pattern of Moroccan sainthood in which the saint is seen as the guardian of more restrained forms of Sufism, somehow detached from the miracle-endorsing beliefs of many of his followers.[27] On many occasions miracle-endorsing beliefs will thus be performed not so much by 'living masters' (i.e. *awliyā'*) but by 'Sufi healers' who are part of the religious traditions of Sufism but often do not hold prominent or active roles within the leadership of a *ṭarīqa,* such as is the case with Bābā.

Healing practices are a case in point of the dichotomy between the leadership's conformity to religious sobriety and the discipleship's beliefs on magic. In healing terms, one can see the efforts of the Būdshīshiyya for its healing practices to be included in what is nowadays hegemonic, be 'normativised', and associated with the *ṭibb al-nabawī* 's tradition, and not with, paradoxically enough, the Sufi healing trend.[28] In this sense, various urban devotees defend the use of healing prayers or the practices undertaken by Bābā by arguing that they are not witchcraft but 'prophetic medicine'. Similarly, I have spoken with a devotee who, after widely criticizing 'the charlatan healers that give a bad reputation to Moroccan Islam', acknowledged having visited one on behalf of a family member affected by paralysis – but 'he [the healer], was not a marabout, but a righteous scholar of the Qur'ān'. A woman who was, in principle, critical of those who have turned to healers on various occasions said that it is always worth trying it out, just in case their methods work.[29]

Another adherent of the order from Agadir, in consonance with the comments made by the woman from Oujda, told me that people who visit healers do not publicly acknowledge it, and in fact some of the women I found in the lodge sitting next to Bābā did not want to talk about it. There seems, overall, to increasingly be a dichotomy between discourses and practices in relation to healing: what people more commonly publicly 'defend' is not actually what they in some cases end up doing. This is evidence that discourses are more adequately understood as resources for representation that serve different interests, rather than as descriptive images of particular social practices; in other words, discourses may be sometimes dissociated from practice, and, in those cases, the same discourses may therefore be used in relation to different social contexts (van Leeuwen, 2008). In this regard, it is not only those 'sympathetic' to the work of healers who seek the healer's intercession, nor even just those without the financial means to access allopathic treatment; on the contrary, the clientele of healers is diverse and permeates boundaries of ethnicity, class and levels of literacy (Flueckiger, 2006: 3) and includes people with varying degrees of 'publicly stated' support for the practices of healing.

In fact, support for healing practices of this kind is not divorced from support for allopathic medicine, and this Sufi order is an interesting example in this regard. This organization, which has expanded not only but also throughout professional networks[30] surprisingly well, has found a very fertile ground for potential devotees in hospitals in Morocco and France; in certain contingents, like those of Casablanca or Limoges, the percentage of people from the medical sector (nurses and doctors) is surprisingly high. Among them, I have met people whose support for allopathic treatments does not contradict but rather supplements an understanding of spiritual issues, which are believed capable of exerting an impact in the physical world, to the extent that these afflictions may be simultaneously treated with 'allopathic' and 'religious' techniques. In some cases, healing practices are resorted to in addition to the treatment provided by conventional medicine; saintly curative abilities are not seen as incompatible with those provided by the hospital or the medical centre.

Cultural permeability and healing

The belief in miraculous healing practices has not been toned down by audiences in Europe; on the contrary, numerous are the cases that attest to the significance of magic in the belief system and attendant practices of the European adherents of this organization – which contrasts with what earlier scholarship predicted in the matter (e.g Westerlund, 2004), but coincides with more recent studies' suggestion that the phenomenon of healing among Muslims is experiencing a revival thanks to its popularity outside the Muslim world (e.g. Khedimellah, 2007; Mateo Dieste, 2013), particularly among 'a younger generation of Muslims and those with higher educational attainment' (Eneborg, 2013: 1080). European devotees of the Būdshīshiyya are an illustration of this. It is also common to see, in the domed mausoleum (*qubbā'*) in Madāgh, small groups of devotees staying overnight within the premises of the *qubbā'*,[31] for it is believed that some of the *baraka* in the ambience is transferred to those pernoctating. Whereas this is typically requested by peasant women, a case was reported in which a group of European *fuqarā'* asked for permission to stay overnight inside the *qubbā'*, an act one of them believed was a way of becoming impregnated with 'saintly energies'[32] and 'being healed inside'.

Besides, I was told by informants at the lodge and in the surroundings of Madāgh that Bābā is not only visited by Moroccans but by 'people from all creeds and backgrounds', although from what I saw most of the European devotees present at Madāgh are in any case unaware of who Bābā is. This is an order in which a significant number of members have a short-lived commitment to the organization (see Chapter 3 for further discussion on this matter), and it does not advertise or publicize healing in any way, so devotees generally do not know of the existence of Bābā and his alleged powers before visiting the lodge for the first time. The (unverified) claim that Bābā is visited by non-Moroccans would, nevertheless, coincide with what happens to other healers in the borderland region between Morocco and Spain, it being quite common to meet Muslim clients at the consultancies of 'Christian' and 'New Age' healers, and Spaniards requesting the services of Muslim healers as well. In that sense, healing verifies the porosity of what is often called 'vernacular' Islam,[33] 'a practice [that is] negotiable, creative, and flexible […] and depends on a worldview shared across religious boundaries represented by its participants' (Flueckiger, 2006: 8).

The flexibility of healing practices is also attested to by the fact that there seems to be no correlation between the relationship of healer-suppliant and the suppliant's religious affiliation; in other words, many of those who seek the assistance of Bābā are not formal adherents of the *ṭarīqa* and, on various occasions, I was told, they have been to more than one healer (not necessarily Būdshīsh) with the same request. Similarly, devotees of this organization that demonstrate an interest in faith healing methods may not necessarily be looking to the Būdshīshiyya, or even to Islamic sources, for treatment.

For example, within the order, the number of adherents interested in alternative therapies is remarkable. I have met various Moroccan and European *fuqarā'* that are themselves practitioners of non-allopathic therapies. The British devotee Muhammad Sajad Ali defines himself on his website as a 'Sufi Webmaster, Instructor, Herbalist and Healing Therapist'.[34] A convert from Spain is pursuing a four-year degree programme in Chinese medicine with a one-year training element in China with traditional Chinese doctors. There is also a Moroccan therapist who heals with crystals, and another who defined as 'superstition' the healing practices employed by Bābā, yet who regularly attended yoga classes and believed in the curative power of certain 'magical' stones.[35] There was a British revert Muslim of Pakistani origin who pursued studies in shiatsu, and an acupuncturist member of the organization who has applied needles to several peer members. Another European *faqīra* told me she is studying kinesiology, and yet another was part of a programme on chiropractics to become a massage therapist.[36] A French disciple in her forties farms according to the techniques of bio-agriculture,[37] producing food she believes has 'curative effects', and another two are nurses, who, despite their profession, told me they regularly use Bach flower remedies.

Whereas most of those using alternative therapies combine their use with allopathic treatments, a few have reported rejection of using medical drugs, including vaccinations. This seems to show that an experiential approach to Sufism is characteristic of the 're-sacralized' contexts typical of western societies, a re-sacralization that commenced in the 1970s and is deeply impregnated with New Age ideas, including those that have led to the conceptualization of Sufism as a 'therapy' (Klinkhammer, 2009: 135); some of the cases presented above would definitely fit into this phenomenon.

The boundaries of religious allegiance may sometimes be tested by the interest in non-Islamic practices. A *faqīr* who wanted to travel to Peru to learn healing techniques with a shaman from the Andes Mountains asked for Hamza's permission to do so and the *shaykh,* it is reported, did not approve. The case generated intense controversy within the *ṭarīqa,* and it seems he ended up leaving the order, critical of what he considered to be an excessive 'jealousy' of religious affiliation. Other *fuqarā'* tried to persuade him to reconsider his decision, by trying to meet him outside formal gatherings and encouraging him to rethink his position and 'understand the meaning of such impositions'. In a series of conferences organized by the organization in Casablanca on 25 December 2000, the *muqaddim* of that city considered the use of non-Islamic practices perilous, and warned of the danger of Christian and Hindu influences in the *ṭarīqa,* defining them as 'temptations to de-islamise Sufism by assimilating philosophies of Christian or Hindu influence' (Ben Rochd, 2002: 115).[38] Issues of religious exclusivity are frequent among devotees and constitute a basis for heated debates; healing issues are often at the forefront of these discussions, which seems to suggest that healing practices as instances of embodied subjectivity may have the proclivity to subvert normativity more than other forms of expression.[39]

Mental health

Several ideas derived from 'the Moroccan understanding of ethnopsychiatry' can be identified within the order. This is of course an oversimplification.

> Just as they [Moroccans] have many different forms of therapy, so they have many theories of causation. Their 'pathologies' are often self-contradictory.

> They appear to be an amalgamation of various folk beliefs and popularizations of traditional Arab and modern Western medicine. Since theories of causation vary from tribe to tribe, family to family, it is impossible to form a systematic Moroccan pathology.
>
> (Capranzano, 1973: 134)

Nonetheless, some commonalities can be identified countrywide: 'a supernatural element will enter either directly or indirectly into the Moroccan's explanation of any disease [and] it is possible to divide Moroccan theories of causation roughly into two categories: Naturalistic and preternaturalistic explanations' (Capranzano, 1973: 134). Whereas natural causes are those with a mechanistic component (e.g. a particular substance intake causes an illness), preternatural ones are those invisible to the naked eye (e.g. caused by spirit possession).[40] The latter is often associated with diseases that in allopathic terms are considered of a 'psychological' nature. Within the Būdshīshiyya, for example, various are the references to the positive effect that the practice of Sufism or the intercession of a *walī* can have on conditions with a preternatural origin. Insanity, and the healing power attributed to Hamza, is recurrently used as a mechanism to turn people to the order. Ben Rochd explains the story of a man who recalls the need to find a master: 'if I do not find a shaykh I will go mad'. Rochd thinks this was a turning point that made the man join the *ṭarīqa*, a case Rochd compares to his own (2003: 11).

For one of the female converts, entering the organization provided an answer to her search for psychological stability.[41] Sāra (a pseudonym) reports her long-lasting battle against the bipolar disease with which she has been diagnosed and the repeated failures of psychiatric doctors to help her. A similar feeling of dissatisfaction with psychiatry is conveyed by Ifra (not her real name) who was diagnosed as suffering from paranoid episodes, and who found release in the Sufi 'wider, more comprehensive, less simplistic understanding of mental diseases': not only of those phenomena often considered as 'disorders', but also of feelings simply of emotional unease, such as bereavement or other situations that may lead people to embark on this kind of spiritual quest.

See, for example, the case of the hip-hop singer and boy of the *banlieue,* who narrates the pain caused by the deaths of many friends who were the victims of overdoses, police abuses, and knife and gun crime, and develops an acknowledged coping mechanism by joining the Būdshīshiyya (Malik, 2004). On two different occasions I have met psychotherapists who started to think of their profession in new terms after joining the organization, which is presented as a different form of understanding physical and mental balance.[42] Joining the order is related to self-awareness: whereas some (not only European devotees) think of Sufism as a detour of self-discovery, a notion which either imports from or coincides with New Age ideas of disease as a lack of contact with one's natural selfhood (Heelas, 1996: 209), sometimes the opposite is also argued, i.e. the practice of Sufism as a process of de-individuation, and of losing self-awareness. In these cases, the de-emphasizing of personal needs that comes with their experience of being Hamza's disciples is considered helpful, a growth that stems from the progressive abandoning of egocentrism. In this sense, thinking of problems as if they do not belong to you is praised, as explained by a devotee:

> People generally give to states[43] of depression and feelings of loneliness too much importance, and these are things that do not belong to you and that will pass, are states that will end and come back over and over again, they are of no relevance if you detach from the ego, the *nafs*.

Also recurrent is the appearance of adherents who lean into the psychological/emotional causation of physical illness. Illnesses in this view can result from states of psychological/emotional imbalance – e.g. colds would be caused by stress; a loss of voice means that one is preventing oneself from expressing feelings. Others, particularly Europeans, may support ideas of 'spiritist' causation of certain illnesses, and thus believe that 'extramundane attributes' can have healing benefits in those instances, similar to what Capranzano (1973) sees in Morocco. One does not know, however, if the natural/preternatural dichotomy in disease causation is exclusive to Moroccan culture, in which case its usage by European members of the Būdshīshiyya can be seen as a form of 'cultural borrowing'; or if, on the contrary, it responds to emic perspectives also typical of European religion; after all, spiritualism and its more recent offshoot, Spiritism, have been part of Western Europe's religious landscape since the nineteenth century.[44]

The set of ideas initiated by Hypolite Léon Denizard Rivail appeared both as a reaction to materialist science and as an extreme product of positivism, and postulates that spirits have both the ability and the inclination to interact with the living, very similar to the stances of some of the European adherents I have met. Spiritism was later incorporated into various versions of New Age ideology (including what is often defined as Harmonial Religion, characteristic, again, of various disciples' understanding of the otherworldly)[45] and to some New Religions.[46]

Khādīja (a pseudonym) explained to me that she lost 30 kg after splitting up with her former boyfriend – a convert to Buddhism who was living in the *Zāwiya* in Paris[47] – and she was 'diagnosed' by an iridologist as having an energetic channel which was too open. Because of this she was susceptible to 'negative influences' that made her lose weight, change her mood and fight with her ex-boyfriend. She was receiving treatment from a 'holistic therapist' in order to regain her original weight. Another devotee told me she travelled to Senegal where she got seriously ill, the problem, according to her, having to do with 'malign spirits'. She successfully recovered after staying in 'an energetically clean environment' for quite a long while, a place that she cleansed of 'bad energies' every day by burning incense and placing small piles of salt in each corner.

When compared, the remedies provided, and more relevantly the vocabulary employed to refer to them, may not be the same in Europe and Morocco; thus, in Csordasian terms, the 'somatic images' (Csordas, 1990) vary according to location. One may think of this as evidence of the internal diversity existing in the order, which may possibly end up posing a threat to the cohesiveness of the organization. On the other hand, the belief system that sustains the rationale of pathological causation endorsed by *faqīrāt* worldwide is remarkably and quite surprisingly similar. Both in Morocco and Europe, 'preternatural' maladies – terminology that is not emic among either Moroccan or European devotees – are believed to be cured with the intercession of 'mediums'. Whereas in Morocco, either a Sufi or a *faqīh* may be called on to intervene, instead of, or in addition to, the doctor, some European devotees refer to non-Muslim mediums rather than turning to the 'spiritual' services offered by the order, or within Islam.

In conclusion, healing techniques used by members of this *ṭarīqa* evidence interesting intercultural cross-pollinations regarding notions of the body, ontological cosmologies and bodily anatomies, yet they more powerfully evidence the mechanisms through which sacred knowledge is perpetuated via normative constrictions of religious exclusivism and by using 'somatic images'; these are icons that preserve the cultural pool of what healing practices constitute in Morocco and what is that they can do and the precise terms of how they do it. Healing practices are also instances of embodied subjectivity, and as such show a proclivity to subvert what it is normative, denoting that, whereas discourses are ways in which people represent themselves, practices may sometimes manifest in a dissociated manner, so *la notion du personne* is something that often operates independently from *les techniques du corps* (Mauss, [1938] 1950).

Notes

1 See Ibn al-Kalbī's *Kitāb al-Aṣnām* ([1343] 1924) for an early account of Islamic sorcery including healing. Later medieval accounts of Sufi healing can be found in Bürgel (1988).

2 This is evidenced in a rich body of scholarship. There are some comprehensive studies on healing in South India (Flueckiger, 2006) and Morocco (Capranzano, 1973; Mateo Dieste, 2013) and various studies that contain sections dealing with healing practices. Bowen (1993) reports healing practices among Sumatrans (Indonesia), and Saheb has explored *pir* devotion dealing with healing practices in South India (1998: 72–3); the reputation of the Punjabi Mama Ji Sarkar as a healer has been noted by Frembgen (1998); and Egyptian Sufi healers have been studied by Hoffman (1995: 155, 179, 216–17). Other cases have been reported in Pakistan (Pratt Ewing, 1997; Werbner, 2005; Rozehnal, 2007).

3 References to healing among members of the Būdshīshiyya are common; healing is a recurrent metaphor, for Hamza is seen as the healer of the sick soul of the disciple. The healing metaphor is also used to refer to non-medical situations, for example, the need to be a member of the order to practise Sufism was once argued by a devotee in the following terms: 'Sufism is our hospital', he told me, 'the same way one does not take medicines without consulting the doctor, one does not take

spiritual medicines without consulting a spiritual doctor, therefore do not perform *dhikr* without the guidance of Hamza'.

4 The Būdshīshiyya is a sub-branch of the Qādiriyya; for further information on the *silsila* see Appendix 1.

5 Today, Sufi orders that have reached Europe frequently highlight Sufism's similarities with the Christian tradition, thus making it look more familiar to European audiences who are assumed to be Christian or at least to have a Christian heritage (which can be seen as a strategy to attract converts). Thus Jesus is held to be one of the initiators of the Sufi tradition, and miracle-performance is presented as 'proof' of that connection (Skali, 2004: Ch. 9).

6 This is of particular relevance – although not exclusive – to members of the Qādirī lineage. One of the many famous cases of Qādirīs performing miracles is that of the Tunisian Abū al-Ghayth al-Qashshāsh (d.1622); see for instance Wiegers (1994). The tomb of the Shādhilī Sayyida 'Ā'isha al-Manubiyya (d. thirteenth century), in Tunis, for example, was a place (up to 2012, when it was burnt in an alleged 'Salafi' attack) frequently visited not only by Shādhilī *fuqarā'* but by people who came even from neighbouring countries in search of divine blessing and cure (Kugle, 2007: 99). She is only one of many examples that we could use to illustrate the still-powerful belief in curative powers associated with Sufi *personages* in the region. The healing aspect of *ziyāra* in Morocco has been described in detail in the as yet unparalleled work of Westermarck (1926). One of the many famous cases of Qādirīs performing miracles is that of the Tunisian Abū al-Ghayth al-Qashshāsh (d.1622); see for instance Wiegers (1994).

7 For further explanation of this particular formula in Sufi litanies of *dhikr,* see Glossary. For more information about *dhikr* as performed by Būdshīshī *fuqarā',* see Chapter 6.

8 The alley today is known as al-Qalia, though at that time it was called al-Ṣirāwiyyīn. An historical approach to Fes architecture can be found in Cambazard-Amahan (1989). However, today there are no actual remains of 'Alī Ibn Abī Ghālib's body or tomb and we really do not know if he was indeed an historical figure (Kugle, 2007: 69).

9 It is the pain produced by seeking pleasure beyond 'the pleasure principle' that compels the subject to constantly attempt to transgress the prohibitions imposed on his/her enjoyment. Since there is only a certain amount of pleasure that the subject can bear, the result of transgressing the pleasure principle, according to Lacan, is not more pleasure but pain. Beyond this limit, pleasure becomes pain, and this 'painful principle' is what Lacan calls *jouissance.* A more detailed discussion on the Lacanian use of the term is contained in Evans (1996).

10 The shrine complex contains the tombs of some of the members of the *silsila,* whereas the cemetery has the bodies of relatives of the Būdshīshiyya family who are not believed to have inherited the *sirr* (spiritual secret only granted by God to those who lead the order).

11 It is typical of Moroccan shrines that they are to be placed in association with landmarks, such as trees or water springs.

12 *Jinn*; pl. *junūn* (Ar.): literally meaning 'invisible' – beings created by God believed to live in a parallel universe. They are not, strictly speaking, supernatural, because they are believed to be material, made of matter, although humans are unable to see them.

13 The use of water for healing purposes is common throughout the Muslim World, since it is mentioned in the Qur'ān as a purifying element; it is often deemed to have a detox function on the body (thence the cleansing character associated with steam baths, and the central role fountains and springs often have in shrines in Morocco). An example of water usage for healing purposes among members of the Bangladeshi community in London can be found in Muslim Eneborg (2013).

14 *Dunyā* (Ar.) literally means 'lower'. In the Qur'an, *dunyā* is presented as the antithesis of *ākhira*, the former representing this world and the latter the hereafter (7: 156).

15 Available online at www.deenislam.co.uk/sufinotes/sufijourney1.htm (accessed 13 January 2013).

16 Available online at www.deenislam.co.uk/sufinotes/DhikrofTariqah.html (accessed 13 January 2013).

17 The same practice has been seen among Sufis in Rajpur (Pakistan); see Werth (1998: 81).

18 Email communication, 12 December 2008. Praying is typically credited with healing powers; for example, in Egypt, Sengers has analysed the cases of people who visit *shaykhs* who say prayers for them both during these visits and at night (2002: 136); and Javaheri (2006) has assessed this very common practice among cancer patients in Iran. Skipping prayers or performing them inadequately or without intention is commonly believed to bring the potential for being possessed by spirits (Sengers, 2002: 149). Whereas on most occasions Hamza disciples understand the healing power of prayers as being exclusively applied to living organisms, a woman once suggested me that prayers can also be said to intervene in wars. This brings us back to the similarities between the Būdshīshiyya and several New Religious Movements, with this type of group behaviour closely resembling, for example, the practices of the Transcendental Meditation (TM) programme, operated by a group that promotes a particular set of meditation techniques developed by Maharishi Mahesh Yogi – practices which are believed to have a positive effect in solving conflicts of all types; people in these groups travel to war zones to practise meditation in order to 'help solve' such conflicts. The group is generally regarded among scholars as a New Religious Movement (e.g. Wallis, 1984), although some authors (e.g. Hanegraaff, 1996) highlight the fact that the movement is sometimes misleadingly considered to be part of the New Age phenomenon, and it is grouped together with organizations such as the International Society for Krishna Consciousness (ISKCON) and the Osho Organisation. For more information about the group visit the official website available online at http://tm.org/ (accessed 22 January 2013).

19 My own translation from the French: '*Sīdī Jamāl vous demande de prier avec lui dans toutes vos invocations pour qu'il soit rétabli rapidement*'.

20 Fifty-two per cent of the rural population compared with 88% of the urban population have the use of adequate sanitation facilities. 90% of the urban population use improved drinking water sources, compared with 56% in rural areas; see the UNICEF 2004 census, available online at www.unicef.org/infobycountry/morocco_statistics.html#44 (accessed 19 January 2009). After years of planning, Morocco officially launched the EU-funded Medical Assistance Regime (RAMED) in November 2008. The programme was aimed at rural populations not covered under the employer-based mandatory health insurance system. It was estimated that the programme would extend medical coverage to 62% of the population. Today, however, coverage is still insufficient. Lack of health coverage was seen by scholars studying Sufi *ziyārāt,* either in Morocco (Crapanzano, 1973) or in Lebanon, as a cause of recurrence to faith healing; see for instance Howell (1970).

21 Morocco has a very strong tradition of healers and sorcerers, a custom that has been recently reinforced by diaspora communities (Mateo Dieste, 2013), and is not always free of controversy. See the case of a Moroccan healer accused of killing an 18-year-old girl in Belgium (a report of the case available online at www.deredactie.be/cm/vrtnieuws.english/News/1.624404 (accessed 14 January 2014); and of another accused of murder after the bleeding to death of a girl in Vic, Spain (Mateo Dieste, 2013: 6). Most of the accounts are by no means tragic, however, and Moroccan healers remain very popular among both Moroccans and non-Moroccans. The case of a disabled American who was back to walking after being cured in Morocco turned out to be a viral video available online at www.lisamharrison.com/2013/06/28/bobs-journey-to-healing-in-morocco/ (accessed 10 January 2014). Another case is that of a famous Moroccan healer who toured the Balkans and was met with a great ovation; see an account of this case

available online at http://janissaire.haut etfort.com/archive/2010/10/28/mekki-torabi-le-guerisseur-marocain-qui-fait-tourner-la-tete.html (accessed 15 January 2014).

22 This belief has been fiercely criticized as 'associating partners with God' (*shirk*) since its origins go back to pre-Islamic times in the Arabian Peninsula, according to early sources. The most comprehensive accounts are detailed in Ibn al-Kalbī's *Kitāb al-Aṣnām* ([1343] 1924), or 'Book of Idols'. In that work the concept of *siḥr* is described as an umbrella term that includes believing in *jnūn* possession and exorcisms, use of talismans, cursing, and the curing of others by extirpating malign forces from their bodies. According to O'Connor (2009) it was not until the tenth century that a distinction between acceptable and illicit *siḥr* was developed and certain forms of exorcism related to healing were forbidden. Today, these criticisms are also very common in other countries (e.g. Flueckiger, 2006: 13).

23 *Faqīh*; pl. *fuqahā'* (Ar.): an expert in Islamic law; the term is often translated as 'Jurist'. In popular parlance, however, people considered articulate in religious matters are often referred to as *faqīh*. For example, healers who argue in favour of their practices by citing the Qur'ān are often referred to in this way.

24 The use of the term 'orthodoxy' is problematic with regard to Islam, as there is no centralized clergy. It should be made clear that what is being referred to here is 'orthodoxy' in Asad's (1986) sense of the term; that is, the exercise of power in consolidating agreement on certain practical issues – what is commonly known as *orthopraxis*. Historically speaking, Islam has witnessed various attempts to reach or impose agreement, but they have never been completely successful, making problematic the use of the categories orthodox and unorthodox. As Werbner has pointed out, this false dichotomy of Islam upheld by scholars – Sufi Islam *vs* Orthodox Islam – has been influenced by the opinions of some Islamic reformist movements, especially those that are critical of Sufism (Werbner, 1998).

25 A collection of articles that masterfully illustrate these cross-pollinations is Ridgeon's (forthcoming) edited volume *Sufis and Salafis in the Contemporary Age: Partners in Purity*.

26 Although there are some exceptions in Morocco; see for instance Spadola (2008).

27 For example, although not related to healing, the love Hamza has for his disciples is believed to be so strong that he miraculously appears to them in different locations. Many devotees, for instance, have reported having seen his face in the full moon. Other cases of reports of Sufis' appearance have occurred in Africa; for instance, in September 2013 a Sufi was said to appear on the walls of a small mosque in Lagos, which consequently lured crowds of believers from across Nigeria and neighbouring West African nations to the mosque, amid criticisms by other Muslims of idolatry. The report on the apparition is available online at www.onislam.net/english/news/africa/464433-sufi-scholars-apparitions-lures-nigerians.html (accessed 16 January 2014).

28 The case of the Dandarawiyya is similar. The *ṭarīqa*'s leader during the 1970s denied any sort of miracle-performance, whereas his followers were fervently at odds with his position; see Sedgwick (2000).

29 The persisting vitality of beliefs in miraculous healing is manifested not only in Moroccan Islam but in Sufi orders throughout the world. Ballard, when discussing the Sufi religiosities of Punjabi Muslims in Pakistan, has noted that most people explore the utility of such remedies (2006: 166).

30 In Morocco the order is in some circles known as the '*zāwiya* of the [medical] doctors', while in France there are groups where doctors and nurses are predominant, with the Būdshīshiyya finding the workplace of the hospital a fertile ground for new members. The 'quasi-corporativist' (Haenni and Voix, 2007: 249) structure of this *ṭarīqa* among the Moroccan elites results in particular professional sectors becoming affiliated to it, while professional networks are partly related to the order's expansion in the cities of Western Europe as well. This is another element that

allows us to compare the Būdshīshiyya with movements categorized as New Religious Movements. The corporate structure is one remarkable characteristic, for example, of Japanese New Religious Movements, among others; see Matsunaga (2000).

31 *Qubbāʿ* (Ar.): doomed mausoleum, or more generically any Muslim shrine complex used for *ziyāra*.

32 Westerlund (2004: 34) has suggested that European Sufism has toned down several aspects of this religiosity which nevertheless remain typical of it in the Muslim World – matters such as the veneration of saints and forms of healing using exorcism; yet this does not seem to be the case with the Būdshīshiyya, where belief in healing practices seems to be quite widely held. Similarly, orders established in Europe have an increasing number of Sufi healers living in European countries; see for example, Werbner (2009).

33 The term famously coined by Flueckiger (2006), however, may be called into question on the basis that, not only are other understandings of Islam deemed to be more 'normative' also 'idioms' that represent specific negotiations of textual traditions and participations and/or reactions to discursive hegemony, but also, cultural borrowings and intercultural participation are common in both Sufi-oriented and Reformist versions of Islam.

34 Available at http://unsfoundation.co.uk/ (accessed 20 January 2014).

35 Haenni and Voix have explained the pejorative attitude of these elites towards popular religious beliefs as the result of the lack of religious education that these urban groups have received: 'Religion is often problematic for them. As a result of what is often a minimal or otherwise impoverished traditional religious education, they soon develop a relationship with the sacred that is distant or even outspokenly hostile. They are highly critical of the religiosity of their parents, which they consider as "ritualistic", associated with the "Islam of the *jinn*", and unattractive because it is too "mechanical" and, in a nutshell, "too superstitious"' (Haenni and Voix, 2007: 243).

36 Another example of these borrowings, although not related to healing, is that back in 2008 classes teaching martial arts were held in the *Zāwiya* of Birmingham.

37 Bio-agriculture, she explained to me, is not the same as organic agriculture. Bio-agriculture tries to profit from the natural qualities of each soil type by applying 'natural' techniques to it that optimize its productivity. Some peasant members of the order in Morocco have become interested in this technique and the first pilot experiments are being conducted in the north-eastern region of the country. Several European devotees are interested in bio-agriculture and/or organic food culture; Eatwell, a young British disciple of the *ṭarīqa*, exposed the contrast between the peasant Moroccan and the middle-class European approaches to 'organic' food when he visited Madāgh: 'The midday sun caught the tips of the corn, turning the leaves a golden yellow. A larger cloud of dust rose in front of us, and I looked to see the wholegrain wheat being winnowed and gathered for our bread. […] We tipped the wheat slowly into a basket, carefully avoiding spillage. We carried it over to a large rustic sieve, and sitting on crates, sorted slowly through it, looking for small rocks (and anything else for that matter!). This is as organic as it gets, I thought. Ironically though, in Morocco this is not considered any great asset, and it is only used because it is the cheapest available. This reminded me of the barley we used to eat in Tangier because it was so cheap, whereas the exact same product in England costs twenty times as much (simply because it is organic and from Morocco)'; available online at www.sufiway.net/ar_Sufism_cornerstone-zawiya.html (accessed 21 January 2013).

38 My own translation from French.

39 The process undergone by the Burhāniyya during the 1980s in Germany seems to be somehow similar to what we are seeing in the Būdshīshiyya today. There was among the Burhāniyya's devotees considerable interest in yoga, tantra and shamanism and in the teachings of other Sufi and non-Sufi masters. As is the case

with some of Hamza's followers, for these people (Burhāniyya's disciples), 'the Burhāniyya had appeared as one option among others' (Lassen, 2009: 153). With time, however, the Burhāniyya evolved into a more solid order in which devotees' commitment became stronger, something that is yet to occur in some of the urban strands of the Būdshīshiyya, both in Morocco and Europe. In the Būdshīshiyya, there are still plenty of examples of followers who mix their adherence to the *ṭarīqa* with religiosities of a wider eclectic nature and 'universalistic' scope.

40 For an interesting study of *jinn*-related beliefs in Morocco and the resulting discourses on power, see Maarouf (2007). Rozehnal explains the case of someone who suffered from tuberculosis of the spine and who went to see the Chīstī *shaykh* Zauqi Shah when the treatments prescribed by his medical doctors failed (2007: 56).

41 The search for psychological stability by joining *ṭuruq* in Europe has been highlighted by Köse (1996: 173) and Geaves (2000: 157).

42 This was the case, for example, of a psychotherapist from London, who joined the order after going on a Būdshīshiyya retreat in Southern Spain as a participant in the BBC2 reality programme *The Retreat*, broadcast in February 2007. Further discussion on this is provided in Chapter 3.

43 They relate these 'states' to the Sufi *aḥwāl* (sing. *ḥāl*), a notion used in early mystical sources (e.g. Sulamī, Safī ad-Dīn) to denote the realization of an encounter with the Divine, a moment described as acquaintance with perfect balance of the soul due to the acceptance of this encounter.

44 An interesting analysis of the historical development of spiritist ideas within western thought can be found in Hanegraaff (1996: 411–513).

45 Although never referred to in those terms, one can identify instances of 'harmonial' ideas among some European devotees. We define 'harmonial religion' following Ahlstrom's definition: 'Harmonial religion encompasses those forms of piety and belief in which spiritual composure [and] physical health […] are understood to flow from a person's rapport with the cosmos' (Ahlstrom, 1972: 1019). Some forms of New Age Religion incorporate harmonial ideas by stressing a harmony with 'the spiritual forces' (Ahlstrom, 1972: 8; Fuller, 1989: 51).

46 Spiritism has been and still is central to monotheisms. There are quite a number of Spiritualist churches, which are explicitly Christian in theology, forms of worship and praise, and liturgical orientations. Some of the more sizeable ones are African American denominations such as the Spiritual Church Movement. Some 'new religions', such as Wicca, incorporate spiritist ideas and perform various forms of magic through which devotees engage with these entities. It is common for Wiccans to use spells for healing, protection or fertility, or to banish negative influences.

47 The Buddhist found himself jobless and homeless in Paris and the people from the order offered him shelter and food in the *Zāwiya* where he stayed, according to some accounts, for almost a year. He was never asked for money. Hospitality is central to the moral code of this organization and of other forms of Moroccan Sufism, something I address in Chapter 5.

References

Ahlstrom, S. E. 1972. *A Religious History of the American People*. New Haven, CT: Yale University Press.

Asad, T. 1986. *The Idea of an Anthropology of Islam*. Washington, DC: Georgetown University, Center for Contemporary Arab Studies.

Ballard, R. 2006. 'Popular Islam in Northern Pakistan and its Reconstruction in Urban Britain', in J. R. Hinnells and J. Malik (eds) *Sufism in the West*, 160–87. London; New York: Routledge.

Ben Rochd, R. 2002. *Le soufisme. Patrimoine universel, méthode d'épanouissement et doctrine d'harmonie.* Oujda: Déchra.

Ben Rochd, E. R. 2003. *Le soufre rouge.* Casablanca: Dechra.

Bouasria, A. 2011. 'The Boutchichi Order and the Politics of *Jouissance*', *Middle East Studies Journal* 3(6): 421–7. Washington, DC: Middle East Institute.

Bowen, J. R. 1993. *Muslims through Discourse: Religion and Ritual in Gayo Society.* Princeton, NJ: Princeton University Press.

Bürgel, J. C. 1988. *The Feather of Simurgh: The 'Licit Magic' of the Arts in Medieval Islam.* New York: New York University Press.

Cambazard-Amahan, C. 1989. *Le décor sur bois dans l'architecture de fès: Époques almoravide, almohade et début mérinide.* Paris: Editions du Centre National de la Recherche Scientifique.

Capranzano, V. 1973. *The Ḥamadsha: A Study in Moroccan Ethnopsychiatry.* Berkeley, CA: University of California Press.

Cornell, V. J. 1998. *Realm of the Saint. Power and Authority in Moroccan Sufism.* Austin, TX: University of Texas Press.

Csordas, T. J. 1990. 'Embodiment as a Paradigm for Anthropology', *Ethos* 18(1): 5–47. Berkeley, CA: University of California Press.

Draper, M. 2002. 'Towards a Postmodern Sufism: Eclecticism, Appropriation and Adaptation in a Naqshbandiyya and a Qadiriyya Tariqa in the UK', unpublished PhD thesis. Birmingham: University of Birmingham.

Eneborg, Y. M. 2013. 'Ruqya Shariya: Observing the Rise of a New Faith Healing Tradition amongst Muslims in East London', *Mental Health, Religion & Culture* 16(10): 1080–96. London: Routledge.

Evans, D. 1996. *An Introductory Dictionary of Lacanian Psychoanalysis.* London: Routledge.

Flueckiger, J. B. 2006. *In Amma's Healing Room: Gender and Vernacular Islam in South India.* Bloomington, IN: Indiana University Press.

Frembgen, J. W. 1998. 'The Majzub Mama Ji Sarkar. A Friend of God Moves from One House to another', in H. Basu and P. Werbner (eds) *Embodying Charisma: Modernity, Locality, and Performance of Emotion in Sufi Cults,* 140–59. London; New York: Routledge.

Fuller, R. C. 1989. *Alternative Medicine and American Religious Life.* New York: Oxford University Press.

Geaves, R. 2000. *The Sufis of Britain: An Exploration of Muslim Identity.* Cardiff: Cardiff Academic Press.

Ridgeon, L. (ed.) (forthcoming). *Sufis and Salafis in the Contemporary Age: Partners in Purity.* London: Bloomsbury Continuum.

Haenni, P. and Voix, R. 2007. 'God by All Means … Eclectic Faith and Sufi Resurgence among the Moroccan Bourgeoisie', in M. Bruinessen and J. Day Howell (eds) *Sufism and the 'Modern' in Islam,* 241–56. London: Tauris.

Hanegraaff, W. J. 1996. *New Age Religion and Western Culture: Esotericism in the Mirror of Secular Thought.* Leiden: Brill.

Heelas, P. 1996. *The New Age Movement. The Celebration of the Self and the Sacralization of Modernity.* Cambridge, MA: Blackwell.

Hoffman, V. J. 1995. *Sufism, Mystics and Saints in Modern Egypt.* Columbia, SC: University of South Carolina Press.

Howell, D. 1970. 'Health Rituals at a Lebanese Shrine', *Middle East Studies* 6(1): 179–88. Abingdon: Routledge.

Ibn al-Kalbī, H. [1343] 1924. *Kitāb al-Aṣnām*. Cairo: Dār al-Kutub al-Miṣrīyah.
Javaheri, F. 2006. 'Prayer Healing: An Experiential Description of Iranian Prayer Healing', *Journal of Religion and Health* 45(2): 171–82. New York: Springer.
Khedimellah, M. 2007. 'Une version de la ruqiya de rite prophétique en France', in C. Hamès (ed.) *Coran et talismans: Textes et pratiques magiques en milieu musulman,* 385–407. Paris: Karthala.
Klinkhammer, G. 2009. 'The Emergence of Transethnic Sufism in Germany. From Mysticism to Authenticity', in R. Geaves, M. Dressler and G. Klinkhammer (eds) *Sufis in Western Societies. Global Networking and Locality*, 130–47. London; New York: Routledge.
Köse, A. 1996. *Conversion to Islam: A Study of Native British Converts*. London: Kegan Paul International.
Kugle, S. A. 2007. *Sufis and Saints' Bodies. Mysticism, Corporeality and Sacred Power in Islam*. Chapel Hill, NC: University of North Carolina Press.
Lassen, S. C. 2009. 'Growing Up as a Sufi. Generational Change in the Burhaniya Sufi Order', in R. Geaves, M. Dressler and G. Klinkhammer (eds) *Sufis in Western Society. Global Networking and Locality*, 148–61. London; New York: Routledge.
Maarouf, M. 2007. *Jinn Eviction as a Discourse of Power: A Multidisciplinary Approach to Moroccan Magical Beliefs and Practices*. Leiden: Brill.
Malik, A. 2004. *Qu'Allah bénisse la France*. Paris: Albin Michel.
Mateo Dieste, J. L. 2013. *Health and Ritual in Morocco: Conceptions of the Body and Healing Practices*. Leiden: Brill.
Matsunaga, L. 2000. 'Spiritual Companies, Corporate Religions: Japanese Companies and Japanese New Religious Movements at Home and Abroad', in P. B. Clarke (ed.) *Japanese New Religions: In Global Perspective*, 35–73. Richmond: Curzon.
Mauss, M. [1938] 1950. *Sociologie et anthropologie*. Paris: Presses Universitaires de France.
O'Connor, F. 2009. *History of Islam*. New York: Rosen Publishers.
Pratt Ewing, K. 1997. *Arguing Sainthood: Modernity, Psychoanalysis, and Islam*. Durham, NC: Duke University Press.
Rozehnal, R. T. 2007. *Islamic Sufism Unbound: Politics and Piety in Twenty First Century Pakistan*. New York: Palgrave Macmillan.
Saheb, S. A. A. 1998. 'A "Festival of Flags". Hindu-Muslim Devotion and the Sacralizing of Localism at the Shrine of Nagore-e-Sharif in Tamil Nadu', in H. Basu and P. Werbner (eds) *Embodying Charisma: Modernity, Locality, and Performance of Emotion in Sufi Cults*, 55–76. London; New York: Routledge.
Schimmel, A. 1975. *Mystical Dimensions of Islam*. Chapel Hill, NC: University of North Carolina Press.
Sedgwick, M. 2000. 'The Primacy of the Milieu: The Dandarawiyya's Unsuccessful Attempt to Change its Identity', in D. G. Rachida Chih (ed.) *Le saint et son milieu ou comment lire les sources hagiographiques,* 203–13. Cairo: Institut Français d'Archéologie Orientale.
Sengers, G. 2002. *Women and Demons: Cultic Healing in Islamic Egypt*. Leiden: Brill.
Skali, F. 2004. *Jésus dans la tradition soufie*. Paris: Albin Michel.
Spadola, E. 2008. 'The Scandal of Ecstasy: Communication, Sufi Rites, and Social Reform in 1930s Morocco', *Contemporary Islam* 2(1): 119–38. New York: Springer.
van Leeuwen, T. 2008. *Discourse and Practice, New Tools for Critical Discourse Analysis*. Oxford: Oxford University Press.
Wallis, R. 1984. *The Elementary Forms of the New Religious Life*. London: Routledge & Kegan Paul.

Werbner, P. 1998. 'Langar: Pilgrimage, Sacred Exchange and Perpetual Sacrifice in a Sufi Saint's Lodge', in H. Basu and P. Werbner (eds) *Embodying Charisma: Modernity, Locality, and Performance of Emotion in Sufi Cults*, 95–116. London; New York: Routledge.

——2005. *Pilgrims of Love. The Anthropology of a Global Sufi Cult*. Karachi: Oxford University Press.

——2009. 'Playing with Numbers. Sufi Calculations of a Perfect Divine Universe in Manchester', in R. Geaves, M. Dressler and G. Klinkhammer (eds) *Sufis in Western Societies. Global Networking and Locality*, 113–29. London; New York: Routledge.

Werth, L. 1998. 'The Saint Who Disappeared. Saints of the Wilderness in Pakistani Village Shrines.' in H. Basu and P. Werbner (eds) *Embodying Charisma: Modernity, Locality, and Performance of Emotion in Sufi Cults*, 77–91. London; New York: Routledge.

Westerlund, D. 2004. 'The Contextualization of Sufism in Europe', in D. Westerlund (ed.) *Sufism in Europe and North America*, 13–35. London: Routledge Curzon.

Westermarck, E. 1926. *Ritual and Belief in Morocco*. London: Macmillan.

Wiegers, G. 1994. *Islamic Literature in Spanish and Aljamiado*. Leiden: Brill.

8 Final Caveats

The present research contributes to a yet-incipient scholarly trend that has emerged in the last decade,[1] one that aims to comprehensively scrutinize Sufism as a living tradition, and in order to do so prioritizes the study of religious practices over that of texts (e.g. Geaves, 2000; Raudvere, 2002; Werbner 2005). Fieldwork-based research has revealed the current vitality enjoyed by Sufism and its capacity to keep adapting to the changing social conditions of the modern world. Until recently, most of the existing studies on Sufism relied mainly on textual analysis as a form of data collection, arguably producing a distorted image in which Islamic mysticism becomes a remnant of the past and an almost extinct tradition (Geaves et al., 2009).

In this study I have attempted to deconstruct the romanticized idea (sometimes endorsed by both Orientalist scholars and practitioners) that depicts Modern Sufis as other-worldly people, unaffected by social or historical change. Instead, I have discovered a *ṭarīqa* that is eminently modern, and whose study is illustrative of some of the major changes that have occurred in Western European and Moroccan religious life during the course of the twentieth century and the beginning of the twenty-first century. Rather than instances of continuity between pre-modern and modern Moroccan forms of Islam as well as between the medieval Qādiriyya and that of today, this book has tried to show how these forms have not remained intact, but have instead been re-appropriated, re-imagined, and expressed in eminently new ways. The study of *ziyāra*, for example, demonstrates how this well-established pilgrimage tradition takes place today, with people coming by car, bus, taxi and plane, in a highly securitized setting, with a high turnover of public attendees, in a locale with limited infrastructure. Its study also reveals that it serves a variety of purposes, from the more spiritually oriented, to the mercantile, from renovating and reinforcing Berber ethnicity, to authenticating the belonging of those who have recently joined; it even serves to try to sell property or conduct partner-matching.

This *ṭarīqa*'s very modernity has allowed us to define the order (and not only its European contingents) as a World-accommodating New Religious Movement (Wallis, 1984) for several reasons, among which we may concisely underline: (a) its organization ethos; (b) its not demanding substantial life changes in adherents as a requisite to join; and (c) the conviction that although ritual performance must be collective and regulated by the organization, individual spiritual transformation derived from it is indeed individual. Surely, *fuqarā'* would disagree with that categorization, as adherents may claim their *ṭarīqa* is part of the Qādiriyya which originated at the end of the eleventh century, and in that they will also share another feature with other members of World-accommodating New Religious Movement (e.g. Neo-Pentecostalism),[2] who, being mainly offshoots of major religious traditions, tend to oppose the idea of being 'new'.

The newness of this *ṭarīqa* has been understood as resulting from its interaction with the 'modern' contexts in which it has settled down. In the case of Morocco, 'modernity' is referred to in the study to denote some of the processes of social transformation which have taken place in that country since independence in 1956. I have particularly considered certain aspects of modernity that have been influential in the process of identity formation within the order – namely, the gradual appearance and consolidation of a middle class with access to higher education, the restructuring of the maraboutic system, the emergence of cosmopolitan ties among privileged urban minorities and their participation in New Age culture as well as the rise and consolidation of Reformist Islam in Morocco and the resulting varied ways in which it has engaged with Sufi ideologies and practices, always in transformation. While examining 'modernity' in relation to the Būdshīshiyya in Europe, one can identify social determinants that typically affect European youth – disillusionment with political ideologies, lack of interest in community issues and the voluntary sector (if not related to religion), no identification with other youth movements.

The *ṭarīqa* (not only in Europe) often serves individuals as a way of overcoming loneliness, feeling connected, and developing amity and a feeling of *camaraderie* with a close community; it may even entail social mobilization and participation. In terms of why and how people born or at least raised in Europe relate to an organization that is Moroccan, issues of Islamophilia/Islamophobia are often present, signifying a reversal of Said's 'postcolonial gaze' (1979). Whereas the 'postcolonial gaze' implies that the colonizer–colonized (i.e. European–Moroccan in this case) relationship is determined by 'otherness', and the inferiority once assumed in the colonized was viewed as justificatory of the domination exerted on him/her, its reverse implies that moral superiority is assumed in Muslim culture (I shall add, in this case for the very fact of being Muslim).

In essence, however, both models are brutally essentialist and denote that Europeans acquire the quality of being subjects thanks to, and at the expense of, objectivizing 'the other'. In the postcolonial gaze (and in its reversed version adopted by adherents of the order) the colonizer–colonized encounter is at the core of how Europeans understand their own identity. Thence, European disciples of Hamza sometimes have a romanticized approach to the 'otherness' represented by Moroccan culture and see it as a source of (often unquestionable) moral excellence. Identities are construed in a reactive manner, in which Moroccans represent what Europeans are not. But sometimes, paradoxically, the pattern is subverted, and Moroccans are approached in a pejorative manner, for in this view they represent the cultural backwardness that is antithetical to the European devotees' views on gender, class and society. Overall, identity is framed in reactive ways and dithers between an essentialist pair of contraries, easily oscillating between devotion for the exotic and the discriminatory – and in either case displaying a weak interest in understanding the culture in which the Sufi order to which they belong originates.

Besides, the expansion and consolidation of this *ṭarīqa* beyond the Moroccan province of *l'Oriental* can only be understood in relation to two key aspects: (a) the 'deterritorialisation of Islam' (Roy, 2004) by which Muslims in their everyday lives have access to an incredibly wide array of choices in matters of religion, thus becoming familiar with a multiplicity of approaches to Islam that may be borne out of or at least informed by ideas coming from distant corners of the world; and (b) the 're-sacralisation' that Western societies (and, I would add, secular elites in places like Morocco too) have experienced since the 1960s (Geaves et al., 2009: 2). Both phenomena, despite being very different, coincide in that the notion of a 'pick and mix' approach to religion (Hamilton, 2000) is always in the background.

Thus, with regard to the Būdshīshiyya, the individual's possibility of adhering to a *religion à la carte* both in Morocco and in Western Europe results in a kaleidoscopic portrayal of the *ṭarīqa*'s religious identity(/identities). Thence, some devotees have highly eclectic religious identities; others react against the permeability between religious traditions and develop a 'strictly Islamic' and/or 'strictly traditional' approach to Sufism (emic definitions that may mean many different things according to the context), yet a majority end up navigating between forms of puritanism and eclecticism. Moreover, the research concludes, both puritanical and eclectic styles are the fruit of processes of *melange* between diverse religious choices. Eclectic positions typically evidence an amalgam of Muslim and non-Muslim (mainly westernized versions of oriental) doctrines and practices; puritanism, on the other hand, represented for instance by the 'Quietist' followers, often displays a mixture of ideas that stem from various Muslim traditions, a *potpourri* that includes those popularly presented as opposing understandings of Islam (e.g. 'modern' Reformism *vs* 'classical' Moroccan Sufism).

In this sense, the findings of this research could not agree more with Geaves's statement that 'it is always good to remember that living religions are not the coherent, ordered packages found in theological or philosophical understandings of the sacred […]. In the field, religions are messy, paradoxical and chaotic […]' (Geaves, 2014a: 244). In fact, a series of oxymora are not only apparent in the identity of the order but a key component to understanding its surprisingly swift navigation between cultural niches that are diametrically different. Several are the issues that attest to an existing contrast between the integrity we find in the official line of discourse and its, on occasion, paradoxical *mise en scène*. First, the 'mechanisms' they propose in order to access the Divine fluctuate between the textual and the anti-textual, the experiential and the intellectual. The group publicly promotes a 'sensorial' engagement with religion, with the typically Būdshīshi motto, 'Sufism is a science of tastes'.

However, both leadership and discipleship produce a rich body of Būdshīshiyya-themed textual culture, in the form of books, booklets (assessed in Chapter 3) and websites (assessed in Chapter 4). This output will be seen both as a means to promote the order and gain adepts, and as a tool to communicate to devotees what is deemed normative by the leadership (in an organization, it will be remembered, in which face-to-face encounters between the grassroots and the higher echelons are very unusual). Second, the 'Quietist' approach that some devotees embrace, and that the order publicizes, clashes with their political involvement. 'Quietism' represents a 'contemplative' understanding of religion characterized by intellectual stillness over a more vocal position on societal matters, a form of piety that is not only sober in ritual terms but also advocates adopting a similar stance in society and politics. On the contrary, this *ṭarīqa* in Morocco is overtly outspoken on political matters, from the active involvement it had in local politics in north-eastern Morocco, to the more recent actions in support of the monarchy at a national level, as discussed in Chapters 2 and 3.

Last but not least, as a result of its expansion, the *ṭarīqa* has developed an often contradictory position on matters of religious inclusivism/exclusivism. On the one hand, the order advocates respect for other religious traditions, not only in 'theory' but in 'practice', as evidenced in ideas of religious tolerance that circulate among disciples, and the *de facto* acceptance of actual borrowings from other religious cultures, as well as the fact that some adherents are part of interreligious initiatives (e.g. Fes Festival of Sacred Music). Among these views are those asserting that the Būdshīshiyya is 'one path among many' and that all human attempts to access the Divine, including the one they have chosen, are, in their human condition, incomplete and tentative.

On the other hand, various practices within the order point towards an exclusivist approach that invalidates the former claims: devotees' assertions of belonging to the 'right Path', claims of 'authenticity' and views that other religious choices as 'misunderstandings', 'ignorance' or instances of holding the Truth 'incompletely' are recurrent among *fuqarā'*. A stricter approach towards eclecticism from the leadership, warning or even expelling from the organization those interested in religious groups or practices other than those of the Būdshīshiyya, is also identifiable as part of the exclusivist pattern.[3] Exclusivism, in the Būdshīshiyya, is also more likely to occur in contexts where other 'religious choices', Islamic and/or not, are also available to the disciple and, therefore, one may suggest that these are 'techniques' developed to neutralize the potential threat posed by these other options, techniques commonly known as 'nihilation' (Geaves, 2014b: 307).

Fieldwork has enhanced my understanding of this *ṭarīqa*, by enabling me to witness their living practices and, as a result, the study of emplaced and embodied religion brings about interesting outcomes. This research definitely backs Appadurai's (1996) belief that the nation state as an icon to which individuals *feel* identified is at a critical juncture and that identities progressively tend to be disconnected from territories. I also coincide with him in considering that globalization works multidimensionally. Referring to cultural borrowings, Appadurai suggests that globalization can be defined in terms of 'the tension between cultural homogenization and cultural heterogenization' (2011 [1990]: 588). 'Westernization theories' often argue that globalization is a mere process of westernization, in which global forces operate to impose western cultural imperialism on the non-western world. Such voices contend that westernization is destroying cultural diversity (see for example Holton, 1990). By contrast, Appadurai criticizes these theories on the grounds that they consider only one facet of cultural globalization. He instead proposes to understand patterns of cultural influencing in the context of globalization as multifocal rather than dominated by a single centre.

Cultural cross-pollinations are evident throughout this *ṭarīqa* and work out in a multiplicity of directions. Whereas European devotees sometimes adopt quite straightforwardly deeply culturally rooted 'Moroccan' practices (such as the respect for gender segregation in rituals and its associated rationale), ideas originally born in Europe are also becoming integrated into the mainstream doctrinal fabric of the order (with, for example, 'spiritist' or 'harmonial' concepts of various kinds typical of Western Esotericism being integrated into Moroccan worldviews). In Appadurai's view, we need not only to look at how 'western' ideas have colonized the world but also at the increasing relevance that identity markers of local cultures such as those articulated though religion have gained in recent times. Besides, global culture is to be viewed not merely as 'westernized' but also in its heterogenized, decentralized, localized and re-tribalized components.

In the Būdshīshiyya, this is evident in how several 'typically Moroccan' elements are kept surprisingly intact in most locations – for example, the integrity displayed throughout the *ṭarīqa* in terms of ritual performance styles, as *dhikr* is fairly homogeneously enacted in most locations. The study of rituals elucidates the extent to which unity is maintained. Rituals have been shown to have a key function in intra-*ṭarīqa* bonding among adherents, and are central to the permanence of the order transnationally, as evidenced in Chapters 5 and 6.

Another example of the ways in which Moroccan culture has been preserved can be seen in the shared lexicon used by members of the organization. Despite not being able to communicate with one another, I have noted, Hamza's followers from different origins use the same Arabic terminology when referring to religious issues, a lexicon I have devoted a substantial part of this research to exploring and understanding. The ways in which these phrases and terms are used by devotees of this organization make of the

Būdshīshiyya, I would contend, a 'speech community'. They are a 'speech community' in the sense of being a group of people who share a series of understandings and expectations regarding the use of a particular vocabulary; a glossary worth noticing is in *fuṣḥā,* and that enhances a sense of intra-*ṭarīqa* unity difficult otherwise to maintain by (the lack of) other means (e.g. personal interaction with people from other enclaves, face-to-face encounters with the order's leadership). People that use the same terms feel they are part of the same world, strengthening, thus, feelings of companionship *inter pares* within the organization.[4]

Moroccan culture is, however, not unequivocally transplanted; it is reinterpreted, reframed and overtly questioned in not a few instances. I have found interesting throughout the course of this research the fact that, whereas discursive questionings of *la marocanité* are mostly overlooked by the order's leadership, those interrogations that occur at the level of religious praxis (both in Morocco and in Europe) are not easily accommodated, demonstrating how embodied subjectivities are often deemed to hold a subversive power less commonly associated with 'words'; in terms of discrepancy, a lot more can be said than done, embodied, in*corpo*rated. In the information-saturated societies in which we live, this case would suggest that sometimes ideas that are perceived as threatening may be taken less seriously than equivalent actions; faith healing is a case in point: a devotee can say they are interested in shamanistic healing, but visiting a shaman brings about consequences at another level.

I also find interesting the fact that 'global appeals' can be formulated by local actors. For example, an underlying ideology that stresses the *ṭarīqa*'s universal and transcendental character, likely to be enunciated from the order's leadership, has been helpful in consolidating its international success. Because of this episteme, organizations such as the Būdshīshiyya can have an appeal that goes beyond their mere locality. Madāgh, a dormant village known only to local people in the region, becomes all of a sudden a 'mini-Benares' (or at least this is how it is perceived by a Moroccan *faqīr* and journalist). Sufi ideology in Morocco and elsewhere tends to have a universal flavour that is conducive to its expansion beyond the original *milieu*. And, as has happened with other Islamic trends and other world religions, the possibility is opened up for outsiders to join the organization, whether they are already Muslims or whether they convert to Islam in order to join.

All these elements contribute to building up a certain degree of unity and cohesiveness within the organization. Besides, the *ṭarīqa* has also developed certain tactics to enhance cohesiveness and alleviate differences in approach and ease intra-*ṭarīqa* relations. In particular, the order recommends that members avoid meeting with devotees whose approaches to Islam are markedly different from their own. Sincere engagement between people with different opinions is often avoided. National and international encounters are times of continuous and intense ritual performance, but they are also occasions when there is an evident absence of talk and debate. This is so much the case that most members know hardly anything about devotees from other groups. The dynamics within any particular group of *faqīrāt* are likely to contrast with this wider picture of alienation between groups. In the course of the weekly congregational *waẓīfa* sessions there will be a degree of gossip and chat after the performance of ritual obligations, which also helps to build amity. Of course members of the same group get to know each other over time. The leadership's idea is to try to make each group homogenous with regard to the worldview and Islamic understanding of its members. However, it is difficult to achieve a great degree of homogeneity among devotees, particularly in groups where there are only a few members, and tensions do occur. The leadership of the order always recommends that like-minded people should gather together, and that groups whose members show no affinity for one another should be split up. Ideally, this ensures that divergences of opinion do not lead to definite breakaways from the central *ṭarīqa*. This delicate equilibrium facilitates the perpetuation of the 'hybridity' that characterizes the modern Būdshīshiyya. This study has explored how different narratives can coexist without decisively damaging the cohesion of the order.

Each manifestation of Islam creates its own 'web of meaning' which is fluid and dynamic (El Zein, 1974: 250). In the course of the present research, I found out just how diverse the webs of meaning within the Būdshīshiyya can be. For this reason I have attempted to explore this *ṭarīqa* as an amalgam of diverse ways of embodying Sufism. The issue of plurality led me to discover the dynamics of adaptation of a Sufi order into new environments. Thus I have scrutinized the ways in which the Būdshīshiyya has changed in order to adapt to the particularities of the host *milieu*. For instance, an exploration of the ways in which healing is understood and embodied by different people has elucidated some of the central dynamics involved in negotiating identities and interests within and between the various groups and between them and the central lodge.

This research has found that differences between various strands of the Būdshīshiyya not only result from cultural factors but also from disparate economic conditions. For example, the inaccessibility of medical care in certain Moroccan rural areas may account for the relatively higher success of faith healing techniques in peasant communities, although issues of social etiquette and the fact that some healing practices are looked at pejoratively can also be taken as a proof of why wealthier Moroccans tend to be more secretive about visiting healers. Differences – whether cultural or economic, individual or collective – have been in evidence throughout this research, with plurality emerging as perhaps one of the strongest *leitmotifs* in the study.

Diversity is also eloquently manifested in the various understandings different followers of Hamza have of their relationship to the *walī*. Among rural devotees, membership is a vaguer concept, and it remains connected to Berber culture, with Hamza being looked at as an *Agourram*, and not implicatory of religious exclusivity in terms of allegiance to the organization; many among the peasants participate in the activities of this order *vis-à-vis* those of other *ṭuruq*. Their adscription to the organization is somehow loose, less defined, as evidenced in a different understanding of the notions of initiation and affiliation from that of the rest of the devotees. On the other hand, in settings where the Būdshīshiyya is one among many religious 'choices' (e.g. cities in Morocco and Europe), the order operates more clearly as a religious 'organization', one in which 'voluntarism' has been made the basis of discipleship.[5]

In these settings, strategies to gain adherents are evident, and have been discussed throughout the book: trying to ensure participation in rituals (Chapter 6) and pilgrimage activities (Chapter 5); disseminating disciples' narratives of 'salvation' (Chapter 3) and of 'recovery' (Chapter 7); participation in the World Wide Web (Chapter 4); organizing events with a missionary appeal (Chapter 3); and even a reality TV programme; and regulating interaction between the various contingents and with other religious sources. Besides, with numbers of devotees steadily rising, this research has discovered that, by often adopting an apparent attitude of *laissez-faire*, the Būdshīshiyya leadership has managed to ensure that a wide range of people with different ideas of what they want to achieve are by joining the *ṭarīqa* somehow conciliated. However, this ought not to be seen as antithetical to the existence of an 'orthodoxy'. Indeed, this book has explored the diverse and more or less subtle means the *ṭarīqa* uses to exercise control over its members. We noted a certain degree of surveillance over devotees' attitudes.

Despite the fact that the measures adopted by the leadership are deliberately attuned to the different types of followers, the existence of a homogeneous 'official' discourse that is the same for everybody may be taken to imply a sense of 'orthodoxy' (in the Asadian sense) (Asad, 1986). Būdshīshiyya orthodoxy is of an embodied nature, as it requires from members, not the adherence to specific beliefs and doctrines, but rather the performance of specific religious practices and adherence to certain codes of behaviour. In light of this it seems not unreasonable to suggest that in the Būdshīshiyya 'orthodoxy' has become 'orthopraxis'. For whereas Gellner (1969) and others discerned doctrinal imposition in their studies of other *ṭuruq*, this study has found a *ṭarīqa* more concerned that certain religious practices be performed in specific ways, and that certain behaviours be observed, than with the endorsement of a particular religious discourse: the Būdshīshiyya leadership provides an exemplary practice (orthopraxis) which embodies what is perceived to be appropriate in the Būdshīshī behavioural code, while the doctrinal dimension of Islam is often looked on with a less meticulous eye. The importance attributed by devotees to the notion of *iḥsān* – behavioural excellence – seems to bear this out.

Partially responsible for the success of the order beyond its original enclave are the ways in which religious authority is being recreated and reinvented. Religious authority in the Būdshīshiyya has a dynamic, twofold nature, a combination of 'traditional' charisma with modern methods of decentralizing power. It could perhaps be debated whether 'traditional' is quite the right way to characterize this particular manifestation of religious authority, since (a) it is partly sustained and preserved via its reinforcement through the dissemination of images in non-traditional media such as the internet (as discussed in Chapter 4); and (b) it is widely accepted by followers who would themselves appear to be antithetical to such 'tradition' – for example, Moroccan urban devotees influenced by New Age ideas, critical of the *ṭuruq* system.

The study has also presented new forms of *de facto* decentralized power in the Būdshīshiyya, and the way in which these forms are being enacted. Thus it has identified two types of religious authority. One is represented by the personage of Hamza Būdshīsh, and the other by people like Skali. Whereas Hamza does not talk to followers, does not address large audiences, does not publish any books and only rarely leaves Madāgh, people such as Skali, on the other hand, epitomize the most visible side of the leadership – he is a public personage in Morocco, has published several books, and often appears in the media in Morocco, Spain and France. He embodies a new type of charisma that, when articulated orally (talks, conferences, and short courses), is proving to be effective in helping the *ṭarīqa* to garner new adherents. I argue that Hamza's charisma also appeals to many, despite being distant and often somehow diffuse. In fact, because it is relatively uncommon for devotees to meet Hamza, it would appear that he acts as an image to be admired but not as an actual role model. Other people within the locality of each small group embody the type of daily guidance that many devotees are seeking when they join. Such figures tell fellow *faqīrāt* how to behave in accordance with the order's standards, how to perform rituals. Various stories are also circulated with the idea of transmitting this sacral knowledge. I have referred to them as 'somatic images' (see Chapter 7, using Csordas's 1990 term); these fables tell devotees what it is considered permissible, detailing the imaginable, the thinkable, the avoidable, the manifest, and the form in which these rituals shall be expressed to reproduce knowledge and maintain the ritual stylistic integrity of the *ṭarīqa*.

The study has seen how non-indigenous ideas have influenced the process of identity formation in all enclaves of the order. Contrary to the idea of an original 'pristine' religiosity to be found in the original enclave and a series of mimetic expressions beyond this central focus, we have encountered people whose views of religion have been shaped by an extraordinary variety of influences, evidencing the 'glocal' character of the communities considered in this research.

It has been pointed out that 'glocalization' implies worldwide exchange of social and cultural ideas and has contributed to the transformation of local realities and cultural behaviour (Geaves et al., 2009: 4). The Būdshīshiyya is becoming ever more 'glocal', manifesting what Beyer found in other 'glocal' groups: the prioritization of a new *multi-centre scenario* (2009: 13). This means that all the branches of the Būdshīshiyya exercise a certain influence over all the others – a stronger influence than that exerted by the centre in the traditional centre–periphery model, a model in which it would be Madāgh that determined the religious character of the branches.

This process has brought about new hybrid forms of religion. Likewise, each group of devotees not only develops particular ways of construing their religious identities in accordance with their personal life trajectories and cultural frames, but also redefines, in accordance with their religious stances, the ways in which they relate to their societal contexts. This fascinating exchange presents challenging new directions for future research into Sufism in the modern world.

As is the case with other forms of hybrid Sufism that have partly maintained their 'Islamic' character while incorporating followers whose approach to religion tends to be more eclectic (e.g. Burhāniyya), two main questions remain unanswered with regard to the Būdshīshiyya, and they deserve consideration for further research. First, will the central locus of authority remain in the hands of the Būdshīshī family, or will the newly emerging leadership gain a more central role in deciding the future development of the *ṭarīqa*? In other words, it remains unclear whether the order will develop into a new type of Sufi organization which leaves aside traditional *ṭarīqa* ties, or whether the force of *maraboutism* will maintain its vitality and continue to govern the power relations of the *ṭarīqa* in the future. Second, also unanswered, is the question of how new members are going to be recruited. If the current missionary strategy is perpetuated, the original vigour of the traditional leadership might be eclipsed in favour of a new, more cosmopolitan leadership. This research indicates that the commitment of the type of follower who is attracted by the order's proselytizing tends to be volatile; thus, although the missionary outlook might generate a more rapid growth of the organization, it might also bring about a more unstable body of disciples. How the *ṭarīqa* will deal with these challenges remains to be seen. A comparative perspective with other 'hybrid' orders could produce future lines of research.

Notes

1 There are some pioneering works that were produced before the 2000s, notably Geaves (1995).

2 An interesting introduction to neo-Pentecostalism that serves as a point of comparison to the Būdshīshiyya is Hunt (2002).

3 A similar dichotomy has been observed in other Muslim leaders that have shown a different attitude towards these issues in public and in private. As Frishkopf has argued: 'In public, Muslim leaders tend towards tolerance and liberality […] but […] out of the public eye, a different [more restrictive] atmosphere often prevails' (2009: 49).

4 As an exception to that pattern I have identified that the consistent use of a determinate ritual style and a shared lexicon have also been challenged by some 'external' influences, particularly by accepting borrowings from South Asian styles and terminology, atypical of Moroccan Sufism among members of the order in Britain, an issue that is not discussed in detail in the monograph but has been addressed elsewhere (see Dominguez Diaz, 2012).

5 Similar processes have been reported in other Sufi organizations; for example, the Turkish Gülen movement presents a trajectory resembling that of the Būdshīshiyya: ethnic restrictions have been lifted in an attempt by this organization to reach new markets of potential devotees who do not necessarily fit the traditional ethnic parameters (Hermansen, 2009: 29).

References

Appadurai, A. 2011 [1990]. 'Disjuncture and Difference in the Global Cultural Economy', in I. Szeman, and T. Kaposy (eds) *Cultural Theory: An Anthology*, 282–95. Chichester: Wiley-Blackwell.

——1996. *Modernity at Large: Cultural Dimensions of Globalization*. Minneapolis, MN: University of Minnesota Press.

Asad, T. 1986. *The Idea of an Anthropology of Islam*. Washington, DC: Georgetown University, Center for Contemporary Arab Studies.

Beyer, P. 2009. 'Globalization of Religions. Plural Authenticities at the Centres and at the Margins', in R. Geaves, M. Dressler and G. Klinkhammer (eds) *Sufis in Western Societies. Global Networking and Locality*, 13–25. London; New York: Routledge.

Csordas, T. J. 1990. 'Embodiment as a Paradigm for Anthropology', *Ethos* 18(1): 5–47. Berkeley, CA: University of California Press.

Dominguez Diaz, M. 2012. 'Performance, Belonging and Identity: Ritual Variations in the British Qadiriyya', *Religion, State and Society* 39(2–3): 229–45. London: Routledge.

El Zein, A. H. M. 1974. *The Sacred Meadows: A Structural Analysis of Religious Symbolism in an East African Town*. Evanston, IL: Northwestern University Press.

Frishkopf, M. 2009. 'Globalizing the Soundworld. Islam and Sufi Music in the West', in R. Geaves, M. Dressler and G. Klinkhammer (eds) *Sufis in Western Societies. Global Networking and Locality*, 46–76. London; New York: Routledge.

Geaves, R. 1995. 'Sectarian Influences within Islam in Britain: With Reference to the Concepts of "Ummah" and "Community"', Community Religions Project Monograph Series. Leeds: University of Leeds.

——2014a. 'Fieldwork in the Study of Religion', in G. D. Chryssides and R. Geaves (eds) *The Study of Religion: An Introduction to Key Ideas and Methods*, 241–74. London; New York: Bloomsbury.

——2014b. 'The Question of Truth', in G. D. Chryssides and R. Geaves (eds) *The Study of Religion: An Introduction to Key Ideas and Methods*, 303–38. London; New York: Bloomsbury.

——2000. *The Sufis of Britain: An Exploration of Muslim Identity*. Cardiff: Cardiff Academic Press.

Geaves, R., Dressler, M. and Klinkhammer, G. 2009. 'Introduction', in R. Geaves, M. Dressler and G. Klinkhammer (eds) *Sufis in Western Societies. Global Networking and Locality*, 1–12. London; New York: Routledge.

Gellner, E. 1969. *Saints of the Atlas*. London: Weidenfeld & Nicholson.

Hamilton, M. 2000. 'An Analysis of the Festival for Mind-Body-Spirit, London', in S. Sutcliffe and M. Bowman (eds) *Beyond New Age: Exploring Alternative Spirituality*, 188–200. Edinburgh: Edinburgh University Press.

Hermansen, M. 2009. 'Global Sufism. "Theirs and Ours"', in R. Geaves, M. Dressler and G. Klinkhammer (eds) *Sufis in Western Societies. Global Networking and Locality*, 26–45. London; New York: Routledge.

Holton, R. J. 1990. *Globalization and the Nation-State.* New York: St Martin's Press.
Hunt, S. 2002. 'Deprivation and Western Pentecostalism Revisited: Neo-Pentecostalism', *PentecoStudies, Online Journal for the Interdisciplinary Study of Pentecostalism and Charismatic Movements* 1(2), available online at www.glopent.net/pentecostudies/online-back-issues/2002/hunt2002–2.pdf/download (accessed 22 January 2014).
Raudvere, C. 2002. *The Book and the Roses: Sufi Women, Visibility and Zikir in Contemporary Istanbul.* Istanbul: Swedish Research Institute in Istanbul.
Roy, O. 2004. *Globalised Islam: The Search for a New Ummah.* London: Hurst & Co.
Said, E. W. 1979. *Orientalism.* New York: Vintage Books.
Wallis, R. 1984. *The Elementary Forms of the New Religious Life.* London: Routledge.
Werbner, P. 2005a. *Pilgrims of Love. The Anthropology of a Global Sufi Cult*. Karachi: Oxford University Press.

Appendix 1 – Būdshīshiyya's saintly genealogy

Muḥammad
Abū al-Ḥasan 'Alī ibn Abī Ṭālib
Ibn al-Haytam
al-Ḥussayn
Zīna al-'Ābidīn 'Alī
Muḥammad al-Bakr
Ja'far as-Sādiq
Mūsā al-Kāẓim
'Alī ibn Mūsā al-Riḍā
M'arūf al-Karkhī
Abū al-Ḥassan Sarī Saqtī
Abū al-Qāsim Junayd
Abū Bakr 'Abdullāh Shiblī
Rāzī ad-dīn Abū Faḍl 'abd al-Wāḥid 'abd al 'Azīz
Abū Farāh Muḥammad Yūsuf Tartusī
Abū al-Ḥassan 'Alī Āḥmad Qureyshī al-Ḥanqarī
Qādī Ābī S'ayd 'Alī Mubārak al Mukhramī
'Abd al-Qādir Jīlānī
'Abd ar-Razzāq (the first)
Sīdī Ismā'īl
Sīdī 'Abd ar-Razzāq (the second)
Sīdī Muḥammad (the first)
Sīdī Muḥammad (the second)
Sīdī 'Abd al-Qādir
Sīdī 'Alī Sīdī Shūayb
Sīdī al-Ḥassan
Abū Dakhīl
Sīdī Muḥammad (the third)
Sīdī Muḥammad (the fourth)
Sīdī Muḥammad (the fifth)
Sīdī 'Alī
Sīdī Muḥammad (the sixth)
al-Mukhtār (the first)

Sīdī al-Mukhtār al-Kabīr
Ḥājj Muḥyī ad-dīn
Sīdī al-Mukhtār al-Būdshīshī (Sīdī Hamza's grandfather)
Sīdī Abīmadyan Qādirī al-Būdshīsh
Ḥājj al-'Abbās ibn al-Mukhtār al-Qādirī al-Būdshīshī
Sīdī Hamza al-Qādirī al-Būdshīshī

Appendix 2 – Būdshīshiyya's central lodge

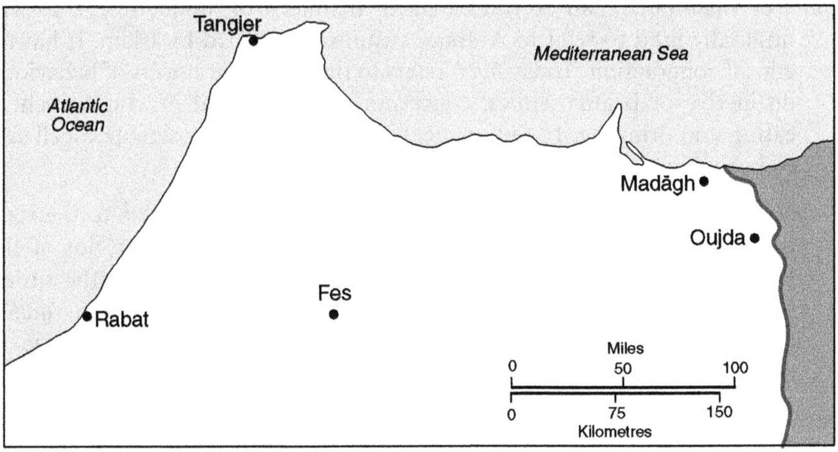

Glossary

ādab; pl. *ādāb* (Ar.): can be translated as 'manners' or 'etiquette'. *Ādāb* was originally used to refer to Arabian customs, as refined by Islam. It has an ethical connotation. Today *ādāb* refers to the particular norms of behaviour, distinctive of Islamic ethics, concerning several social practices, such as eating and drinking. In Sufi contexts it also serves to designate excellence of behaviour.

'ādhāb (Ar.): can be translated into English as 'torment'. It refers to the state of separation from God and association with those who are not of the Path. For some Sufis *'adhāb* is relating with people outside the order; but more generally, as in the case of the European Būdshīshiyya, *'adhāb* only refers to associating with people who are atheist or agnostic in orientation.

āgourram; pl. *igourramene* (Ber.): generally translated as 'Sufi saint'; see also *marabout* and *walī 'Allāh.* For females the term used is *tagourramt.*

'ālim; pl. *'ulamā'* (Ar.): generally translated as 'religious scholar'. It designates an expert in the sciences of *ḥadīth*, *fiqh* and/or *sharī'a.*

'Allāh (Ar.): the name of God in Islam. Also used by Arabic-speaking Christians and Jews.

'āql (Ar.): generally translated as 'intellect'.

āwliyā' 'Allāh (Ar.): see the singular form, *walī 'Allāh.*

baraka (Ar.): generally translated as 'blessing'. It refers to the spiritual potency or power that holy individuals, places and/or objects are believed to have. Since its existence is believed to be tangible, it is believed that it can be transmitted to those who come into contact with the person or thing that possesses it.

bāṭin (Ar.): generally translated as 'inner'. In Islam the term has been used to designate the inner aspect of religion or the knowledge of the inner dimension of reality (*'ilm ab-bāṭin*) as opposed to the external dimensions (*zāḥir*) or exoteric knowledge (*'ilm az-zāḥir*).

bay'a (Ar.): generally used to refer to an 'oath of allegiance' pledged to a religious or political institution or leader. In the Būdshīshiyya, it signifies a vow of allegiance to the Sufi saint (*walī 'Allāh*), in this case Sīdī Hamza. Most of the Būdshīshiyya's European members refer to it as *the pact*.

chorfa (Ar. *dārija*): see *sharīf.*

da'wa (Ar.):religious proselytization in Islam.

dhikr (Ar.): generally translated into English as 'remembrance'. Ritual commonly performed by Sufis that consists of mentioning a previously memorized formula. *Dhikr djāli* refers to the performed ritual when the formula is uttered aloud, whereas *dhikr khāfi* refers to the one practised either in silence or in a low voice. Both can be performed either individually or collectively.

dunyā (Ar.): literally means 'lower'. In the Qur'ān, *dunyā* is presented as the antithesis of *ākhira*, the former representing this world and the latter the hereafter (7: 156).

faqīh; pl. *fuqahā'* (Ar.): an expert in Islamic Law; the term is often translated as 'Jurist'. In popular parlance, however, people considered articulate in religious matters are often referred to as *faqīh*. For example, healers that argue in favour of their practices by citing the Qur'ān are often called in this way.

faqīr/a; pl. *fuqarā'/faqīrāt* (Ar.): in Arabic it means 'poor', and in popular parlance it is used for a homeless person, a pauper or a beggar. Among North African Sufis, the term is used as a synonym for disciple. The traditional connotations of the term describe someone who entirely accepts the will of God and has no private property, considered to be indispensable attributes of the *faqīr*. Today reformed Sufi orders such as the Būdshīshiyya use the term simply to refer to a member of the *ṭarīqa*, irrespective of his/her degree of spiritual commitment.

fātiḥa (Ar.): it is the first *sūra* of the Qur'ān, literally meaning 'the Opener', also known as 'the Opening of Scripture' (*fātiḥat al-kitāb*). Its recitation is part of the prayer (*ṣalāt*) and of most of the *formulae* in Sufi litanies or *dhikr*.

hadīth (Ar.): sometimes translated as 'Tradition'. An account of the acts and sayings of Muḥammad, and of His Companions' acts and sayings that received the Prophet's tacit approval. These have been compiled and are used as a secondary textual source (after the Qur'ān) from where *sharī'a* prescriptions derive.

haḍra (Ar.): term used to refer to congregational *dhikr* sessions; see *waẓīfa.*

ḥāl; pl. aḥwāl (Ar.): generally translated as 'condition' or 'state'. In medieval Sufism it meant the state of realization of an encounter with the Divine, a moment described as acquaintance of perfect balance of the soul due to the acceptance of this encounter. Today the term is used to refer to states of ecstasy attained during *dhikr* sessions.

hijāb (Ar.): literally meaning 'cover', though it is more generally translated as veil. Non-Muslims use it generally to refer to the type of veil that covers all or most of the hair leaving the face uncovered. In Arabic-speaking countries it is also used to refer to the Islamic code of dress for women that prescribes full body coverage with the exception of face and hands.

iḥsān (Ar.): generally translated as 'excellence in behaviour'. For Sufis, it specifically connects spiritual perfection and excellence in worship with right behaviour in social relations. Within the Būdshīshiyya, it is believed to be the most fundamental of the forms of worship.

jilāba (Ar.): traditional loose fitting, North African garment used by men and women, though there are slight differences between the sexes in texture and form – i.e. the male *jilābāt* tends to be made of wool, whereas finer textiles are used in the female *jilābāt.*

jīnn; pl. *junūn* (Ar.): literally meaning 'invisible' beings created by God, believed to live in a parallel universe. They are not strictly speaking supernatural, because they are believed to be made of matter, although humans are unable to see them.

karāma, pl. karāmāt (Ar.): supernatural interventions in the physical world. *Karāmāt* generally refer to miracles ascribed to *awliyā' 'Allāh,* often presented as proof of their saintly nature. Miracles are present in the Qur'ān in a threefold sense: in sacred history, in connection with Muḥammad himself and in relation to revelation. However, generally speaking, miracles ascribed to the Phophet are called *mu'jiza* (pl. *mu'jizāt*) and not *kārāma.*

Madāgh (Ar.): village where the central lodge or *Zāwiya* of the *ṭarīqa* Qādiriyya al-Būdshīshiyya is situated. It is located in the north-eastern region of Morocco, 52km north of Oujda and 60km from the North African Spanish enclave of Melilla. See Appendix 2.

maḥabba: generally translated as 'love', believed to be central in the relationship between a Sufi *shaykh* and God and between the *shaykh* and his disciples.

makhzān (Ar.): literally meaning 'storehouse'. It is a term used since colonial times to denote the centre of authority in Morocco.

Mālikī (Ar.): one of the four schools of Islamic jurisprudence borne out of the teachings of the medieval scholar Mālik ibn Ānas. He was the author of al-Muwaṭṭa, one of the first written compendiums of law which became the primordial source of the *Mālikī* school. Although Mālik ibn Ānas was from Medina and followed by people in Egypt and Mecca, the *Mālikī* madhab mainly developed in North and West Africa.

marabout (Fr.): French adaptation of the Arabic word *murābiṭ*, the term is used to refer to the *walī 'Allāh*. It was coined in colonial times to describe the phenomenon of sainthood in North African Sufism – particularly in studies dealing with Algeria and Morocco – and it has progressively extended to designate West African Sufi authorities too. In Berber languages a *marabout* is called *agourram*.

mawlid (Ar.): celebration that commemorates the birthday of the prophet Muḥammad. It is also known as *mawlid an-nabī* and it occurs during the third month of the Islamic calendar (*rabī' al-awwal*). In the Būdshīshiyya, the *mawlid* is considered a major festival, consisting of an entire week of celebrations. Followers from all over the world go to Madāgh to visit Sīdī Hamza.

moussem; pl. *muassīm* (Ber.): religious festivity that combines pilgrimage to a saint or a saint's tomb visitation (*ziyāra*) with mercantile activities. Thus, every time a *moussem* occurs, a market is set up in the lodge's surroundings. The relevance of the *moussem*'s commercial dimension is such that some people use the term to refer to the market rather than the religious festivity.

muqaddim/a (Ar.): spiritual leader; in many orders the term is used to designate secondary authorities within the *ṭarīqa*, that is to say, local representatives of the supreme leading *shaykh*.

murīd (Ar.): literally meaning 'desirer'; but the term is commonly used to refer to disciples of a Sufi *shaykh*.

nafs (Ar.): often translated as 'inner self', soul or ego. The Qur'ān presents it in three different phases; in its initial phase, it is considered an unrefined state of being, as it represents the animal side of humans, the instinctive aspect of us that leads us to behave evilly. Individuals are supposed to awaken their conscience in a second phase, and to accuse themselves, repent and ask for forgiveness, in order to reach the final stage, one in which the *nafs* is at peace. Sufism is all about the perfecting of the *nafs* by means of attempting to overcome phase two in order to enter phase three.

niyyā (Ar.): often translated as intention. It refers to the will of a person to do something for the sake of *'Allāh*. It is, among others, a prerequisite to the performance of *dhikr*.

qalb (Ar.): literally meaning 'heart'. In Sufism it is perceived as the locus of man's good and evil aspirations and of religious apprehension and divine visitations.

Qaṣīda (Ar. sing); *qasā'id* (pl.): form of musicalized classical Sufi poetry

qubbā': (Ar.): doomed mausoleum, or more generically, any Muslim shrine-complex used for *ziyāra*.

Qur'ān (Ar.): Sacred Scripture of Islam that contains the revelations Muḥammad received from the archangel Gabriel, preserved in a fixed, written form.

salāt (Ar.): the five canonical daily prayers.

samā' (Ar.): type of music used in Sufi rituals of *dhikr*. Today it has become a musical style in its own right and is performed in non-religious settings. *Samā'* literally refers to the act of hearing, but more precisely denotes 'that which is heard'. In Sufism, *samā'* is often used to refer to the hearing of music, the spiritual concert, in a more or less ritualized form. In medieval Sufi writings *samā'* is perceived as a means of enriching the soul that often induces pronounced emotional states (*aḥwāl*), including episodes of trance.

Sayyid (Ar.): literally meaning 'descendant of the Prophet'. The term is used by followers of Sufi orders to address the supreme leader in a way that shows spiritual love and respect for him.

sharī'a (Ar.): set of norms and regulations that contains a code of morality and conduct for Muslims. These rules are mainly derived from interpreting the Qur'ān and *Ḥadīth*.

sharīf, pl. shurafā' (Ar.): terms used to designate nobility; in Morocco, a descendant of the Prophet of Islam. Sharifism is an ideology in which religious and political authority is legitimated on the basis of such a genealogical link. In Moroccan dialect the term most commonly used is *Chorfa*.

shaykh (Ar.): generally used to address someone in a respectful way. It means elder, wise person, religious scholar. In a religious context is used to refer to a scholar, the head of a religious group or of a Sufi order.

shifā' (Ar.): literally means 'healing'.

shirk (Ar.): generally translated as associationism, or simply as polytheism or unbelief. It signifies the act of 'associating' with God, therefore accepting the existence of other deities along with her/him/it.

Sīdī (Ar.): Arabic term that Būdshīshiyya devotees use before the name to refer to male members of the group, and expressing affection. For females, the term used is Lālā.

Silsila (Ar.): the chain of authority that traces the genealogy of a Sufi order back to the Prophet. The *silsila* of the Būdshīshiyya can be found in Appendix 1.

subḥa (Ar.): rosary generally used when performing silent *dhikr*, to keep count of the number of times particular phases have been recited. Every order has its distinctive *subḥa*, and in some it is given to the aspirant when s/he enters the order. In others, such as the Būdshīshiyya, *subḥāt* are available for purchase at the central lodge in Madāgh.

sunna (Ar.): generally translated as custom. Set of practices introduced by Muḥammad and his Companions during the formative period of Islam, and compiled in the *Hadīth*. In Islamic law, this set of practices is regarded as a textual basis from which *sharī'a* prescriptions are derived. Thus, *Sunna*, generally speaking, stands for an all-encompassing code of conduct to be observed by Muslims.

tabarruk (Ar.): one attaining *baraka*.

tarbiyya (Ar.): literally means 'education' or 'upbringing'.

tarīqa; pl. *ṭuruq* (Ar.): Sufi order.

tawāḍū'(Ar.): Islamic embodied notion of humility that must be shown through modesty in dress and gentleness in manners.

ulamā' (Ar.): see the singular form *'ālim*.

Umma (Ar.): generally translates as the community of believers in Islam. In the Qur'ān it appears to designate any community of people sharing religious beliefs, whether Muslim or not. However, its meaning is later limited to refer only to the Muslim community.

uṣūl (Ar.): a methodological tradition that began with Muḥammad ibn Idrīs ash-Shāfi'ī. It aims to unify Islamic practice by deriving legal reasoning only from standardized sources of tradition. Accordingly, the roots (*uṣūl*, sing. *aṣl*), or sources, to be used have to be the Qur'ān and the *sunna*, and the methods applied, analogical reasoning (*qiyās*) and the consensus of the community (*ijmā'*). This legal hermeneutical approach was called *uṣūl al-fiqh*, and it has inspired similar procedures applied to religious dogma (*uṣūl ad-dīn*) and Qur'ānic interpretation (*uṣūl at-tafsīr*).

walī 'Allāh; pl. *awliyā' 'Allāh* (Ar.): *walī* can be translated as manager, guardian, protector, and also intimate or, most commonly, friend. *Walī 'Allāh*, generally translated as 'friend of God', is the term used to designate a Muslim 'saint', one who intercedes for others as God's deputy or vice-regent on earth. It is (especially in North-Africa) also commonly referred as *marabout* (a French adaptation of *murābiṭ*, the one at the *ribāṭ*, the lodge or retreat); Berbers often call it in Amazigh, *Agourram* (masc.), *tagourramt* (fem.).

waẓīfa; pl. *waẓīfāt* (Ar.): litany consisting of various *formulae* chanted and/or recited in repetitive ways, either individually or collectively during *dhikr* sessions. They are distinctive to every order and are generally kept in secret by the followers of each group. Members of the Būdshīshiyya use the term to refer to collective *dhikr* sessions, although technically speaking not all the constituent parts of a ritual session of this type are the *waẓīfa* proper. In this study, we will nevertheless use the two terms 'collective *dhikr*' and '*waẓīfa*' interchangeably, in accordance with their use by followers of the Būdshīshiyya. It can also be called *Haḍra*.

wird (Ar.): recitation of particular passages of the Qur'ān. The term is often used as a synonym of *dhikr*.

zāḥir (Ar.): literally meaning outer or apparent, it is generally used in Islam to refer to exoteric knowledge (*'ilm aẓ-ẓāḥir*) as opposed to inner (*bāṭin*) or esoteric knowledge (*'ilm al-bāṭin*).

zakāt (Ar.): tax on property, livestock, agriculture, etc. It is one of the five pillars of Islam.

Zāwiya (Ar.): term used in the Būdshīshiyya and other Moroccan Sufi orders to refer to the central lodge where the highest authorities of the *ṭarīqa* reside. It might also be used in a more generic way to designate any of the places where a group of followers gathers together to perform collective ritual sessions. The *Zāwiya* of the Būdshīshiyya is located in the town of Madāgh (north-eastern Morocco).

zawj (Ar.): from the classical Arabic term meaning 'one of a pair or couple'. It denotes the idea of duality, hence it has also come to designate 'spouse' ('husband' in its masculine form – *zaw*j – and 'wife' in its feminine one – *zawjāt*).

ziyāra; pl. *ziyārāt* (Ar.): Sufi pious visitation, pilgrimage to a holy place, generally a *Zāwiya,* or tomb or shrine.

Index

2002 elections, Moroccan 25
2003 Casablanca Bombings 58 n. 51, 108
2008 CESNUR International Conference 1
2009 elections, Moroccan 25
2011 elections, Moroccan 25
9/11 4, 5, 48, 90, 99, 108

à la carte, religion 143
'Abbadī, Muḥammad 25
'Abduh, Muḥammad 24
ablution, ritual (*see also wuḍū*) a101, 113 n. 21
Abū al-Quṭūt's lodge 121
Abū Shish 106
academic interest in Sufism 5, 27, 48, 58 n. 50
action, Hamza's 106
acupuncturist 129
adaptability of *ṭuruq* (*see also* plasticity) 88, 98, 105, 110
adaptation, Būdshīshiyya's 32, 57 n. 43, 107, 147
adaptation, social 32
ad-du'ā prayer 101
adept, Būdshīshiyya's 144
adherent (*see also* devotee) 9, 34 n. 29, 49, 79, 105, 106, 114 n. 29, 115 n. 41, 123, 127, 128, 131, 142, 144, 145, 148, 149
affiliation, religious (*see also* membership) 42, 73, 82, 84, 100, 128, 129, 135 n. 30
affliction 127
African American, Christian denomination 137 n. 46
African follower 53
Agadir 40, 81, 123, 127
Agde 40
age, devotees' 5, 44, 78, 114 n. 21
age, Hamza's 28, 45, 91, 122
agourram (*see also marabout, tagourramt*) 80, 92 n. 2, 147, 156, 159, 161
agricultural calendar 80
agricultural cycle 106
Ahfir 2, 32 n. 6, 40
Ahlstrom, Sydney E. 137 n. 45
aḥwāl (*see also ḥāl*) 99, 102, 112 n.12, 137 n.42, 158
'aīd al-fiṭr 107
ailment 125
Ain Reggada 32 n. 6
airport 35 n. 43, 85, 90, 105
Aissati, Abderrahman 75 n. 3
Aix-en-Provence 40
Ajārūm, Ibn 34 n. 24
Ajiba, Ibn 28
ajr (*see also* religious merit) 103
Akhmisse, Mustapha 9
al-'Adl wal-iḥsān (movement) 23
al-'Arabī, ibn 8
al-Būdshīsh, Abīmadyan Ibn Munawwar Qādirī 23, 45, 154
al-Būdshīsh, Boumediene 28, 154
al-Būdshīsh, Ḥajj al-'Abbās al-Mukhtār al-Qādirī 45, 154
al-Būdshīsh, Mukhtār 23, 45, 154
al-Ḥassania, school in Rabat 46
al-Jīlānī, 'Abd al Qādir 22, 23, 32 n. 3, 120
al-Jīlānī, band 110, 116 n. 51
al-Kabīr, Mukhtār 23, 154
al-Kattānī, Muḥammad ibn Ja'afar 124 Aleppo 112 n. 15
al-Makkī, Hamza's uncle 45, 57 n. 33
al-Manubiyya, 'Ā'isha 133 n. 6

al-Mīrghanī category, of Sufi religious authority 33 n. 19
al-Murid, Sufi Journal 48
al-Qādirī, Alī 106
al-Qalia alley 133 n. 8
al-Qashshāsh, Abū al-Ghayth 133 n. 6
al-Quṭūt, Abū 121
al-Razzāq, 'Abd 23
al-ṣirāwiyyīn alley 133 n. 8
al-Sulamī, Abū 'Abd-al-Raḥmān 58 n. 59
'Alawī devotee 76 n. 11
'Alawī text 76 n. 11
'Alawīyya 41, 76 n. 11
Albirini, Abdulkafi 75 n. 2
Algeria 8, 23, 35 n. 35, 41, 159
'Alī Ibn Abu Ghālib 121, 133 n. 8
'Allāh 98, 99, 101, 103, 104, 106, 112 n. 13, 156, 159
allegiance, religious 2, 41, 42, 66, 69, 80, 129, 147, 157
allopathic 123, 124, 127, 128, 129, 130
Alqueria de los Rosales 83
altered state of consciousness (*see also* ecstasy) 13
alternative religiosity 29, 65
alternative therapy 128, 129
amazement, narratives of 82, 83
Amazigh (*see also* Berber language) 92 n. 2, 161
American follower 53 n. 4
American lifestyle 115 n. 32
American Muslim 114 n. 31
American person 134 n. 21
American tourist 58 n. 51
American-Moroccan 48
Amina Trust, organization 55 n. 20, 66
amity (*see also* comradeship) 83, 84, 85, 86, 142, 147
analytical approach to Sufism 47
Andalusia 22, 94 n. 22
Andes Mountains 129
Andezian, Sossie 8
aniconic religion 99
animal side of humans 97, 159
animal/s 82, 97
animosity 99
annihilation 33 n. 20
antagonistic bodily force 101
anthropological 8, 9, 10, 11
anthropologist 9, 82
Anthropology 46, 48
anti-'Islamist' 27
anti-democratic 27
anti-royalist 74
anti-Sufi 33 n. 9, 125
anti-textual 144
anti-textualism 51, 52, 70, 111 n. 4, 113 n. 21, 144
anti-West 60
anti-Western 48, 66
Anway, Carol Anderson 115 n. 32
anxiety 85, 99
apolitisme 24, 27
Appadurai, Arjun 3, 145
apricot 35 n. 40
Arab populations 1, 15
Arab Spring 4
Arab World 75 n. 2, 75 n. 4
Arabian Peninsula 135 n. 22
Arabic grammar 28
Arabic language (*see also Fuṣḥā*) 16 n. 2, 32 n. 3, 53, 55 n. 18, 56 n. 28, 56 n. 30, 64, 69, 75 n. 2, 75 n. 4, 76 n. 5, 100, 145, 156, 157, 158, 159, 160, 162
Arabic script 76 n. 5
Arabicized 108
arbitrator, social 30, 32
Argenteuil 31, 44, 55 n. 21, 55 n. 22, 112 n. 8
article (*see also* literary output) 3, 47, 92 n. 3, 115 n. 42, 135 n. 25
Asad, Talal 111 n. 5, 135 n. 24, 148
ascetic live 26
ash'arite 34 n. 25
'Ashir, Ibn 28, 34 n. 25
aspirant 25, 83, 98, 113 n. 18, 160
'Aṭā 'Allāh, Ibn 53, 59 n. 64, 104, 114 n. 28
Athens, US 53 n. 3
Atlanta 53 n. 3
Atlas, High 80, 81
Atlas, Middle 81
atonement 110
attitudes in public service 23
attitudes towards fasting 15
attitudes towards women 89
audience 28, 62, 64, 149
audience, 'Western' 108
audience, European 127, 133 n. 5
audience, international 58 n. 51
audience, Moroccan 34 n. 27
audience, new 63, 67, 98
audience, non-Reformist 125
audience, urban 25, 33 n. 18
audience, wealthier 108
audience, youngster 63
audiovisual material 3

aura, saintly 46, 58 n. 56, 78
authentic 47, 85, 88
authenticating 26, 103, 141
authenticity, of the Būdshīshiyya's Path 42, 43, 88, 97, 144
authoritarian 12, 56 n. 23
authority, female 40, 50
authority, Moroccan 29, 32, 158
authority, non-consanguineal 47
authority, political 158, 160
authority, religious (*see also* leadership) 6, 10, 26, 27, 41, 33 n. 19, 34 n. 31, 43, 45, 46, 47, 49, 56 n. 27, 58 n. 48, 58 n. 53, 70, 103, 111 n. 4, 148, 149, 150, 160
authority, secondary (*see also* *muqaddim/a*) 49, 159
autobiographical 34 n. 29
autonomy, contingent's 55 n. 19
avalanche of people 91, 112 n. 16
Avignon 40
awakening, spiritual 97, 109, 159
awliyā' (*see also* *walī*) 14, 22, 56, 78, 92, 94, 106, 120, 121, 125, 126, 158, 161

Bābā 15, 123, 124, 126, 127, 128, 129
Bach flower remedy 129
back to walking 134 n. 21
Badran, Margot 94 n. 18
Baghdad 22, 121
Balkans 134 n. 21
Bangladeshi 133 n. 13
banlieue 44, 52, 109, 116 n. 51, 130
baraka (*see also* *walaya*) 30, 33 n. 19, 45, 46, 49, 70, 72, 78, 91, 93 n. 5, 94 n. 23, 102, 106, 120, 121, 122, 128, 156, 161
Barcelona 40
barefoot 99
barley 136 n. 37
bathe the sick 123
bay'a (*see also* initiation) 2, 16 n. 3, 25, 26, 42, 54 n. 9, 109, 113, 157
Bayonne 40
BBC 53, 83, 137 n. 42
Beckford, James A. 89
bedroom 93 n. 15
befriending 76 n. 11, 83
behaviour, offensive 90
behaviour, social 51
behavioural code 148
Belgium 1, 2, 40, 55 n. 19, 134
belief 4, 6, 8, 12, 13, 16 n. 11, 42, 56 n. 23, 69, 89, 111 n. 4, 121, 122, 125, 126, 127, 130, 133 n. 6, 135 n. 22, 135 n. 29, 136 n. 32, 136 n. 35, 137 n. 40, 137 n. 45, 145, 148, 161
belief system 9, 127, 132
Ben Aïssa *moussem* 80
Ben Driss, Karim 10, 23, 25, 26, 30, 34 n. 30, 45, 58 n. 50, 106
Ben Rochd, Rachid 10, 34 n. 29, 34 n. 30, 45, 97, 99, 103, 104, 130
Benares 78, 146
Ben-Brahim, Naoufel 21
benevolence 106
Béni-Snassen 23, 32 n. 6
Berber 'nation' 81
Berber area (*see also* Berber zone) 29
Berber culture (*see also* *Berbérité*) 18
Berber devotee (*see also* Berber *fuqarā'/faqīrāt*) 42
Berber dialect (*see also* Riffian Berber) 75 n. 5
Berber diversity 81
Berber *fuqarā'/faqīrāt* (*see also* Berber devotee) 1, 42, 63
Berber identity (*see also* Berber culture) 64, 75, 80
Berber language (*see also* dialect) 75 n. 3
Berber movement 76 n. 6
Berber people (*see also* Berber population) 32 n. 6
Berber population (*see also* Berber people) 23, 25, 90
Berber pride 81
Berber zone (*see also* Berber area) 9
Berbérité (*see also* Berber identity) 64, 75
Berberized 108
Berkane 1, 2, 27, 30, 31, 32 n. 6, 32 n. 7, 35 n. 35, 35 n. 36, 40, 45, 57 n. 34, 115 n. 40
Berque, Jacques 29
bewilderment 82
Beyer, Peter 4
Bidwell, Robin Leonard 29, 32 n. 6
Bilgili, Özge 54 n. 6
Bilu, Yoram 72
bio-agriculture 129, 136 n. 37
biographical 10, 46, 53, 57 n. 36, 109
biological 101
Birmingham 8, 40, 44, 54 n. 10, 55 n. 21, 66, 94 n. 19, 108, 136 n. 36

birth, dates of 57 n. 35
birth, rite of 114 n. 21
black clothes 108, 109
blé concassé 106
blended character 46, 48
blessed 93 n. 5, 123, 125
blessing, saintly (*see also baraka*) 56 n. 29, 102, 121, 133 n. 6, 156
blog 3, 65, 82, 92 n. 3
Bocking, Brian x
bodily experience 111 n. 4
bodily force 101
bodily function 113 n. 21
bodily practice 49
bodily religious enactment 15, 16 n. 10, 55
bodily ritual 48
bodily saintly power 47
bodily search (*see also* frisking) 80
body 7, 13, 15, 16 n. 11, 98, 121, 123, 126, 132, 133 n. 13, 158
body, saint's 70, 78, 121, 133 n. 8
body-bouncing 101
bond among peers 85
bond, Berber community's 80
bond, disciple/master 100
bonding among peers 102, 103, 110, 145
book x, 1, 2, 3, 6, 8, 11, 14, 15, 16 n. 3, 16 n. 7, 24, 32 n. 7, 34 n. 29, 43, 45, 48, 52, 53, 56 n. 28, 56 n. 30, 57 n. 30, 57 n. 32, 58 n. 50, 58 n. 57, 62, 63, 64, 69, 70, 98, 104, 109, 110, 111 n. 4, 120, 123, 135 n. 22, 141, 144, 148, 149
booklet 3, 33 n. 11, 57 n. 34, 58 n. 60, 93 n. 60, 93 n. 12, 100, 110, 144
Bordeaux 40
border 23, 35 n. 35, 35 n. 43, 41, 54 n. 5, 86, 90, 92 n. 4
borderland 9, 54 n. 5, 128
borderland communities 9
borderland economy 54 n. 5
Boujad 115 n. 37
boundary between insiders and outsiders 89
boundary between Reformism and Sufism 125
boundary, class 110, 127
boundary, ethnic 1, 127
boundary, gender 87, 110
boundary, religious 128, 129
bourgeoisie 44, 108
Bowen, John Richard 132 n. 2
boyfriend 131
Bradford 40
Brasher, Brenda E. 63
Brazil 41
breathing 123
breathing pace, in *dhikr*'s performance 98
Brett, Michael 29
Britain (*see also* United Kingdom) 11, 16 n. 1, 35 n. 45, 40, 105, 114 n. 26, 116 n. 47, 150 n. 4,
British devotee 9, 33 n. 16, 43, 44, 55 n. 19, 85, 94 n. 26, 105, 123, 128, 136 n. 37, 150 n. 4
British group 43, 55 n. 16, 58
broker, function (*see also* brokerage) 23, 32 n. 8, 47, 104, 122
brokerage 48
Brotherhood, Muslim 33 n. 9, 52
Brunel, René 9
Bruner, Edward M. 17 n. 14
Brussels 40
Buddhism 35 n. 44, 131
Buddhist 137 n. 47
Būdshīsh, Asiya 50
Būdshīsh, Hamza 2, 5, 10, 15, 16 n. 4, 22, 24, 25, 26, 28, 29, 30, 33 n. 16, 33 n. 19, 34 n. 31, 41, 42, 43, 45, 46, 47, 48, 49, 50, 51, 52, 54 n. 11, 56 n. 28, 57 n. 44, 58 n. 50, 58 n. 53, 59 n. 65, 63, 64, 69, 70, 71, 72, 78, 79, 80, 82, 84, 85, 86, 87, 91, 92 n. 3, 94 n. 26, 97, 98, 100, 102, 103, 104, 106, 107, 108, 109, 110, 111 n. 3, 112 n. 12, 112 n. 17, 113 n. 17, 113 n. 20, 113 n. 21, 120, 121, 122, 124, 126, 129, 130, 131, 132 n. 3, 133 n. 3, 134 n. 18, 135 n. 27, 137 n. 39, 142, 145, 147, 149, 154, 157, 159
Būdshīsh, Hmida 30
Būdshīsh, Jamāl 46, 47, 49, 50, 51, 57, 124, 134 n. 19,
Būdshīsh, Munīr 6, 46, 47, 48, 49, 58 n. 53
Būdshīsh, Murād 45
Buehler, Arthur F. 33 n. 17, 112 n. 17, 113 n. 17
Buitelaar, Marjo 106, 115 n. 40
Bunt, Gary 76 n. 8
Bürgel, Johann Christoph 132 n. 1
Burhāniyya *ṭarīqa* 115 n. 33, 136 n. 39, 137 n. 39, 150
Burhāniyya's devotee 136 n. 39
bus 85, 141
business 5, 23, 94 n. 21
bypassing Hamza's authority 103

Cairo 94 n. 19
calendar 16 n. 4, 79, 80, 107, 115 n. 41, 159
California 53 n. 3
call to prayer 121
call, initial, to the Būdshīshiyya 68
camaraderie among devotees (*see also compagnonnage*) 15, 96, 87, 114 n. 24, 142
Cambazard-Amahan, Catherine 133 n. 8
Campbell, Heidi A. 72
Camus, Albert 53
Canada 1, 41
Canadian Muslim 115 n. 45
Capranzano, Vincent 124, 130, 131
car 79, 80, 81, 85, 141
caretaker of the shrine complex 123
Casablanca 27, 40, 47, 58 n. 51, 85, 108, 127, 129
cash (*see also* money) 90, 91, 92
Catalan 65
celebration 3, 16 n. 4, 25, 30, 35 n. 41, 50, 79, 80, 87, 90, 93 n. 5, 102, 115 n. 41, 124, 159
celebrity 49, 52
Cembrero, Ignacio 33 n. 13
cemetery 82, 121, 133 n. 10
censorship 74
centralized *ṭarīqa* 88
ceremony 99, 101
Cesari, Jocelyne 54 n. 9, 65
CESNUR, Center for Studies on New Religions 1
channel, energetic 13, 28, 125, 131
channelling 13, 14
chant 102, 108
chanting 46, 99, 100, 161
chanting style 107
chaotic aspect of religion 143
charisma, religious 14, 49, 71, 72, 73, 75, 148, 149,
charismatic 50, 72
charity 55 n. 20, 66, 91
charlatan (*see also* charlatanism) 126
charlatanism (*see also sha'wada*) 124
Charlottesville 53 n. 3
chest 101
Chicago 53 n. 3
Chih, Rachida 10, 26, 34 n. 34, 35 n. 40, 94 n. 19, 94 n. 23
childhood 81
children 26, 80, 82, 87, 92, 114 n. 21, 121
Chile 41
China 41, 128
Chinese doctor 128
Chinese medicine 128
Chishtī Sabīrī order 8, 16 n. 8, 111 n. 4
chivalry, spiritual 58 n. 59
Chlyeh, Abdelhafid 112 n. 12, 115 n. 43
choice, religious 28, 42, 62, 65, 73, 74, 105, 143, 144, 148
Christian 14, 59, 111 n. 7, 115 n. 41, 128, 129, 133 n. 5, 137 n. 46, 156
Christian calendar 115 n. 41
Christian healer 128
Christian heritage 133 n. 5
Christian pilgrimage 82
Christian tradition 133 n. 5
Christianity 16 n. 11
Christmas 115 n. 41
circumcision, rite of 114 n. 21, 121
citrus fruits 35 n. 40
civil servant 30, 33 n. 10, 45
civil service 34 n. 33
civil society 66
civil status 123
civilization 94 n. 22
civilizational dialogue 108
Claisse, Pierre-Alain 9, 112 n. 12, 115 n. 43
clandestineness 24
class, social 41, 84, 86, 110, 127, 143
classical Sufism 33 n. 19, 57 n. 44, 58 n. 59, 143
clean 28, 50, 79, 87, 99, 101, 113 n. 21, 123, 131, 133 n. 13
cleanliness 113 n. 21
clergy 135 n. 24
client, healer's 124, 125, 127, 128
client-patron relationship 35 n. 40
cloistered lives 26
CNRS, France's *Centre national de la recherche scientifique* 58 n. 50
coexistence 63, 85
Coffey, Amanda 53
Cohen, Shana 34 n. 21
cold 131
Coleman, Simon 84
collect money 91, 92
collective *dhikr* 15, 54 n. 10, 58 n. 57, 98, 102, 103, 104, 110, 112 n. 10, 114 n. 22, 142, 157, 161, 162
colloquium 71
colonial 9, 32 n. 5, 32n. 6, 158, 159
colonized 142, 145
colonizer 142

colonizer-colonized encounter 142
commercial 93 n. 5, 159
commercial exchanges 54 n. 5
commercial ties 29
commitment to Islam 26
commitment to the Būdshīshiyya 2, 5, 26, 44, 82, 83, 85, 100, 102, 137, 150
commitment, religious 25, 56 n. 28, 157
communalism 83
communication, within the Būdshī shiyya 62, 68, 86, 103
communitas 84, 85, 87, 89
community (*see also Umma*) 26, 44, 66, 79, 80, 83, 84, 87, 90, 100, 103, 114 n. 24, 142, 161
community belonging 103
community, agricultural 30, 41
community, gendered 87
community, religious 30
compagnonnage (*see also* companionship) 84, 102, 114
Companions 157, 161
companionship (*see also* amity) 29, 34 n. 30, 84, 102, 103, 146
competitive context 73
complementary bodily force 101
computer screen 65
comradeship (*see also camaraderie*) 83
concert 6, 81, 92, 108, 115 n. 42, 116 n. 48, 160
condition, social 125, 142
conference, organized by the Būdshīshiyya 28, 47, 129, 149
confidential 100
congregation (*see also* contingent) 54 n. 10, 102
congregational meeting, Būdshīshiyya's (*see also* ritual session) 4, 31, 40, 41, 100, 158
consanguine relation, to Hamza Būdshīsh
conscience 97, 159
consideration (*see also* kindness) 84
consumer, Būdshīshiyya texts' 52, 67, 71
contemplative understanding of religion 27, 144
content, book's ix, 14, 17 n. 12
continental Europe 55 n. 16, 105
contingent (*see also* enclave) 2, 4, 31, 41, 42, 43, 50, 53 n.3, 59 n. 61, 69, 73, 76 n. 12, 79, 86, 87, 89, 90, 91, 98, 100, 102, 103, 104, 107, 113 n. 20, 127, 141, 148
contribution, monetary (*see also* donation) 91
controversy 57 n. 41, 109, 110, 122, 129, 134 n. 21
convention 107
conventional medicine 123, 127
conversion, religious 10, 11, 17 n. 13, 42, 54 n. 11, 54 n. 15, 55 n. 15, 55 n. 17, 68, 83, 93 n. 9, 105, 115 n. 32, 116 n. 51
convert devotee 53
convulsion, bodily 101
cooking 50, 79, 83, 87, 106
Coon, Carleton Stevens 9
Cornell, Vincent J. 9, 33 n. 8, 126
corporate character, Būdshīshiyya's 47, 135 n. 30, 136 n. 30
corporate structure, religious organization's 47, 136 n. 30
corporeal 14, 70, 71, 91
corporeality (*see also* embodiment) 7, 9
corpus of believers, Būdshīshiyya's 107
correction, social 74
corruption 30
cosmopolitan 142, 150
cosmopolitanism 10
counter-hegemonic status of healing practices 124, 125
courtesy (*see also* consideration) 35 n. 43, 51
couscous 79
Cowan, Douglas E. 76 n. 8
crazy, person 30, 68
creed 35 n. 44, 128
critical of healers 127
critical of Moroccan culture 87
critical of Sufism 135 n. 24, 136 n. 35, 149
critical of the Būdshīshiyya 34 n. 27, 73, 74, 92, 100, 122, 129
criticism 3, 35 n. 44, 74, 75, 86, 112 n. 16, 122, 135 n. 22, 135 n. 27
crop 92, 106
cross-legged 99
cross-pollination 10, 33 n. 9, 132, 135 n. 25, 145
crowd 50, 79, 80, 89, 99, 100, 135 n. 27
crying 101, 102
Csordas, Thomas J. 121, 132, 149
cultural association 65
cultural background 22, 26, 42, 66, 76 n. 11, 128
cultural backwardness 143
cultural barriers 5
cultural borrowing 131, 136 n. 33, 145
cultural differences 79

cultural heterogenization 145
cultural homogenization 145
cultural permeability 127
cultural stranger 5, 31, 42
curative power 121, 122, 128, 129, 130, 133 n. 6, 134 n. 18
cure 100, 120, 121, 122, 123, 132, 133 n. 6, 134 n. 21
Curtis, Maria F. 108
cyberspace 62, 63, 64, 66, 68, 71, 73, 74, 75

da'wa (*see also* proselytization) 8, 14, 26, 28, 47, 51, 52, 53, 68, 157
Daadaoui, Muḥammad 27
daily life 7, 89, 103
dance 107
Dandarawiyya order 135 n. 28
Dar al-Hassania institute, Rabat 46
dārija (*see also* spoken Arabic) 41, 157
Darqawiyya order 34 n. 26
data 3, 4, 5, 6, 10, 44, 46, 47, 55 n. 16, 55 n. 21, 55 n. 22, 57 n. 34, 57 n. 36, 57 n. 41, 62, 66, 68, 74, 76 n. 9, 141
daughter xi, 30, 33 n. 12, 43, 50, 51
Dawson, Lorne L. 76 n. 8
de Vitray-Meyerovitch, Eva 58 n. 50, 109
deafness 120
death 24, 33 n. 10, 53, 57 n. 35, 114, 121, 130, 134 n. 21
death, dates of 57 n. 35
death, rite of 114
debate 9, 16 n. 8, 108, 115 n. 45, 129, 146, 149
de-Berberization 28
decentralized power 145, 149
decentralizing power 148
decision maker 109
decision making 93 n. 16
de-individuation 130
delegation 89
democratic character, internet's 73
democratic ideals 108
demon 115 n. 39
Denizard Rivail, Hippolyte Léon 131
depressed 104
depression 131
desire 97, 112 n. 12, 123, 159
deterritorialisation, Islam's 143
de-territorialization of Islam 143
deviant religiosity 65, 76 n. 11
devotee (*see also faqīr/a*) 1, 2, 3, 4, 5, 6, 10, 11, 12, 14, 15, 22, 26, 27, 28, 29, 31, 35 n. 40, 35 n. 43, 40, 41, 42, 43, 44, 46, 48, 49, 50, 51, 52, 54 n. 11, 55 n. 18, 55 n. 19, 56 n. 23, 56 n. 24, 56 n. 28, 57 n. 36, 58 n. 50, 58 n. 53, 62, 64, 67, 68, 69, 70, 71, 72, 73, 78, 79, 83, 84, 85, 86, 87, 88, 88, 99, 100, 102, 104, 105, 106, 107, 111 n. 4, 111 n. 5, 113 n. 21, 114 n. 24, 115 n. 41, 116 n. 49, 126, 127, 128, 129, 131, 132, 135 n. 27, 137 n. 39, 137 n. 46, 143, 144, 145, 146, 147, 148, 149, 150, 160
devotion, religious 5, 8, 34 n. 31, 40, 42, 45, 49, 63, 72, 132 n. 2, 143
devotional 43, 72, 79
dhikr (*see also waẓīfa*) 8, 15, 48, 49, 50, 58 n. 48, 58 n. 53, 58 n. 57, 81, 94 n. 19, 97, 98, 99, 100, 102, 103, 104, 107, 111 n. 4, 111 n. 5, 112 n. 10, 112 n. 11, 112 n. 13, 112 n. 17, 113 n. 18, 114 n. 25, 114 n. 26 115 n. 44, 123, 133 n. 3, 133 n. 7, 145, 157, 158, 159, 160, 161, 162
dhikr djali 98
dhikr khāfi 98
dialectical persuasion 47
diaspora 2, 10, 31, 35 n. 45, 36, 54 n. 6, 54 n. 7, 84, 94 n. 24, 134 n. 21
differences, social 79, 85
digital 14, 62, 63, 65, 67, 70
digital appearance (*see also* online appearance) 62, 74, 76 n. 9
digital content 64, 67, 73
digital devotion 63
digital era 62, 63, 75
digital imagery 71
digital literacy 69
digital literature 52
digital material (*see also* digital output) 3, 14, 57 n. 36, 64, 71
digital output (*see also* digital production) 71
digital production (*see also* internet output) 69
diglossia 75 n. 2
Dilday, Katherine A. 33 n. 12
diplomatic body 108
directing *shaykh* 112 n. 17, 113 n. 17
dirham 30, 92
dirigeant, Būdshīshiyya's (*see also* upper echelon) 71
disaffiliation, religious 73, 75
disciple (*see also* adherent) 2, 6, 14, 24, 26, 33 n. 15, 41, 42, 43, 44 46, 47, 50, 52, 53, 58 n. 48, 59 n. 61, 59 n. 64, 67, 68, 69, 70, 72, 83, 84, 85, 86, 91, 93,

n. 8, 97, 98, 100, 101, 102, 104, 108, 109, 111 n. 2, 111 n. 4, 111 n. 5, 112 n. 12, 112 n. 14, 113 n. 17, 122, 123, 129, 131, 134 n. 18, 135 n. 27, 136 n. 37, 137 n. 39, 142, 144, 148, 150, 157, 158, 159
disciplehood (*see also* discipleship) 22, 25, 80
discipleship (*see also* disciplehood) 5, 16 n. 3, 40, 41, 42, 44, 111 n. 5, 126, 144, 148
discipline, spiritual 28, 51, 104, 105, 109
discrimination 52, 143
discrimination, gender 90
discriminatory 143
discursive 70, 88, 125, 136
discursive hegemony 136 n. 33
disease 82, 1220, 121, 124, 130, 131
disorder 104, 123, 130
dissatisfaction with psychiatry 130
diversity within the Būdshīshiyya 1, 3, 7, 15, 22, 132, 147
division, social 84
dizzy 102
doctor 100, 122, 123, 127, 128, 130, 132, 132 n. 3, 133 n. 3, 135 n. 30, 137 n. 40
doctor, spiritual 133 n. 3
doctrine, religious 6, 14, 26, 32, 33 n. 18, 40, 53 n. 1, 57 n. 43, 63, 92, 97, 98, 111 n. 5, 112 n. 17, 126, 143, 145, 148
dogma, religious 111 n. 5, 161
domed mausoleum (*see also qubbā*) 128
Dominguez Diaz, Marta 35 n. 44, 54 n. 7, 55 n. 16, 56 n. 23, 56 n. 24, 112 n. 9, 115 n. 41, 150 n. 4
donation, monetary (*see also* contribution) 91, 92, 94 n. 25, 106
Douglas, Malti 16 n. 10, 110
Doutté, Edmond 7
download 62
downloaders 71
Draper, Mustafa 4, 9, 23, 26, 45, 58 n. 50, 98, 112 n. 12, 116 n. 47, 120
dress 31, 81, 82, 90, 100, 158, 161
Dumont, Paul 36 n. 47
dunya 123, 133 n. 14, 157
duration, *dhikr's* 99
duty, canonical 78
duty, moral 92
duty, religious 50, 58 n. 55
duty, spiritual 34 n. 30, 51, 80
Dwyer, Kevin 9
Eade, John 84
ear, deafness cured 120
East-West narrative 48
Eatwell, Abdarrahman 81, 82, 84, 136 n. 37
eclectic 4, 10, 29, 76 n. 11, 116 n. 52, 137 n. 39, 143, 150
eclecticism, religious 14, 17 n. 17, 53, 143, 144
economic background 22, 29, 40, 44, 55 n. 18, 86, 103, 147
economic benefits 89
economic crisis 55 n. 22
economic differences 79, 85
economic dimension 8, 15, 89, 90
economic improvement 94 n. 21
economic support 30
ecstasy (*see also* ecstatic experiences) 28, 101, 112 n. 12, 158
ecstatic experience (*see also* trance) 13, 14, 99, 112 n. 12
educational attainment 128
egalitarian 85, 86
egalitarianism 85, 86
ego 97, 99, 112 n. 11, 123, 131, 159
egocentrism 131
egoistic 91
Egypt 33 n. 9, 34 n. 34, 94 n. 23, 132 n. 2, 134 n. 18, 159
Egyptian healer 132 n. 2
Eickelman, Dale F. 9, 29, 57 n. 32, 82, 84, 86, 87, 93 n. 14, 115 n. 37
El Abar, Lahlou 9
El Zein, Abdul Hamid M. 147
Elahmadi, Mohsine 24, 33 n. 10
electrical work 87
elite 27, 29, 44, 86, 108, 135 n. 30, 136 n. 35, 143
embodied subjectivity 129, 132, 146
embodiment, religious (*see also* corporeality) 6, 14, 40, 54 n. 15, 69, 111 n. 5, 121, 145, 146, 147, 148, 149, 161
emic 13, 25, 131, 132, 143
Emirates 41
emotional causation of illness 131
emotional devotion 34 n. 31
emotional experience 102
emotional imbalance 131
emotional state 160
emotional suffering 108
emotional support 103
emotional unease 130
emotional veneration 71

emplacement, study of 6, 7, 69, 111 n. 5
enclave (*see also* congregation) 2, 3, 4, 5, 14, 29, 41, 42, 49, 55 n. 19, 58 n. 53, 66, 79, 84, 86, 91, 93 n. 16, 99, 107, 116 n. 52, 146, 148, 149, 158
Eneborg, Yusuf Muslim 133 n. 13
energetic blockage 13
energetic channel 131
energy 101, 128, 131
Engelund, Sara Rismyhr 59 n. 63
England 55 n. 21, 136 n. 37
English 33 n. 16, 35 n. 44, 54 n. 12, 56 n. 26, 57 n. 44, 64, 67, 69, 94 n. 26, 113 n. 19, 156, 157
English-speaking 10, 56 n. 30
enlightenment, spiritual 66
Ensel, Remco 9
entering *hal* 99, 101
entering the Būdshīshiyya 4, 10, 33 n. 10, 42, 43, 52, 83, 92, 94 n. 18, 103, 110, 111 n. 5, 113 n. 18, 113 n. 21, 122, 130, 161
episteme 146
equality, ethos of 84, 93 n. 16
equalizing ethos 87
Ernst, Carl W. 98, 111 n. 6
Escaffit, Jean-Claude 58
esoteric 35 n. 44, 100, 112 n. 14, 162
essentialist 142, 143
ethical 94 n. 24, 112 n. 16, 156
ethics 103, 156
ethnic boundary 1
ethnic melange 44
ethnic, ethnicity 11, 34 n. 22, 41, 55 n. 21, 84, 86, 127, 141, 151 n. 5
ethnicity 11, 34 n. 22, 41, 84, 86, 127, 141
ethnographer 3, 53
ethnographic 3, 8, 14, 16 n. 6, 111 n. 6
ethnography 3, 54 n. 5
ethnopsychiatry 129
ethos, Būdshīshiyya's 24, 27, 28, 69, 84, 85, 86, 87, 88, 109, 141
etiquette, social 147
euro 30
Europe 1, 2, 3, 8, 10, 15, 16 n. 1, 31, 32, 41, 42, 43, 44, 46, 49, 54 n. 6, 55 n. 16, 58 n. 53, 65, 74, 76 n. 11, 80, 82, 83, 85, 87, 88, 89, 91, 94 n. 21, 99, 100, 105, 111 n. 4, 115 n. 32, 115 n. 33, 115 n. 41, 116 n. 47, 116 n. 52, 123, 127, 131, 132, 133 n. 5, 135 n. 30, 136 n. 32, 137 n. 39, 137 n. 40, 142, 143, 145, 146, 148
European Būdshīshiyya 2, 8, 12, 31, 43, 46, 55 n. 16, 55 n. 19, 56, 67, 93 n. 16, 99, 103, 105, 107, 112 n. 9, 114 n. 27, 115 n. 41, 127, 141, 156
European devotee 31, 35 n. 42, 54 n. 9, 74, 81, 88, 90, 107, 113 n. 21, 127, 128, 130, 131, 132, 136 n. 37, 137 n. 45, 143, 145, 157
European expatriate community in Morocco 29
European Islam 54 n. 9
European languages 41, 54 n. 5, 57 n. 44, 59 n. 64, 64, 67, 74, 75, 114 n. 28
European Sufism 14, 136 n. 32
Europe-Maghrib institute, Paris 46
Evans, Dylan 133 n. 9
event 15, 48, 78, 79, 80, 81, 82, 92, 99, 100, 102, 103, 106, 108, 113 n. 21, 148
Evers Rosander, Eva 91, 93 n. 6
evil 97, 159
Ewing, Katherine Pratt 116 n. 51, 132 n. 2
excellence of behaviour (*see also* courtesy) 58 n. 59, 84, 88, 106, 143, 148, 156, 158
exceptional character of pilgrimage 81, 85, 89
exclusivism, religious 132, 144
exclusivist 144
exclusivity, religious 129, 147
ex-devotee (*see also* ex-member) 73
exemplarity (*see also iḥsān*) 52
existential 97
ex-member (*see also* former disciple) 5, 7
exorcism (*see also siḥr*) 135 n. 22
exotic, devotion for
expansion, Būdshīshiyya's 14, 27, 28, 47, 52, 63, 135 n. 30, 143, 144, 146
experience x, 3, 4, 5, 7, 8, 17 n. 14, 47, 51, 52, 53, 79, 81, 82, 83 84, 85, 86, 87, 102, 110, 116 n. 51, 121, 125, 131
experience, 'ground-breaking' 82
experience, religious 11, 17 n. 14, 40, 101, 102, 111 n. 4
experiencing the Divine 102, 112 n. 12, 137 n. 43, 144, 158
experiencing 52, 70, 71, 102, 128
experiential, approach to Sufism 6, 12, 51, 56 n. 23, 68, 69, 70, 71, 97, 111 n. 4, 129, 144
expression, emotions' 101
expression, the Divine's 115 n. 41
extinct tradition, Sufism 79, 141

extremism, religious 59 n. 65, 74, 108, 114 n. 31
extremist 68

face, God's 99
face, Hamza's 83, 135 n. 27
face, scary 103
Facebook 45
face-to-face, religious instruction 72, 144, 146
facial expression, in *dhikr*'s performance 98
faction 84, 86
factionalism 84, 86
faith healing 124, 125, 128, 134 n. 20, 146, 147
faith x, 16 n. 11, 82
faith, Muslim 43
false religiosity 109
false *shaykh* 104
family member 68, 79, 104, 127
family xi, 2, 22, 23, 26, 29, 30, 31, 35 n. 40, 35 n. 42, 40, 43, 45, 46, 47, 48, 50, 51, 54 n. 5, 56 n. 28, 57 n. 323, 57 n. 34, 57 n. 36, 57 n. 38, 64, 68, 72, 79, 80, 81, 84, 87, 89, 92, 93 n. 15, 102, 103, 104, 115 n. 41, 120, 121, 123, 124, 125, 127, 130, 133 n. 10, 143, 150
famine 106
faqīh 132, 135 n. 23, 157
faqīr/a (*see also* member, *fuqarā'/faqīrāt*) 1, 6, 7, 14, 15, 25, 26, 28, 34 n. 30, 34 n. 31, 35 n. 42, 42, 44, 45, 46, 48, 49, 50, 51, 52, 53, 55 n. 18, 68, 78, 80, 81, 82, 83, 85, 86, 88, 89, 90, 91, 99, 100, 102, 103, 104, 105, 106, 107, 109, 113 n. 21, 114 n. 24, 123, 129, 132, 146, 147, 149, 157
fasting (*see also Ramaḍān*) 15, 105, 106 107, 115 n. 40
fātiḥa 50, 58 n. 57, 120, 124, 157
fear 97, 99
feeling connected 142
feeling God 83
feet, Hamza's 83
female devotee (*see also faqīra*) 8, 51, 78
female member (*see also* female devotee) 4, 50, 58 n. 54, 78, 87
Fentress, Elizabeth 29
fertility 137 n. 46
Fes 44, 45, 47, 48, 108, 120, 121, 133 n. 8, 155
Fes Sacred Music Festival 48, 58 n. 51, 108, 144
festival 16 n. 4, 48, 58 n. 51, 78, 79, 108, 144, 159
festivity 107, 115 n. 36, 115 n. 41, 159
Fezouane 32 n. 6
fieldwork x, xi, 2, 3, 4, 5, 8, 35 n. 37, 46, 47, 56 n. 24, 57 n. 36, 58 n. 54, 62, 66, 67, 68, 74, 76 n. 9, 79, 108, 115 n. 40, 116 n. 51, 120, 121, 124, 141, 145
financial exploitation 94 n. 25
financial means 127
fitra 42
flag 81
flexibility of healing practices 128, 129
Florida 53 n.3
Flueckiger, Joyce Burkhalter 127, 128, 132 n. 2, 135 n. 22, 136 n. 33
fluid membership 5, 76 n. 9
folk belief 130
folk Islam 34 n. 22, 130
follower 1, 2, 3, 4, 5, 6, 11, 12, 13, 14, 15, 16 n. 4, 17 n. 15, 22, 26, 28, 31, 32, 40, 41, 42, 44, 47, 49, 53, 54 n. 10, 55 n. 19, 63, 64, 66, 69, 70, 71, 73, 75, 76 n. 11, 78, 79, 80, 85, 86, 89, 93 n. 6, 94 n. 23, 103, 105, 106, 111 n. 2, 114 n. 26, 114 n. 27, 115 n. 33, 121, 122, 126, 135 n. 27, 143, 145, 147, 148, 149, 150, 159, 160, 161, 162
following, religious 22, 26, 29, 34 n. 32, 41, 44, 65, 66, 67
food (*see also* meal) 15, 30, 31, 35 n. 41, 41, 79, 85, 86, 87, 90, 105, 106, 129, 136 n. 37, 137 n. 47
foreigner 42, 86, 90, 92 n. 4, 93 n. 5, 108
forgiveness 97, 159
formal devotee (*see also* formal member) 2
formal member (*see also* formal devotee) 83
former disciples (*see also* ex-devotees) 2, 23
formulae, dhikh 100, 104, 112 n. 16, 157, 161
forum, internet 3, 34 n. 27, 65, 73, 76 n. 17
fountain 121, 133 n. 13
France 1, 2, 10, 29, 31, 40, 44, 46, 52, 53, 54 n. 11, 55 n. 21, 55 n. 22, 85, 102, 105, 127, 135 n. 30, 149
Francophone 48
free will, belief in 29
freedom of expression 68, 73, 105

Frembgen, Jürgen Wasim 132 n. 2
French 29, 35 n. 44, 44, 46, 84, 105, 109
French colonization 23
French devotee 31, 49, 54 n. 13, 82, 129
French language 29, 35 n. 38, 35 n. 39, 41, 42, 54 n. 12, 56 n. 30, 58 n. 49, 58 n. 58, 59 n. 62, 59 n. 64, 64, 67, 69, 92 n. 2, 92 n. 3, 111 n. 9, 112 n. 11, 114 n. 25, 114 n. 28, 114 n. 30, 115 n. 46 116 n. 50, 134 n. 19, 136 n. 38
French occupation of Oujda 23, 32 n. 5
French philosophy 53
friend of God (*see also agourram*) 14, 92 n. 2, 161
friend xi, 2, 44, 53, 68, 81, 84, 85, 89, 92 n. 2, 103, 104, 109, 130
friendly 76 n. 11
friendship 29, 84, 114 n. 24
Frishkopf, Michael 115 n. 45, 150 n. 3
frisking (*see also* bodily search) 80
Fuller, Robert C. 137 n. 45
fundamentalism 48, 49, 52
fuqahā' (*see also faqīh*) 125, 135 n. 23, 157
fuqarā'/faqīrāt (*see also faqīr/a*) 1, 5, 7, 14, 15, 25, 29, 31, 35 n. 42, 41, 42, 43, 44, 46, 47, 48, 49, 50, 51, 52, 53, 57 n. 40, 63, 64, 67, 70, 78, 79, 82, 83, 86, 87, 88, 89, 90, 91, 92, 94 n. 22, 99, 100, 102, 103, 105, 106, 107, 108, 110, 112 n. 10, 113 n. 21, 114 n. 24, 124, 128, 129, 132, 133 n. 6, 133 n. 7, 142, 144, 147, 149, 157
Fuṣḥā (*see also* Arabic language) 64, 75 n. 2, 75 n. 4, 146

Gabriel, Theodore 7
gathering area 87
gathering room 87
gathering, ritual (*see also* congregational meeting) 3, 6, 25, 31, 40, 41, 42, 44, 54 n. 7, 54 n. 10, 55 n. 19, 58 n. 54, 63, 67, 68, 76 n. 11, 79, 80, 82, 85, 86, 87, 99, 101, 102, 103, 111 n. 4, 112 n. 8, 114 n. 23, 114 n. 24, 123, 124, 129, 147
Geaves, Ronald Allen x, 4, 7, 8, 11, 16 n. 1, 35 n. 45, 88, 111 n. 4, 113 n. 20, 137 n. 41, 141, 143, 144, 149, 150 n. 1
Geertz, Clifford 9, 56 n. 27, 58 n. 55
Gellner, Ernest 9, 29, 33 n. 8, 98, 148
gender 4, 16 n. 6, 16 n. 7, 26, 51, 58 n. 54, 87, 88, 89, 90, 93 n. 16, 99, 110, 113 n. 20, 143, 145
gender divide (*see also* separation between sexes) 4, 51, 58 n. 53, 87, 88, 93 n. 16
gender equality 93 n. 16
gender mixing 93 n. 16
gender segregation 49, 89, 99, 113 n. 20, 145
gendered 4, 87
gender-mixed 87, 89, 101
genealogical 23, 26, 160
genealogy (*see also silsila*) 26, 153, 160
generosity 51, 90, 91, 97, 106
Genn, Celia A. 34 n. 31
geographical dispersion, Būdshīshiyya's 3, 5, 14, 22, 40, 45, 63, 73, 93 n. 13
geographical origin 86
geographical proximity, of Būdshīshiyya's contingents 8, 41, 43
geography, Būdshīshiyya's 1, 30, 56 n. 24, 74
Georgia, US 53, 3
Germany 40, 114 n. 24, 115 n. 33
ghetto 44, 52, 53, 110
Gilan province, Iran 22
Gilliat-Ray, Sophie 55 n. 15
Gilsenan, Michael 111 n. 6
Girona 40
Glastonbury 9
global appeal 146
globality 89
globalization 10, 46, 58 n. 45, 71, 72, 88, 145
globalizing context 1, 72
glocal 4, 149
glocalization 88, 149
glossary ix, 32 n. 2, 53 n. 2, 54 n. 8, 56 n. 25, 56 n. 26, 56 n. 29
Gnawa 112 n. 12, 115 n. 38, 115 n. 43
goal, spiritual 22, 112 n. 12
goat 92
God 11, 55 n. 18, 70, 88, 97, 98, 99, 100, 104, 122, 125, 133 n. 10, 133 n. 12, 135, 156, 157, 158, 160, 161
God's beneficence 94 n. 23
God's contemplation 34 n. 20
God's disciple 98
God's existence 42
God's knowledge 112 n. 12
God's presence 98
God's quality 98
Godlas, Alan 34 n. 32
gossip 57 n. 41, 87, 147
Goulmina 40
governor of Berkane 30, 45

grace, divine 42
Granada 22
grandchildren 43
gratitude x, xi, 91
Grenoble 40
groaning 102
growth, spiritual 13, 94 n. 24
guardian 15, 92 n. 2, 93 n. 8, 123, 126, 161
Guénon, René 31, 35 n. 44
Guénonian (*see also* Perennialist) 32, 35 n. 44, 115 n. 41
Guénonianism (*see also* Perennial) 32, 115 n. 41
guest 31, 50, 87
guiding shaykh 113 n. 17
Guitouni, Abdelkader 32 n. 7
Gülen movement 33 n. 17, 151
Gulf War, first 58 n. 51
gun 53, 98, 130

Hackney, Jennifer Kay 16 n. 6
Ḥadīth 28, 157, 161
haḍra (*see also dhikr*) 123, 158, 162
Haenni, Patrick 10, 26, 29, 111 n. 4, 135 n. 30, 136 n. 35
hagiographical 121
hair 109, 158
ḥajj 79, 82, 93 n. 14
ḥāl (*see also* altered states of consciousness, *aḥwāl*) 99, 101, 137 n. 43, 158
ḥalāl 125
Halaqa, association 65
Halstead, J. Mark 115 n. 45
Hammoudi, Abdellah 9, 23, 35 n. 40, 82
hand gesture, in *dhikr*'s performance 98
hands, Hamza's 83
Hanegraaff, Wouter J. 17 n. 16, 134 n. 18, 137 n. 44
Haqqaniyya *ṭarīqa* 116 n. 47, 116 n. 52
ḥarām 125
harassment 35 n. 43, 89
Hare Krishna 109
Harmonial Religion 131, 137 n. 45, 145
Hart, David M. 9
Hassān II, former King of Morocco 24
healer 93 n. 8, 120, 121, 122, 123, 124, 125, 126, 127, 128, 132 n. 2, 132 n. 3, 134 n. 20, 134 n. 21
healing (*see also shifā'*) 8, 9, 13, 15, 28, 48, 120, 121, 122, 123, 124, 125, 126, 127, 128, 129, 130, 131, 132, 132 n. 1, 132 n. 2, 133, 133 n. 6, 133 n. 13, 134, 134 n. 18, 134 n. 20, 134 n. 21, 135, 135 n. 22, 135 n. 27, 135 n. 29, 136, 136 n. 32, 136 n. 36, 137, 137 n. 46, 138, 146, 147, 160
healing technique 124, 125, 127, 129, 132, 147
healing therapist 128
healing-related assistance 122
healing-related issue 120
healing-related pilgrimage 121
healing-seeking supplicant 124
health 7, 9, 15, 33 n. 10, 101, 104, 120, 124, 134 n. 20, 137 n. 45
health coverage 134 n. 20
health effect 104, 129
health insurance system 134 n. 20
health, mental 129
heart (*see also qalb*) 48, 51, 70, 83, 84, 85, 97, 123, 126, 159
heavy metal 109, 110
Heelas, Paul 13, 130
helping to conceive 121
herbalist 128
heretical 65
Hermansen, Marcia 11, 17 n. 15, 31, 33 n. 17, 35 n. 44, 54 n. 7, 88, 93 n. 17, 116 n. 52, 151 n. 5
heterogenization, cultural 145
hierarchical 29, 110, 114 n. 24
hierarchy, religious (*see also* religious authority) 45, 49, 50, 75, 85, 110
higher echelon, of religious authority (*see also* hierarchy) 45, 144
higher education 128, 142
high-ranked woman in the Būdshīshiyya 51
ḥijāb 158
hip-hop 52, 53, 130
historical study of Sufism 6, 7, 13, 14, 15, 22, 23, 24, 25, 26, 27, 28, 29, 30, 31, 32 n. 6, 33, 33 n. 8, 34, 35, 35 n. 44, 36, 37, 38, 39, 40, 97, 111 n. 6, 115 n. 34, 126
Hoffman, Valerie J. 79, 132 n. 2
holistic therapist
holy individual 56 n. 29, 156
holy place 92 n. 1, 162
home, devotee's 31, 42, 44, 55 n. 18, 55 n. 19, 72, 74, 79, 81, 85, 88, 98, 99, 102, 113 n. 21, 123
homeland, Moroccan 31, 41
homeless 137 n. 47
homeopathy 13

homogeneity, within Būdshīshiyya's groups (*see also* uniform group) 41, 147
homogeneous, Būdshīshiyya's group 41, 103, 147, 148
homogenization, cultural 145
hospital 24, 82, 122, 123, 124, 127, 132 n. 3, 135 n. 30
hospitality 15, 31, 50, 58 n. 55, 137 n. 47
Howell, Julia Day 7, 94 n. 19, 111 n. 4, 134 n. 20
hub, Moroccan 41
human 7, 13, 42, 91, 97, 99, 100, 115 n. 39, 116 n. 51, 122, 133 n. 12, 144, 158
Human Rights 27, 108
humankind 35 n. 44, 109
Hunt, Steven 150 n. 2
husband 36 n. 46, 54 n. 7, 113 n. 20, 162
Hutson, Alaine S. 114 n. 22
hybrid, group 17, 31, 42, 43, 44, 88, 89, 150
hybridity, religious 4, 10, 11, 105, 147
hygiene 113 n. 21, 124

Iberian Peninsula 22, 120
ibn al-Kalbī 135 n. 22
ibn Ja'afar al-Kattānī, Muḥammad 124
Ibrāhīm, *shaykh* 22
iconographic 72
identity formation, process of 142, 149
identity marker 145
identity, ethnic 35 n. 45
identity, group 7, 78
identity, Muslim 107, 115 n. 33, 116 n. 52
identity, religious 6, 7, 8, 28, 42, 46, 54 n. 15, 64, 67, 69 71, 75, 79, 98, 105, 107, 110, 116 n. 51, 121, 142, 143
identity, social 41
identity, transnational 48
ideological 3, 25, 32, 41, 74, 116 n. 51
ideology 24, 25, 49, 86, 116 n. 51, 131, 142, 146, 160
idhn 45, 48, 58 n. 48
idiom, Islam's 136
idolatry 122, 135 n. 27
ignorance 144
iḥsān (*see also* excellence of behaviour) 84, 85, 97, 148, 158
illiteracy 63
image 45, 48, 66, 74, 88, 108, 114 n. 22, 126, 127, 141
image recording 3
image, of Hamza Būdshīsh 63, 71, 72, 99, 149
imitating behaviour 46, 85, 100
immaterial creature (*see also jinn*) 115 n. 39
imperialism, cultural 145
Inayat Khan, Sufi order 34 n. 31, 76 n. 11, 116 n. 52
inclination, religious 103
inclusive 25, 31, 46, 52
inclusivism, religious 48, 144
inclusivist 49
income 80
independence, Morocco's 23, 42
individual *dhikr* 98, 103, 104, 157
individualist 29
Indonesia 132 n. 2
infertility 125
informal disciples 111 n. 4
informal influence 50, 74, 100
information technology 72
in-group ties 86
inhale water 97
initiated, disciple 28, 100, 104, 111 n. 4, 112 n. 17, 113
initiation, rite of (*see also* pact) 25, 33 n. 17, 45, 48, 54 n. 9, 58 n. 48, 58 n. 53, 111 n. 4, 148
inner self
inner transformation
innovation, religious 26
insider 89, 90
insider/outsider problem 5, 16 n. 8
institutional dimension 40, 42
institutionalized religion 12, 16 n. 11, 17 n. 11, 29, 62
instruction, religious 25, 34 n. 32, 47, 51, 52, 104, 112 n. 17
instrument, musical 107
instrumental 107, 110
instrumentalist, musical 107
integrity, official discourse's 144
intellectual 6, 27, 31, 44, 51, 52, 55 n. 17, 69, 70, 102, 144
intellectual stillness 27
intellectualized 47, 67, 69
intention (*see also niyya*) 100, 112 n. 13, 159
interaction, among devotees 3, 42, 62, 86, 87, 89, 90, 93 n. 14, 131, 146
interaction, social 87
interceding 82, 92 n. 2, 121, 161

intercession 93 n. 5, 113 n. 17, 122, 123, 124, 127, 130, 132
intercultural 132, 136 n. 33
interest in 'non-Islamic healing practices' 129, 146
interest in faith healing 128
interest in Sufism 49, 71, 83, 112 n. 14
interest in the Būdshīshiyya 5, 6, 53, 54, 64, 68, 72, 83
interest, devotees' 13, 32, 33 n. 18, 34 n. 20, 90, 108, 109, 110, 136, 136 n. 39, 142, 143, 144, 147
interfaith 51, 108
internal conflict in the Būdshīshiyya 103
international 1, 31, 32, 58 n. 51, 80, 88, 146
international gathering 3, 6, 67, 85, 88, 103, 114 n. 23, 146
international organization 11, 14, 22, 31
internaut 63, 67
internet 14, 15, 62, 63, 64, 65, 67, 68, 69, 70, 71, 72, 73, 74, 75, 75 n. 1, 76, 116 n. 78, 149
internet output (*see also* digital material) 67
internet portal 64
internet use 63, 71, 75 n. 1
internet user 63, 75 n. 1
interpreter, musical 107
interreligious 144
intra-*ṭarīqa* relations 15, 44, 47, 102, 110, 145, 146
invocation 97, 98, 103, 123, 124, 134 n. 19
involvement, in the Būdshīshiyya 2
iridologist 131
ISKCON, International Society for Krishna Consciousness 99, 134 n. 18
Islam x, 1, 5, 6, 7, 9, 10, 12, 15, 16 n. 1, 16 n. 10, 16 n. 11, 17 n. 13, 17 n. 15, 26, 27, 34 n. 32, 36, 42, 43, 47, 48, 52, 53, 53 n. 2, 54 n. 7, 54 n. 9, 54 n. 11, 64, 71, 76 n. 8, 78, 82, 83, 93 n. 9, 94 n. 18, 98, 104, 105, 107, 108, 110, 111 n. 5, 113 n. 21, 115 n. 32, 115 n. 39, 115 n. 40, 115 n. 45, 122, 124, 125, 126, 128, 132, 135 n. 24, 136 n. 33, 136 n. 35, 141, 143, 146, 147, 148, 156, 157, 158, 160, 161, 162
Islamic calendar 16 n. 4, 79, 159
Islamist 1, 23, 24, 25, 29, 32 n. 8, 33 n. 9, 33 n. 12
Islamophilia 142
Islamophobia 4, 52, 142
Islamophobic 48
isolation 42
'Issāwā order 8
Istanbul 8, 115 n. 44
Italian language 64, 69
Italy 40

Jackson, Michael 7
Jakarta 94 n. 19
Javaheri, Fatemeh 134 n. 18
Jazūlī 104
Jerrahiyya *ṭarīqa* 116 n. 52
Jesus 120, 133 n. 5
jilāba, Moroccan dress 31, 41, 100, 158
jinn 107, 115 n. 39, 123, 125, 133 n. 12, 136 n. 35, 137 n. 40, 158
job 29, 30, 82, 92, 103, 123
jobless 137
joining the Būdshīshiyya 11, 26, 28, 31, 35 n. 46, 36 n. 46, 42, 43, 52, 53, 54 n. 7, 56 n. 23, 64, 65, 71, 82, 83, 84, 94 n. 18, 104, 115 n. 41, 122, 130, 137 n. 41, 137 n. 42, 141, 142, 146, 148, 149
Jonker, Gerdien 36 n. 46, 54 n. 7, 114 n. 24
jouissance 122, 133 n. 9
journalist 78, 80, 146
journeying, religious (*see also ziyāra*) 78, 83, 85, 102
junūn (*see also jinn*) 115 n. 39, 123, 133 n. 12, 158
jurist 34 n. 25, 135 n. 23, 157
Justice and Development Party, JDP 25, 27
Justice and Spirituality, movement, JS 23, 24, 25, 27

Kansas City 53 n. 3
Kapchan, Deborah 9, 58 n. 51, 112 n. 12, 115 n. 38, 115 n. 43
karāma (*see also* miracle, *karāmāt*) 26, 158
karāmāt (*see also karāma*) 33 n. 18, 126, 158
Karrar, Ali Salih 33 n. 19, 56 n. 27
Karsmakers, Suzanne 75 n. 3
Katan, Yvette 9, 29, 32 n. 5
Katz, Steven T. 16 n. 10, 101
Khalwātiyya order 34 n. 34, 94 n. 23
Khedimellah, Moussa 128
Khenifra 40
kin group 50, 80
kind-heartedness 85

kindness (*see also iḥsān*) x, 84
kinesiologist 129
king, Morocco's 24, 27, 99
kissing 83
Klinkhammer, Gritt 4, 129
knife crime 53, 130
knowledge x, 6, 7, 10, 42, 46, 57 n. 36, 66, 100, 121, 132, 144, 157, 162
knowledge, of Islam 26, 28, 29, 43, 73, 97, 98, 111 n. 4, 111 n. 5, 112 n. 17, 126
knowledge, of the Būdshīshiyya 2, 65
knowledge, spiritual 47, 70, 112 n. 12
Köse, Ali 17 n. 13, 93 n. 9, 137 n. 41
Kugle, Scott A. 16 n. 10, 58 n. 56, 120, 121, 133 n. 6, 133 n. 8
Kurvers, Jeanne 75 n. 3

L'Oriental, Moroccan province 1, 14, 23, 26, 32 n. 7, 78, 143
Lacan, Jacques 133 n. 9
Lacanian 122, 133 n. 9
Lagos 135 n. 27
laïcité 105
laissez-faire attitude 28, 33 n. 18, 148
Lālā 16 n. 2, 50, 51, 56 n. 28, 160
landowner 30, 45
Langlois, Tony x, 9, 34 n. 33
Latin America 1
Latin characters 76 n. 5
Laurant, Jean-Pierre 35 n. 44
Law, Divine (*see also sharī'a*) 26, 92
Law, Islamic (*see also* Divine Law) 28, 46, 103, 135 n. 23, 157, 158, 161
Lawrence, Bruce B. 98
lawyer 30
lay institutions 27
lay market 93 n. 5
lay minority 29
lay relations 89
lay space 87
leadership (*see also dirigeant*) 6, 12, 14, 16 n. 9, 26, 33 n. 18, 34 n. 28, 46, 47, 48, 49, 50, 56 n. 23, 57 n. 41, 58 n. 48, 62, 64, 68, 69, 70, 71, 73, 75, 85, 86, 89, 90, 92, 94 n. 20, 99, 100, 101, 103, 108, 110, 112 n. 12, 114 n. 23, 122, 123, 126, 144, 146, 147, 148, 149, 150
learning curriculum of the devotee 51
left, political 24, 29
legitimacy, religious 23, 26, 34 n. 27, 41, 100, 120, 124, 160
leitmotif 147
Levant 36 n. 47
Lewisohn, Leonard 36 n. 46, 54 n. 7, 93 n. 16
lexicon 145, 150 n. 4
liberality, religious 150 n. 3
life change 43
life, religious 1, 8, 11, 12, 56 n. 23, 63, 65, 98, 141
life, spiritual x, 12, 56 n. 23
lifecycle, ritual 106
lifestyle 10, 12, 26, 105, 115 n. 32
like-minded devotee 86, 103, 147
līla 107
līlāt 107
Limoges 127
lineage (*see also* genealogy) 2, 22, 23, 24, 133 n. 6
Lings, Martin 7, 76 n. 11, 113 n. 21
linguistic barriers 52
linguistic diversity 22
litany 98, 99, 101, 111 n. 7, 112 n. 16, 120, 123, 124, 133 n. 7, 157, 161
literacy 57 n. 32, 69, 127
literary study of Sufism 111 n. 6
literature, Sufi 57 n. 44, 114 n. 28
living organism 13, 134 n. 18
living religion 51, 141, 143, 145
living *shaykh* (*see also maître vivant*) 22, 78, 94 n. 25, 100, 122, 126
local 6, 25, 26, 29, 31, 49, 82, 88, 89, 90, 93 n. 16, 102, 104, 145, 159
local administration 30, 34 n. 33
local context 2, 4, 149
local government 2
local police 80
local politics 27, 121, 144
local population 23, 25, 34 n. 33, 35 n. 35, 35 n. 43, 45, 80, 90, 146
local saint 22, 32 n. 8, 88
local *ṭarīqa* 14, 23, 32, 33 n. 10
locality 3, 5, 10, 91, 146, 149
Lochhead, David 63
lodge, Sufi (*see also* Madāgh) 3, 8, 15, 25, 30, 32n. 47, 44, 45, 46, 50, 54 n. 10, 55 n. 19, 55 n. 20, 59 n. 64, 69, 72, 74, 78, 79, 80, 81, 82, 84, 85, 86, 87, 88, 89, 90, 91, 92, 92 n. 2, 93 n. 3, 94 n. 21, 94 n. 25, 99, 102, 106, 112 n. 8, 113 n. 18, 114 n. 28, 121, 124, 127, 128, 147, 155, 158, 159, 161, 162
lodging-rooms 86
logic 28
logistics, sainthood's 90

London 1, 16 n. 1, 137 n. 42
loneliness 131, 142
loosely affiliated member 100
loosely institutionalized group 12
Los Angeles 53 n. 3
love, spiritual (*see also mahabba*) 22, 26, 43, 52, 109, 110, 112 n. 17, 122, 135 n. 27, 158, 160
lower authorities (*see also* secondary authorities) 102
lower economic strata 94 n. 21, 103
lowering the *nafs* 97, 100
Lowry, Joseph 113 n. 21
Lyon 40
lyrics 52, 109

Maarouf, Mohammed 9, 115 n. 39, 137 n. 40
mad 130
Madāgh (*see also Zāwiya*) 3, 15, 16 n. 4, 28, 30, 35 n. 40, 35 n. 42, 45, 46, 50, 54 n. 10, 67, 72, 79, 80, 81, 82, 83, 84, 85, 86, 87, 88, 89, 90, 91, 94 n. 21, 100, 102, 103, 104, 106, 108, 109, 112 n. 8, 113 n. 18, 128, 136 n. 37, 146, 149, 150, 158, 161, 162
Maddy-Weitzman, Bruce 76 n. 6
Maghreb 23, 120
magical stone 129
magical vibe 102
maḥabba (*see also* love) 26, 43, 158
Maharishi Mahesh Yogi 134 n. 18
Mahmood, Saba 29
maître vivant (*see also* living *shaykh*) 51, 121
makhzān 10, 24, 25, 27, 158
malaise 123, 124
male devotee (*see also faqīr,* male member) 4
male member (*see also* male devotee, *faqīr*) 4, 16 n. 2, 45, 56 n. 28, 56 n. 28, 58 n. 54, 103, 160
Mali 41
malign spirit 131, 135 n. 22
mālik 115 n. 39
Malik, Abd Al 52, 53, 109, 110, 116 n. 51, 130
Mālik, Ibn 34 n. 23
Malik, Jamal 7, 10
Mālikī 27, 28, 34 n. 25, 158, 159
malleability of *ṭuruq* (*see also* adaptability) 32, 102
Mama Ji Sarkar 132 n. 2
Manchester 40
mandatory 105, 134 n. 20
mapping, of the Būdshīshiyya 14, 40
marabout (*see also walī*) 80, 83, 91, 92 n. 2, 94 n. 23, 127, 156, 159, 161
marabout Cadillac 94 n. 23
maraboutic code 23
maraboutic system 23, 29, 125, 142
maraboutism 150
Marcus, George, E. 3
marginal religiosity 65
market (*see also moussem*) 80, 90, 93 n. 5, 94 n. 21, 159
market, religious 34 n 21, 72, 73, 109, 151 n. 5
marketing 72, 75 n. 1
marocanité 31, 146
marriage 89, 93 n. 17
Marseille 49
martyr 24
Maryland, University of 48
Masbah, Muḥammad 24
Masonry 31, 36 n. 47
massage therapist 129
master, spiritual 22, 24, 26, 51, 67, 68, 70, 100, 104, 109, 112 n. 17, 122, 126, 130, 136 n. 39
Mateo Dieste, Josep Lluís 9, 124, 128, 132 n. 2, 134 n. 21
material culture 6, 69
material goods 93
material, Būdshīshiyya's written (*see also* article) 34 n. 27, 47, 51, 52, 57 n. 36, 64, 65, 67, 68, 69, 71, 73, 74, 84
materialist approach to the study of religion 111 n. 5
materialist science 131
materialistic 91
Matsunanga, Louella 136 n. 30
maturity, spiritual 42
Mauss, Marcel 98, 132
Mawlid (*see also* Prophet Muḥammad's birth) 3, 16 n. 4, 35 n. 41, 50, 79, 81, 82, 90, 91, 102, 106, 124, 159
Mayer, Jean-Francois 68, 73
McLoughlin, Seán 31
McMurray, David A. 9, 54 n. 5
McPhee, Marybeth 9
McPherson, Joseph Williams 111 n. 6
meal (*see also* food) 85, 102, 103, 106
Mecca 78, 159
mechanistic component 130
media 28, 74, 149
mediator 104

mediatory role 123
Medical Assistance Regime (RAMED) 134 n. 20
medical care 147
medical centre 127
medical coverage 134 n. 20
medical drug 129
medical prescription 100
medical sector 127
medical tradition 14
medical treatment 14
medication 104
medicine, Arab 130
medicine, spiritual 133 n. 3
meditation technique 134 n. 18
Mediterranean 75 n. 1, 89, 155
medium 68, 70, 132
Meknès 80
Melilla (*see also* Mīlīlīa) 54 n. 5, 85, 158
member (*see also* disciple) x, 1, 2, 3, 4, 5, 7, 10, 11, 12, 13, 14, 16 n. 3, 17 n. 15, 17 n. 16, 22, 23, 26, 27, 30, 33 n. 18, 34 n. 31, 41, 42, 43, 44, 46, 47, 50, 51, 53, 55 n. 18, 56 n. 28, 58 n. 50, 65, 66, 70, 71, 75, 76 n. 11, 84, 85, 88, 90, 94 n. 18, 98, 99, 101, 102, 103, 104, 105, 106, 108, 109, 110, 112 n. 10, 112 n. 16, 114 n. 24, 120, 128, 129, 132, 132 n. 2, 132 n. 3, 145, 146, 147, 148, 157, 161
membership (*see also* affiliation) 5, 34 n. 33, 41, 44, 76 n. 9
mental balance 130
mental disease 130
mental disorder 104
mental health 15, 129
mental hospital 24
mercantile 93 n. 5
merit, religious (*see also ajr*) 103
message, Hamza's 49, 70, 103, 104
messy aspect of religion 143
meta-narrative, religious 110
metaphor 57 n. 44, 100, 122, 133 n. 3
methodological 9, 53 n. 1, 161
metrics 28
middle class 28, 34 n. 21, 34 n. 28, 44, 63, 67, 124, 136 n. 37, 142
Middle East 63, 75 n. 1
Middle Eastern language 75 n. 2
middle echelon, of religious authority (*see also* secondary authority) 45, 81
Midelt 40
migrant 1, 17 n. 15, 31, 36 n. 46, 41, 42, 54 n. 5, 54 n. 7, 103, 116 n. 52, 117 n. 52
migration 4, 10, 31, 54 n. 6, 55 n. 16, 74
Mīlīlīa (*see also* Melilla) 54 n. 5
military outpost 32 n. 4
millennialism 12, 56 n. 23
minority 29, 43, 47, 67
minority religion 62, 65, 68, 73, 74
miracle (*see also karāma*) 8, 15, 26, 121, 122, 126, 133 n. 5, 133 n. 6, 135 n. 28, 158
mise-en-scène, religion's 144
missionary (*see also da'wa*) 8, 10, 67, 68, 72, 73, 75, 111 n. 4, 114 n. 24, 148, 150
mixing, of Europeans and Moroccans 86, 90, 93 n. 16
mlek (*mluk*) 107, 115 n. 39
mobilization, social 142
modern 27, 46, 47, 48, 51, 109, 123, 141, 142, 148, 150
modern greed 11
modern Islam 46, 141
modern medicine 130
modern network 28
modern Sainthood 72
modern Sufism x, 8, 9, 15
modern *ṭarīqa* 72, 88, 90, 109, 111 n. 4, 114 n. 24, 147
modern technologies 72
modern urban life 8
modern *ziyāra* 78
modernist, Islamic 24, 27, 29, 143
modernity 35 n. 44, 47, 141, 142
modesty 55 n. 18, 161
modifying body conditions 121
Mohsen-Finan, Khadija 33 n. 9, 33 n. 12
monarch 30
monarchy, Moroccan 2, 23, 25, 27, 32 n. 8, 144
money (*see also* cash) 55 n. 18, 86, 90, 91, 92, 137 n. 47
monitored, by the Būdshīshiyya's leadership 100, 108
monitoring digital content 71, 73
monotheism 35 n. 44, 137 n. 46
monster-like face 103
Montpellier 40
Montreal 47, 58 n. 50
moon 135 n. 27
moral capital 91
moral economy 90
moral superiority 142
Moroccan Arabic (*see also dārija*) 31, 41

Moroccan culture 84, 87, 88, 90, 131, 142, 145, 146
Moroccan devotee (*see also* Moroccan member) 63
Moroccan Government 30, 74
Moroccan Islam 22, 26, 45, 135 n. 29, 141, 142
Moroccan living abroad 29, 86, 93 n. 13
Moroccan member (*see also* Moroccan devotee) 31, 34 n. 32
Morocco xi, 1, 2, 3, 9, 10, 15, 16 n. 1, 22, 23, 24, 25, 26, 27, 28, 29, 31, 32, 33 n. 8, 33 n. 9, 34 n. 21, 35 n. 35, 35 n. 40, 40, 41, 42, 43, 44, 45, 46, 48, 49, 50, 53 n. 2, 54 n. 5, 56 n. 30, 57 n. 32, 57 n. 36, 57 n. 43, 58 n. 53, 63, 64, 65, 67, 69, 72, 73, 74, 75, 76 n. 5, 78, 79, 80, 83, 85, 89, 90, 92, 92 n. 1, 93 n. 5, 94 n. 21, 99, 100, 103, 105, 106, 107, 108, 109, 111 n. 4, 115 n. 37, 115 n. 43, 120, 121, 124, 125, 126, 127, 128, 131, 132, 132 n. 2, 133 n. 6, 133 n. 13, 134 n. 20, 134 n. 21, 135 n. 26, 135 n. 30, 136 n. 37, 137 n. 39, 137 n. 40, 142, 143, 144, 146, 148, 149, 158, 159, 160, 162
mosque 28, 99, 135 n. 27
mother tongue 64
motto, Būdshīshiyya's 144
mouassīm (*see also moussem*) 80, 81, 92 n. 1, 159
mouride 94 n. 24
mouridisme 113 n. 17
moussem (*see also* market, *mouassīm*) 80, 92 n. 1, 93 n. 5, 159
Mufti 27
Muḥammad I University, Oujda 45
Muḥammad VI, King of Morocco 2
Muḥammad, the Prophet 16 n. 4, 79, 157, 158, 159, 160, 161
Mūhīdīn, Hamza's cousin 45
multi-centre scenario 4, 149
multicultural 48, 105
multifocal cultural influencing 145
multi-religious 99
multi-sited fieldwork 2, 3, 4, 5, 8, 56 n. 24
Mūluyya River 30
Munson, Henry 9, 24, 33 n. 8
muqaddim/a (*see also* middle echelon, *muqaddimāt, muqaddimūn*) 6, 26, 49, 91, 100, 101, 104, 129, 159
muqaddimāt (*see also muqaddim/a*) 73, 111
muqaddimūn (*see also muqaddim/a*) 49, 58 n. 53
murābiṭ (*see also marabout*) 92 n. 2, 159
murīd 78, 159
music (*see also samā'*) 9, 15, 28, 48, 71, 90, 107, 108, 109, 110, 112 n. 15, 115 n. 42, 115 n. 45, 116 n. 47, 144, 160
Muslim 1, 2, 5, 8, 14, 16 n. 1, 17 n. 15, 28, 31, 32, 36 n. 46, 41, 42, 43, 48, 49, 50, 52, 53, 54 n. 7, 54 n. 14, 55 n. 18, 66, 67, 68, 75 n. 1, 78, 82, 83, 85, 87, 90, 92 n. 2, 93 n. 10, 94 n. 18, 100, 105, 107, 109, 113 n. 21, 114 n. 31, 115 n. 41, 115 n. 45, 116 n. 52, 124, 127, 128, 129, 135 n. 27, 135 n. 29, 136 n. 31, 136 n. 32, 142, 143, 147, 150 n. 3, 156, 158, 160, 161
Muslim country 22, 65, 89
Muslim culture 142
Muslim World 12, 14, 22, 29, 33 n. 9, 34 n. 33, 35 n. 40, 45, 54 n. 9, 78, 80, 89, 90, 105, 111 n. 4, 112 n. 17, 120, 128, 133 n. 13
Muslim-born member 32
mystical 101, 137 n. 43
mysticism 14, 141

Na'īma 30, 35 n. 40
Nador 2, 32 n. 7, 40
Nantes 40
NAP, New African Poets 52, 108, 109
Naqshbandī Mujaddīdī 114 n. 24, 114 n. 26
Naqshbandiyya 9, 33 n. 17, 73, 76 n. 11, 114 n. 27
narrative 3, 7, 15, 16 n. 1, 25, 43, 48, 52, 53, 54 n. 13, 58 n. 57, 59 n. 63, 67, 80, 83, 106, 110, 116 n. 51, 121, 122, 125, 147, 148
nation 30, 81, 135 n. 27, 145
national 2, 32, 55 n. 21, 55 n. 22, 74, 85, 144
nationalist 29
nationality 86
natural/preternatural dichotomy 131
naturalistic explanation for disease causation 130
needle, acupuncture's 129
neighbour 74, 99
neighbourhood 52
neo-Hindu group 109, 116 n. 49
Neo-Paganism 17 n. 16
Netherlands 40
Netton, Ian Richard 111 n. 6

network 28, 30, 31, 68, 75, 80, 84, 89, 91, 127, 135 n. 30
New Age 8, 10, 13, 14, 15, 27, 28, 29, 34 n. 32, 64, 109, 111 n. 4, 116 n. 51, 116 n. 52, 129, 131, 134 n. 18, 137 n. 45, 142, 149
New Age Būdshīshiyya's member 14, 34 n. 32
New Age follower 13, 14, 105
New Age group 11, 17 n. 15, 29, 34 n. 31
New Age healer 128
new devotee (*see also* new member) 52, 63, 68, 113 n. 21
new member (*see also* new devotee) 67, 108, 113 n. 21, 114 n. 21, 135 n. 30, 150
New Religious Movement (NRM) 1, 10, 11, 12, 56 n. 23, 114 n. 29, 134 n. 18, 136 n. 30, 141, 142
New York 53 n. 3
newness, Būdshīshiyya's 142
Nice 40
niche carving 120
niche decoration 120
Nigeria 114 n. 22, 135 n. 27
nihilation 144
niyya (*see also* intention) 100, 112 n. 13, 159
non-allopathic therapy 128
non-Berber 28, 69
non-corporeal relationship 122
non-cybernated 62
non-democratic 30
non-devotee (*see also* non-member) 57 n. 36
non-discursive religious instruction 70
non-English speaking region 10
non-European 54 n. 6, 86
non-hierarchical 65
non-hybrid enclave 42, 43
non-indigenous ideas 149
non-Islamic 129
non-Islamic practice 129
non-judgmental attitude 109
non-member (*see also* non-devotee) 5, 7
non-Moroccan 5, 42, 49, 53 n. 4, 54 n. 11, 67, 128, 134 n. 21
non-Muslim country 22
non-Muslim person 42, 43, 52, 67, 83, 100, 112 n. 15, 115 n. 41, 132, 143, 158
non-observant Muslim 82
non-reductive materialism 6, 69
non-Reformist Muslim 125
non-religious 13, 42, 47
non-Sufi master 136 n. 39
non-*ṭarīqa* Sufi group 8
non-traditional media 149
non-verbal, devotee-*shaykh* relationship 70
non-Western world 145
norm, religious 44, 88, 113 n. 21, 125, 156, 160
normative 27, 46, 125, 126, 132, 136 n. 33, 144
normative *communitas* 84
normative Islam 28
normativity 4, 45, 125, 126, 129
Norris, Rebecca Sachs 54 n. 15
North African Islam 107
North African Sufism 36 n. 46, 45, 54 n. 7, 56 n. 27, 107, 157, 159
North America 35 n. 44, 67, 111 n. 4
North American follower 67
North-eastern Morocco 1, 2, 9, 10, 15, 16 n. 3, 25, 27, 31, 32 n. 5, 35 n. 35, 40, 41, 44, 54 n. 10, 57 n. 43, 69, 72, 78, 136 n. 37, 144, 158, 162
Northern Nigeria 114 n. 22
notion du personne 132
Nottingham 40
nourishment 106
novice, religious (*see also* pupil) 26
number of disciples 5, 26, 33 n. 15, 44, 55 n. 19, 64, 79, 128, 148
Nurbakhsh, Javad 58 n. 56
nurse 82, 127, 129, 135 n. 30
Nwyia, Paul 59 n. 64

Oarzazate 81
objectivizing 'the other' 142
obligation, religious 81, 84
obligation, ritual 105, 147
obligatory 98
observance, religious 88, 105, 113 n. 21
observer, in a ritual 84, 100
offering, act of 91
offering, material 79, 92, 94 n. 24
official discourse (*see also* officialdom)
official' Islam 27
officialdom (*see also* official discourse) 14
offline appearance 74
offline setting 66, 75
offline-online data 62

offshoot, religion's 131, 142
Ojanunga, Durrenda Nash 94 n.25
older member 63
online 14, 15, 33 n. 12, 33 n. 16, 47, 52, 54 n. 13, 55 n. 20, 55 n. 21, 55 n. 22, 57 n. 34, 57 n. 37, 57 n. 39, 57 n. 42, 58 n. 45, 58 n. 46, 58 n. 47, 58 n. 52, 59 n. 66, 62, 63, 64, 65, 66, 67, 68, 69, 70, 71, 72, 73, 74, 75, 75 n. 1, 76, 76 n. 10, 76 n. 13, 76 n. 14, 76 n. 15, 76 n. 16, 77, 92 n. 3, 92 n. 4, 93 n. 7, 93 n. 11, 94 n. 26, 111 n. 3, 114 n. 22, 114 n. 31, 134 n. 15, 134 n. 16, 134 n. 18, 134 n. 20, 134 n. 21, 135 n. 21, 135 n. 27, 136 n. 37
online appearance (*see also* digital appearance) 65
online data 68
online visitor 64
online-offline dichotomy 72
operation, chirurgical 124
opinion about the Būdshīshiyya 30, 73
opinion, devotee's 3, 5, 34 n. 29, 73, 88, 146, 147
opinion, leadership's 69
oral transmission 64, 75 n. 4, 75 n. 5, 76 n. 5, 121, 149
order, Sufi (*see also ṭarīqa*) x, 1, 2, 3, 10, 12, 29, 32, 34 n. 31, 35 n. 44, 44, 47, 54 n. 10, 56 n. 23, 62, 64, 67, 68, 72, 74, 76 n. 11, 78, 88, 90, 93 n. 6, 93 n. 17, 94 n. 19, 106, 109, 113 n. 17, 113 n. 18, 114 n. 26, 116 n. 52, 121, 127, 133 n. 5, 135 n. 29, 143, 147, 157, 160, 161, 162
organic food 136 n. 37
organization, religious x, 1, 2, 3, 4, 5, 6, 7, 10, 14, 16 n. 3, 16 n. 11, 17 n. 15, 22, 23, 24, 25, 26, 29, 31, 32, 33 n. 9, 33 n. 12, 34 n. 32, 40, 41, 42, 44, 45, 46, 47, 48, 51, 58 n. 50, 62, 65, 66, 67, 68, 69, 73, 74, 75, 79, 80, 81, 83, 85, 86, 87, 89, 90, 92, 98, 100, 102, 103, 106, 110, 111 n. 4, 112 n. 17, 114 n. 24, 122, 127, 128, 129, 130, 132, 134, 134 n. 18, 137 n. 47, 141, 142, 144, 145, 146, 148, 150, 151 n. 5
oriental 143
Orientalism 90
Orientalist scholar 142
orientation, religious 25, 86, 88, 137 n. 46, 156
Orlando 53 n. 3
orthodoxy 135 n. 24, 148
orthopraxis 125, 135 n. 24, 148
Osho Organization 134 n. 18
ostentation before God 55 n. 18
otherness 142
Ottoman Empire 23, 33 n. 4, 36 n. 47
Oujda 23, 28, 31, 32 n. 7, 35 n. 35, 40, 45, 46, 54 n. 5, 124, 127, 155, 158
output, digital (*see also* internet output) 71, 74
output, literary (*see also* Būdshīshiyya's written material) 47, 51, 74, 76 n. 7, 144
output, written 33 n. 14
outreach, Būdshīshiyya's 62, 63, 73
outsider 47, 49, 54 n. 7, 84, 89, 90, 146
outward-looking attitude 35 n. 45
overdose, drugs 53, 130

Pact (*see also bay'a*) 2, 54 n. 9, 114 n. 21, 157
Padwick, Constance Evelyn 111 n. 6
pain 51, 123, 130, 133 n. 9
Pakistan 8, 16 n. 8, 43, 111 n. 4, 114 n. 26, 129, 132 n. 2, 134 n. 17, 135 n. 29
Palais Tazi, Rabat's 108
paradoxical aspect of religion 143
paranoid episode 130
paranormal perception 13
parent 43, 63, 114 n. 21, 136 n. 35
Paris 3, 31, 40, 44, 46, 47, 57 n. 39, 62, 88, 124, 131, 137 n. 47
Parliament, Moroccan 25, 33 n. 12
parochialism 86
participant observation 8, 16 n. 5
participant, in a ritual 100, 101, 128
participation social 142
partner xi, 89, 93 n. 17, 94 n. 18, 94 n. 19, 135 n. 22, 141
party, organized by the Būdshīshiyya 92
party, political 24, 25, 33 n. 12
passage, rite of 82
Path, Sufi (*see also* Sufi order) 26, 34 n. 32, 42, 43, 82, 92, 97, 100, 104, 111 n. 5, 144, 156
pathological 132
pathology 129, 130
pathos 122
peasant 26, 81, 82, 85, 89, 91, 124, 128, 136 n. 37, 147, 148
peasantry (*see also* peasant) 1, 86
peer bonding 102, 110
peer support 103
Pennell, C. Richard 23, 24, 29, 30

Pentecostalism 59 n. 63, 142, 150 n. 2
Perennial (*see also* Philosophia Perennis) 17 n. 15
Perennialist (*see also* Guénonian) 35 n. 44
permeability 127, 143
permission, Hamza's 128, 129
pernoctating in the *qubbā* 128
personage, Sufi 15, 133 n. 6, 149
Peru 129
Philadelphia 53 n. 3
Philosophia Perennis (*see also* Guénonianism) 35 n. 44
philosophical 97, 143
philosophical understanding of the sacred 143
philosophy, Būdshīshiyya's 64
philosophy, Christian 129
philosophy, esoteric 35 n. 44
philosophy, French 53
philosophy, Hindu 129
philosophy, Islamic 53
phone 72, 99
physical 3, 13, 26, 71, 91, 102, 121, 122, 126, 127, 130, 131, 137 n. 45, 158
physical approach to Sufism 71
physical balance 130
physical contact with Hamza 121, 122
physicality 70, 111 n. 4
physically 46, 121
'pick and mix' religiosity (*see also religion à la carte*) 14, 29, 143
picture 7, 14, 44, 45, 53 n. 4, 57 n. 36, 63, 67, 72, 73, 74, 85, 89, 99, 112 n. 10, 123, 147
pilgrim 8, 79, 82, 84, 85, 87, 93 n. 5
pilgrimage (*see also ziyāra*) 7, 11, 15, 78, 79, 82, 83, 84, 86, 89, 92 n. 1, 93 n. 13, 93 n. 14, 102, 115 n. 37, 121, 141, 148, 159, 162
Piscatori, James 82, 84
plane 85, 141
plasticity, Būdshīshiyya's (*see also* malleability) 72
plate 86, 106, 113 n. 21
pleasure principle 133 n. 9
pluralistic discourse 52
plurality 147
poetry 53, 57 n. 39
police 52, 53, 80, 99, 130
police abuse 53, 130
police riot 52
political 4, 8, 23, 27, 29, 30, 33 n. 8, 34 n. 20, 64, 73, 75, 80, 90, 103, 108, 142, 144
political activism 33 n. 9
political agenda, Būdshīshiyya's 2, 5
political agenda, Būdshīshiyya's 2, 5
political authority 160
political broker 23
political containment 24
political discourse 33 n. 9
political disillusionment 29, 142
political group 33 n. 9
political institution 23, 157
political involvement 74, 144
political participation 24, 25, 33 n. 9
political power 27, 30, 33 n. 8, 45, 121, 126
political role, Būdshīshiyya's 2, 9, 24, 50, 57 n. 38
political sciences 10
political system 25
politician 106
politicized Islam 52, 110
poor 29, 33 n. 10, 44, 52, 55 n. 18, 81, 85, 103, 106, 110, 124, 126, 157
Popovic, Alexandre 8
porosity, religious 128
positivism 51, 131
postcolonial gaze 142
post-independence context 23
post-modern 14
potency, spiritual 56 n. 29, 83, 156
potential devotee (*see also* potential follower) 47, 127, 151 n. 5
potential follower (*see also* potential member) 114 n. 27
potential member (*see also* potential devotee) 64, 83
potpourri, religious 143
pottery 79, 92
power abuse 30
power relations, within the Būdshīshiyya 150
power, divine 120
power, saintly 47, 56 n. 29, 58 n. 57, 72, 82, 91, 94 n. 23, 120, 121, 125, 126, 128, 156
power, within the Būdshīshiyya 50, 110
practice, healing 15, 28, 120, 121, 122, 123, 124, 125, 126, 127, 128, 129, 130, 132, 132 n. 2, 134 n. 17, 134 n. 18, 135 n. 23, 136 n. 32, 147
practice, non-Islamic 129
practice, religious 6, 12, 13, 16 n. 11, 26, 34 n. 32, 35 n. 45, 43, 56 n. 23, 69, 85, 88, 111 n. 8, 122, 130, 141, 142, 143, 144, 145, 148

practice, ritual 4, 15, 49, 51, 58 n. 57, 93 n. 16, 97, 98, 104, 105, 106, 107, 111 n. 5, 113 n. 21, 114 n. 26, 115 n. 38, 122, 124
praxis, religious 4, 6, 69, 111 n. 5, 146
praxis, ritual 14, 28, 71, 87, 99
praxis, social 116 n. 51
prayer (*see also ṣalāt*) 15, 58 n. 57, 98, 101, 104, 105, 107, 113 n. 21, 114 n. 31, 115 n. 32, 123, 124, 125, 126, 134 n. 18, 157, 160
prayer room 99, 105
prayer, call to 120
praying 81, 83, 99, 105, 124, 134 n. 18
praying room
preacher 47, 48, 52, 110, 116 n. 51
pre-colonial 33 n. 17
predestination, belief in 29, 56 n. 23
pre-digital 63
preferential treatment given to Europeans 86
pregnant woman 101
pre-modern 90, 141
pre-modern Islam 141
present, for Hamza 79
presentation, by a Būdshīshiyya's member 58 n. 46
prestige, social 80
preternaturalistic explanation for disease causation 130, 131, 132
privacy 57 n. 36, 99
procession, Sufi 45
professional 26, 29, 33 n. 10, 66, 108, 109, 127, 135 n. 30
progress, spiritual 104
progression along the Path 104
progressive, Būdshīshiyya's character 46
pro-monarchy 64
Prophet Muḥammad's birth (*see also Mawlid*) 16 n. 4, 79, 115 n. 36, 159
prophetic medicine (*see also ruqiyya*)125
proselytization (*see also* missionary) 10, 14, 26, 42, 52, 53, 62, 66, 67, 68, 83, 100, 116 n. 51, 122, 150, 157
proselytizing 10, 52, 63, 68, 83, 100, 122, 150
protector 92 n. 2
Protectorate, in Morocco 30, 32 n. 5
psychiatry 130
psychological ailment 125
psychological functioning 13
psychological imbalance 131
psychological nature 130
psychological problem 13
psychological stability 130, 137 n. 41
psychological unease 104
psychology 13, 97
psychotherapist 130, 137 n. 42
public 46, 48, 57 n. 36, 57 n. 41, 58 n. 51, 64, 70, 73, 80, 105
public activity, organized by the Būdshīshiyya 106
public administration 2
public image, Būdshīshiyya's 24, 27, 42
public march, Casablanca's 27
public personality 16 n. 2, 56 n. 28
public profile 2, 9, 73
public realm 12
public recognition 50
public reticence 46
public school 75 n. 3
public sector 66
public service 23
public space 93 n. 15, 99, 105
publication 46
publicity 122
publicizing the Būdshīshiyya 26, 30, 48, 108, 110
Punjabi 132 n. 2, 135 n. 29
pupil, religious (*see also* novice) 25, 26
purification, soul's 97, 113 n. 21, 135 n. 25
purifying, soul's
purism, Islamic 53
puritanism, religious 143
purity (*see also ṣafā'*) 108, 113 n. 21, 123
pyramidal structure, of religious authority 45, 49, 85

Qādirī 22, 23, 45, 120, 121, 133 n. 6, 154
Qādirī tradition 15, 121
Qādirīyya 1, 15, 16 n. 1, 22, 23, 26, 33 n. 11, 33 n. 19, 34 n. 27, 56 n. 27, 57 n. 34, 62, 107, 109, 120, 133 n. 4, 141, 142, 158
qalb (*see also* heart) 159
Qantara, association 65
qasā'id (*see also qaṣīda*) 46, 57 n. 39
qaṣīda (*see also qasā'id*, song) 57 n. 39, 160
Quarawīyin, University 28
'quasi-corporativist character' 135 n. 30
'Quasi-Islamic Sufi Organization' 34 n. 32
qubbā (*see also* domed mausoleum) 128, 136 n. 31, 160
quest, philosophical 97
quest, spiritual 51, 70, 130

Quietism, religious 27, 34 n. 20, 144
Quietist' devotee 26, 27, 28, 29, 143, 144
Qur'ān 57n. 32, 81, 97, 97, 111 n. 8, 113 n. 14, 125, 126, 127, 133 n. 13, 135 n. 23, 157, 158, 160, 161, 162
Qur'ānic exegesis 28
Qur'ānic healer 125
Qur'ānic passage 49
Qur'ānic recitation (*see also tajwīd*) 82, 98, 125
Qur'ānic verse 98
Qustas, Aḥmad 10, 45, 47, 48, 49, 56 n. 28, 56 n. 30, 58 n. 50, 58 n. 53, 108

Rabat 40, 46, 47, 48, 94, n. 21, 108, 155
rabi' al-awwal, month in the Islamic calendar 16 n. 4, 79
Rābi'a al-'Adawīyya 108
Rabinow, Paul 9
radio 108, 116 n. 48
Rajpur 134 n. 17
Ramaḍān (*see also* fasting) 106, 107
rap 109
Rationalism 29
rationalistic approach to Sufism 49, 51, 69
rationality 82
Raudvere, Catharina 7, 8, 100, 111 n. 6, 111 n. 7, 115 n. 44, 141
reactiveness 52, 143
reader 11, 40, 52, 53, 54 n. 12, 64, 98, 116 n. 51
readership 73
reading about Sufism 51, 52, 53, 59 n. 61, 64, 66, 67, 70, 71, 76 n. 11, 76 n. 12, 98, 104, 109, 111 n. 5, 123
reading the Qur'ān 57 n. 32, 81, 111 n. 8, 112 n. 14
re-affiliated Muslim 43
re-affiliation, religious 43
realization, spiritual 82, 85, 112 n. 12, 137 n. 43, 158
recitation (*see also* Qur'ānic recitation) 81, 98, 99, 101, 107, 112 n. 16, 125, 157, 162
reciting 50, 98, 100, 101, 104, 113 n. 18, 120, 123, 124, 160, 161
reciting technique 82
reconversion religieuse 54 n. 12
recovery, narratives of 122, 148
recruiting new members 27, 108, 150
recruitment of new members 26, 122
recueillement 101
reform, Būdshīshiyya's 25, 26, 33 n. 18, 112 n. 17, 157
Reformism, Islamic 24, 124, 125, 126, 135 n. 24, 136 n. 33, 142, 143
reformist 24, 27, 125
reform-minded 125
regulated by the leadership 73, 142
relation, social 30 86, 94 n. 19, 158
relationship among devotees 31, 78, 85
relationship between devotees and Madāghians 31
relationship with internet 67
relationship, believer-God 104
relationship, culture-territory 3
relationship, healer-suppliant 128
relationship, personal 31
relationship, *shaykh*-disciple 14, 35 n. 40, 67, 70, 72, 83, 104, 122, 147, 158
reliability, Būdshīshiyya's 68
religiosity 1, 3, 4, 6, 7, 8, 9, 11, 14, 16 n. 11, 27, 29, 31, 48, 52, 53 n. 4, 65, 79, 85, 89, 105, 111 n. 4, 112 n. 10, 113 n. 20, 113 n. 21, 116 n. 51, 120, 126, 135 n. 29, 136 n. 32, 136 n. 35, 137 n. 39, 149
religious background 101
religious-political 23
remembering (*see also dhikr*) 98
remembrance (*see also* remembering) 51, 56 n. 26, 58 n. 57, 98, 157
repertoire, musical 108
reputation 57 n. 32, 83, 91, 121, 126, 132 n. 2
requisite for *dhikr's* performance 112 n. 13, 159
requisite for initiation 111 n. 4, 111 n. 5, 142
re-sacralization, Western societies' 129, 143
research interest x, 7, 9
respectability 81
re-textualization of Sufism 69
re-textualizing 70, 71
retreat 28, 92 n. 2
Retreat, BBC program 83, 93 n. 10, 137 n. 42
re-tribalized component 145
reversion, religious 54 n. 12, 54 n. 15, 55 n. 15, 68, 105
revert Muslim 42, 43, 53, 55 n. 16, 82, 83, 84, 87, 103, 105, 116 n. 52, 129
revival, religious (*see also* revivalism) 65, 76 n. 8, 128

revivalism, religious (*see also* revival) 29, 65
rhythm, in *dhikr*'s performance 81, 98
rhythmic movement 102
ribāṭ 92 n. 2
rich 44, 85, 94 n. 23, 110
Ricoeur, Paul 116 n. 51
Riḍā, Muḥammad Rashīd 24
Ridgeon, Lloyd 33 n. 9, 135 n. 25
Rif 63, 67, 124
Riffian Berber (*see also* Amazigh) 64
righteousness 50, 83, 127
ritual 2, 7, 8, 11, 12, 15, 16 n. 3, 17 n. 15, 26, 27, 42, 46, 48, 51, 54 n. 9, 56 n. 26, 58 n. 53, 71, 79, 88, 93 n. 5, 97, 98, 99, 100, 101, 102, 103, 104, 105, 106, 107, 108, 109, 110, 111, 111 n. 6, 112, 112 n. 15, 113, 113 n. 20, 113 n. 21, 114, 114 n. 22, 114 n. 29, 115, 115 n. 38, 116, 116 n. 48, 117, 118, 119, 120, 121, 123, 124, 144, 145, 147, 148, 149, 150 n. 4, 157, 160, 161
ritual adaptation 107
ritual celebration 30
ritual ceremony 101
ritual exhilaration 33 n. 18
ritual journey (*see also ziyāra*) 79
ritual lifecycle 106
ritual performance 9, 12, 15, 42, 45, 49, 56 n. 23, 97, 99, 103, 107, 113 n. 17, 122, 142, 145, 146
ritual prescription 101, 103, 113 n. 21, 116 n. 48
ritual purity 123
ritual session (*see also* gathering) 6, 54 n. 10, 59 n. 61, 85, 98, 115 n. 42, 162
rivalry, among religious groups 73
Roald, Anne Sofie 115 n. 41
robbery 35 n. 43
Robertson, Robbie 75 n. 1
rock (music) 109
role, Hamza's
Romania 41
Romanian language 64
romanticized idea of Morocco 90, 141
romanticized idea of Sufism 141
roof 85, 87, 93 n. 15
rosary (*see also subḥa*) 72, 93 n. 5, 113 n. 18, 160
routine, spiritual 83
Roy, Olivier
Rozehnal, Robert 8, 16 n. 8, 111 n. 4, 112 n. 17, 115 n. 42, 132 n. 2, 137 n. 40
ruling 109
ruqiyya (*see also ṭibb al-nabawī*) 125
rural members 3, 10, 29, 34 n. 31, 136 n. 37

Saadi dynasty 32 n. 4
sacralising effect 102
sacred 33 n. 8, 35 n. 41, 48, 87, 90, 93 n. 5, 100, 108, 111 n. 4, 136 n. 35, 143, 144, 158, 160
sacred knowledge 132
sacred space 87, 99
sacredness 99
ṣafā' (*see also* purity) 108
safety, during the *Mawlid* 80
Safī ad-Dīn 137 n. 43
Saheb, Shaik Abdul Azeez 132 n. 2
Said, Edward W. 142
Saidia 2, 30, 40
saint (*see also* friend of God) 7, 14, 22, 33 n. 48, 49, 56 n. 25, 70, 71, 72, 79, 80, 88, 90, 91, 92, 115 n. 37, 121, 122, 126, 136 n. 32, 156, 157, 159, 161
sainthood 72, 126, 159
saintliness 106
Sajad Ali, Muḥammad 128
ṣalāt (*see also* prayer) 104, 105, 157, 160
Salé 40, 80
salt 131
salvation, narrative of 52, 53, 59 n. 63, 148
samā' (*see also* music) 6, 108, 109, 110, 115 n. 42, 116 n. 48, 160
San Diego 53 n. 3
San Francisco 53 n. 3
sanctity (*see also walaya*) 26,90
Sartre, Jean-Paul 53
Sater, James 34 n. 21, 63
Saveurs Soufies 54 n. 12, 57 n. 34, 64, 69, 76 n. 16
sayings, Hamza's 33 n. 16, 47, 57 n. 44, 70, 94 n. 26, 97, 111 n. 3
Sayyid 89, 99, 109, 122, 133 n. 6, 160
scary face 103
Schimmel, Annemarie 97, 111 n. 4, 120
schism, religious 11, 116 n. 52, 117 n. 52
school 1, 26, 33 n. 20, 45, 75 n. 3, 75 n. 4, 158, 159
schooling system 64
sciences, Islamic 28, 45, 48, 111 n. 5, 156
scriptural 27
Scripturalism 34 n. 22
Scripturalist 9, 28
Scripture 157, 160

search, spiritual 52, 108
seasonal migrant 54 n. 5
secondary school pupil 26
second-generation Muslim 87, 115 n. 45
secret, spiritual (*see also sirr*) 45, 133 n. 10
sect 43, 83
sectarian 41
secular 16 n. 1, 43, 47, 54 n. 9, 143
secularized context 29, 66
security 68
Seddon, J. David 9, 30
Sedgwick, Mark 10, 26, 33 n. 18, 35 n. 44, 115 n. 41, 135 n. 28
seeker 64, 97, 124
self-discovery 130
selfhood 130
self-representation, narrative of 67
Senegal 41, 94 n. 23, 131
Sengers, Gerda 134 n. 18
sensorial approach to Sufism 6, 69, 144
separation between sexes (*see also* gender divide) 87, 93 n. 16
sequence of verses 100
sermon 70
service, to the community 79, 84
servility 83
sha'wada (*see also* charlatan) 124
Shādhilī 133 n. 6
shahada 42
Shahin, Emad Eldin 33 n. 12
shaman 129, 146
shamanic 13
shamanism 136 n. 39
Shannon, Jonathan Holt 100, 112 n. 15
sharī'a (*see also* Islamic law) 28, 116 n. 52, 156, 157, 160, 161
sharī'a-compliant 116 n. 52
sharīf (see saint, *shurafā'*) 160
sharifism 32 n. 2, 160
shaykh al-tabarruk 33 n. 19, 45
shaykh–disciple relationship 72
sheep 79
Sherani, Saifur Rahman 94 n. 25
shiatsu 13, 129
shifā' (*see also* healing) 15, 121, 160
shirk 135, 160
shisha 106
shoe 79, 113 n. 21
shop 72, 80, 93 n. 5
short-lived commitment to the Būdshīshiyya 44, 128
shouting 101
shrine (*see also* lodge) 23, 82, 92 n. 1, 120, 121, 123, 124, 133 n. 10, 133 n. 11, 133 n. 13, 136 n. 31, 160, 162
Shterin, Marat x, 16 n. 1
shurafā' (*see sharīf*) 22, 40, 45, 53 n. 2, 160
sick person 29, 82, 120, 121, 122, 123, 124, 125, 126, 132 n. 3
sickness 100, 122, 123
Sīdī 2, 6, 15, 16 n. 2, 23, 28, 34 n. 31, 41, 45, 46, 47, 48, 51, 54 n. 11, 56 n. 28, 56 n. 30, 57 n. 44, 80, 106, 123, 134 n. 19, 153, 154, 157, 160
siḥr (*see also* exorcism) 135 n. 22
silent *dhikr* 103, 104, 112 n. 8, 113 n. 18, 114 n. 26, 160
silsila (*see also* lineage) 24, 26, 57 n. 31, 99, 106, 115 n. 35, 133 n. 4, 133 n. 10, 160
Silverstein, Paul A. 34 n. 22
Simenel, Romain 93 n. 5
sin 33 n. 19
sirr (*see also* spiritual secret) 45
Sirriyeh, Elizabeth 23, 33 n. 9
size, Būdshīshiyya's 26, 44, 65, 66, 74, 76 n. 9, 76 n. 11
size, contingent's 42, 67, 74, 102, 107
Skali, Faouzi 36 n. 48, 47, 49, 52, 56 n. 28, 58 n. 28, 58 n. 50, 58 n. 52, 58 n. 53, 58 n. 59, 71, 108, 109, 110, 133 n. 5, 149
slam poetry 53
sleeping quarter, Madāgh's 50, 79, 85, 86
Small Heath 44, 55 n. 21, 55 n. 22
Smith, Margaret 58 n. 56
snack 79, 82
SOAS, University of London's School of Oriental and African Studies 1
sober Sufism 27, 107, 108, 110, 125, 126, 144
social aspect 90
social capital 91
social change 63, 141
social environment 31
social identity 41
social life 34 n. 22, 41, 44, 55 n. 20, 90
social model 30
social structure 78, 86
sociality 31
socializing 31, 42, 94 n. 19, 102
sociological 11, 41
solemnity 99
solidarity 15, 79, 84, 103

somatic image 121, 132, 149
song (*see also qaṣīda*) 43, 52, 57 n. 39, 82, 110
Sorbonne 31, 46, 47, 48
sorcerer 134 n. 20
sorcery 125, 132 n. 1
Soufisme vivant 51
soul 97, 112 n. 12, 122, 132 n. 3, 137 n. 43, 158, 159, 160
South Africa 78
South Asia 14, 36 n. 46, 43, 54 n. 7, 55 n. 21, 78, 112 n. 17, 150 n. 4
Southern India 132 n. 2
Southern Mediterranean 89
Southern Morocco 80
Southern Spain 10, 83, 137 n. 42
space 3, 11, 50, 65, 79, 84, 86, 87, 90, 93 n. 15, 98, 99, 101, 102, 105, 113 n. 21
Spadola, Emilio 135 n. 26
Spain 1, 2, 10, 40, 54 n. 5, 54 n. 11, 55 n. 19, 83, 85, 105, 111 n. 2, 128, 134 n. 21, 137 n. 42, 149
Spanish language 8, 58 n. 60, 64, 65, 69, 111 n. 2, 115 n. 46, 158
speech 6, 47, 70, 73, 116 n. 51
speech community 146
spirit (*see also* immaterial creature) 11, 6, 107, 115 n. 39, 123, 130, 131, 134 n. 18
spirit possession 28
Spiritism 131, 137 n. 46
spiritist 107, 131, 137 n. 44, 137 n. 46, 145
spiritual 12, 13, 33 n. 10, 81, 82, 83, 91, 100, 110, 113 n. 19, 115 n. 42, 122, 123, 132, 137 n. 45, 156, 157, 159, 160
spiritual betterment 91
Spiritual Church Movement 137 n. 46
spiritual development 13
spiritual exercise 111 n. 4
spiritual guidance 90
spiritual harmony 13
spiritual issue 127
spiritual need 47
spiritual perfection 158
spiritual progress 104
spiritual tendency 9
spiritualism 131
spirituality 28, 48, 71, 88, 105, 109
spoken Arabic (*see also* Moroccan Arabic) 41, 75 n. 2
spring, water 133 n 11, 133 n. 13
springboard to Islam 42
standardization, writing system's 75 n. 4, 75 n. 5
state, spiritual 13, 99, 101, 111 n. 2, 112 n. 12, 123, 131, 137 n. 43, 158, 159, 160
status, social 58 n. 55, 106
Steinvorth, Daniel 33 n. 12
Stenberg, Leif 7
story 49, 53, 106, 109, 113 n. 20, 116 n. 51, 121, 130
stranger 5, 31, 42, 74
Strasbourg 40
strata, social 44, 94 n. 21
strategies for attracting potential devotees (*see also* proselytization) 47, 66, 67, 133 n. 5, 148, 150
stress 131
strictly Islamic approach to Sufism 143
strictly traditional approach to Sufism 143
structural aspects, of the Būdshīshiyya 40
struggle to enter Europe 89
subḥa (*see also* rosary) 93 n. 5, 101, 113 n. 18, 160, 161
submission, to the saint 29, 85 (*see also* religious authority)
sub-Saharan influences 108
substance intake 130
successor 24, 46
suffering 108, 130
Sufi community 8
Sufi group 8, 9, 17 n. 15, 29, 36, 64, 73, 74, 75, 116 n. 52
Sufi idea 23
Sufi Islam 9
Sufi movement 11, 33 n. 17
Sufi person 13, 14, 33 n. 9, 41, 50, 53, 56 n. 26, 78, 105, 108, 120, 124, 125, 132, 134 n. 17, 135 n. 27, 141, 156, 157, 158
Sufi structure 23
Sufi thought 8
Sufi tradition 2, 7, 10, 13, 101, 112 n. 13, 133 n. 5, 141
Sufi universe 81, 98
Sufism x, 1, 5, 6, 7, 8, 9, 10, 11, 13, 14, 15, 16 n. 1, 17 n. 15, 17 n. 17, 23, 26, 27, 29, 31, 32, 33 n. 9, 34 n. 22, 34 n. 32, 35 n. 44, 35 n. 45, 44, 46, 47, 48, 49, 51, 52, 55 n. 18, 56 n. 27, 58 n. 45, 58 n. 50, 58 n. 59, 67, 69, 70, 71, 73, 79, 82, 84, 88, 97, 98, 103, 107, 110, 111 n. 4, 111 n. 6, 112 n. 12,

112 n. 17, 115 n. 42, 122, 125, 126, 129, 130, 132 n. 3, 133 n. 5, 135 n. 24, 136 n. 32, 137 n. 47, 141, 143, 144, 147, 150, 150 n. 4, 158, 159, 160
Sum, Maisie 115 n. 38
Sumatran 132 n. 2
summer course 50, 91
supernatural 115 n. 39, 121, 130, 133 n. 12, 158
superstition 124, 129
superstitious 29, 86, 136 n. 35
suppliant, healer's 128
supra-local discourse 2
suspension of judgement 51, 87
Sutcliffe, Steven 13
sweating 101
Switzerland 41
symbol, religious 1, 11
symbolic meaning 15, 72, 83, 85, 86, 91, 106, 110, 113 n. 21
symbolism, Sufi 8, 57 n. 44
sympathisers, of Hamza Būdshīsh 41
symptom 123

tabarruk 33 n. 19, 45, 161
tabarrukiyya 25
taboo 105, 125
Tafoghalt 32 n. 6
Tafraout 80
Taghjirt 23, 106
tagourramt (*see also agourram*) 92 n. 2, 156, 161
Taji-Farouki, Suha 8
tajwīd (*see also* Qur'ānic recitation) 98
tale 104, 106, 110, 116 n. 51, 121
Tangier 136 n. 37
Tan-Tan 81
Taourirt 40
tarbawiyya 26
ṭarīqa (*see also* Path, *ṭuruq*) 1, 2, 4, 7, 8, 11, 12, 14, 15, 16 n. 1, 22, 23, 24, 25, 26, 28, 29, 32, 33 n. 11, 34 n. 30, 41, 42, 43, 44, 46, 47, 49, 50, 57 n. 31, 62, 63, 64, 67, 70, 71, 73, 74, 75, 85, 94 n. 18, 98, 99, 100, 101, 102, 103, 104, 105, 106, 107, 108, 110, 112 n. 12, 113 n. 21, 114 n. 21, 114 n. 2, 121, 126, 142, 145, 146, 147, 148, 150, 158, 159, 161
Taroudant 40
taste, Sufism's 51, 82, 123, 144
tattoo 109
Tawfīq, Aḥmad 2, 27
taxi 35 n. 43, 90, 141
tayammum 113 n. 21
Taza 40
teaching *shaykh* 33 n. 17, 112 n. 17
teaching, religious 6, 10, 22, 23, 28, 33 n. 17, 41, 47, 48, 70, 76, 82, 109, 112 n. 17, 114 n. 26, 158
technique, *dhikr*'s 97, 100
technique, religious 127, 144
technique, spiritual 13, 111 n. 4
techniques du corps 121, 132
temporary curiosity in the Būdshīshiyya 83
temporary worker 10
tension, social 89
terminology, Sufi 111 n. 5, 112 n. 10, 150 n. 4
terrace 87, 93 n. 15
terrorist 52
Tétouan 40
text, Būdshīshiyya's 10, 14, 24, 28, 51, 52, 53 n. 1, 59 n. 61, 62, 64, 69, 70, 71, 72, 73, 76 n. 11, 111 n. 2, 113, 114 n. 28
text, religious 6, 10, 53 n. 1, 62, 69, 111 n. 4, 111 n. 5, 116 n. 51
text, Sufi 28, 52, 59 n. 61, 71, 76 n. 11, 76 n. 12, 111 n. 5, 114 n. 28
text-reliant, spiritual instruction 51, 71
textual 69, 111 n. 5, 126, 136 n. 33, 141, 144, 157, 161
textuality 52
the 'extraordinary' 81, 83, 126
the 'West' 11, 17 n. 15, 29, 34 n. 32, 35 n. 44, 47, 54 n. 9, 64, 74, 75, 88, 90, 93 n. 16, 93 n. 17, 94 n. 22, 113 n. 20, 114 n. 26, 116 n. 51, 143
the net 66, 68, 69, 71, 74
theological understanding of the sacred 143
theology 28, 48, 137 n. 46
theories of causation, disease's 129, 130
theosophical study of Sufism 111 n. 6
therapist 128, 129, 131
thesis, doctoral x, 9, 16 n. 1, 48, 58 n. 50, 112 n. 16
thick description of ritual 111 n. 6
Thrifa 35 n. 35
ṭibb al-nabawī (*see also* prophetic medicine) 125
Tifinagh writing system 75 n. 5
Tijānī devotee 114 n. 22
Tlemcen 8
toilet 80
toilet paper 93 n. 5

tomb 78, 92 n. 1, 121, 123, 133, 162
tombs' complex (*see also Zāwiya*) 15, 93 n. 8, 121
tombs' guardian 123
Touati, Samia 57 n. 32
'touching' Hamza 70, 82, 91, 121, 122
Toulouse 40
tourist 42, 50, 58 n. 51, 79, 81, 90, 92 n. 4
Tozy, Mohammed 9, 24, 26, 27, 33 n. 10
trade unions 23
Tradition 32, 35 n. 44
Traditionalism 32, 35 n. 44
Traditionalist 31, 35 n. 44
training, religious 50, 98, 100, 104, 112 n. 17, 128
trance (*see also ḥāl*) 101, 107, 112 n. 12, 160
Transcendental Meditation (TM) 134 n. 18
transformation 142
transient nature of membership 56 n. 24
transliterated 32 n. 1, 100
transliterating system 56 n. 30, 57 n. 30
transliteration 56 n. 30, 57 n. 30
transnational 1, 3, 4, 8, 10, 26, 31, 43, 45, 47, 48, 63, 64, 69, 73, 76 n. 11, 88, 89, 90, 100, 110, 113 n. 17, 145
transnationalism 63
Transpersonal Psychology 13
Transplant Sufi groups 11, 17 n. 15, 31
trans-regional 90
treatment, medical 14, 30, 123, 127, 128, 129, 131, 137 n. 40
tree 123, 133 n. 11
trembling 103
tribe 81, 106, 130
Trimingham, J. Spencer 8, 22, 84
trip 3, 35 n. 37, 81, 83, 85
True Knowledge 5, 70
trust 84, 85
Truth 35 n. 44, 47, 70, 97, 103, 104, 144
Tuareg 81
tuberculosis 137 n. 40
Tunisian 133 n. 6
Turkey 8, 36 n. 47
Turner, Edith 78, 82, 84, 102
Turner, Victor Witter 16 n. 10, 17 n. 14, 78, 82, 84, 102
turnover of public 141
ṭuruq (*see also ṭarīqa*) 6, 8, 9, 11, 17 n. 15, 23, 29, 32 n. 4, 41, 45, 51, 84, 88, 89, 93 n. 16, 102, 111 n. 6, 113, 115, 137 n. 40, 148, 161
ṭuruq system 30, 149
ulamā' 27, 126, 156, 161
umma (*see also* community) 106, 107, 161
UN 108
unbelief 160
unemployment 44, 55 n. 22
UNICEF 134 n. 20
'uniform' group, of the Būdshīshiyya (*see also* homogeneity) 42, 43
union with God
un-Islamic 24, 53, 76 n. 11
United Kingdom, UK (*see also* Britain) 2, 8, 9, 43, 55 n. 16, 55 n. 20, 55 n. 22
United States, US 1, 34 n. 32, 41, 48, 58 n. 53
universal 110, 146
universalist 29, 137 n. 39
universalistic approach to Sufism 88, 137 n. 39
universalizing 88
university education 34 n. 21, 63
university students 26
university xi, 1, 5, 27, 28, 43, 45, 46, 47, 48, 50, 91
unorthodox 6, 135 n. 24
unregulated digital content 73
un-spiritual 86
upper class 43, 44
upper echelon (*see also* higher echelon) 6, 71, 75, 81, 112 n. 14
Upper Egypt 34 n. 34, 93 n. 23
Upton, Charles 58 n. 56
urban Berber 81
urban devotee (*see also* urban member) 126
urban member (*see also* urban devotee) 91
urbanite 85, 86, 94 n. 21
urbanization 34 n. 21
Urry, John 93 n. 13
uṣūl al-fiqh 45, 126, 156, 161
uṣūl at-tafsīr 28, 45, 161

vacation 81
vaccination 129
value, social 66
van Bruinessen, Martin 7
van Hoven, Ed 113 n. 17
van Leeuwen, Theodoor 127
van Nieuwkerk, Karin 17 n. 13, 116 n. 51
Vásquez, Manuel A. 6, 53 n. 1, 69, 111 n. 5
Vauvert 40

Veinstein, Gilles 8
veneration, saintly 71, 78, 88, 136 n. 32
Vermeren, Pierre 34 n. 21, 63
vernacular religiosity 128
viability, Būdshīshiyya's 92
Vic 134 n. 21
video 63, 71, 72, 134 n. 21
Villalón, Leonardo A. 94 n. 24
violence, religious 24, 52, 58 n. 51
Virginia 53 n. 3
virtual 63, 72
visit, among devotees 29, 46, 47, 57 n. 40, 85, 88
visitation, Sufi pious 63, 78, 80, 92 n. 1, 115 n. 37, 121, 124, 159, 162
visiting a healer 121, 122, 123, 124, 126, 127, 128, 133 n. 6, 134 n. 18, 146, 147
visiting Berkane 31, 90
visiting Madāgh 15, 16 n.4, 25, 35 n. 42, 42, 46, 70, 71, 72, 78, 80, 82, 83, 84, 86, 89, 91, 92, 102, 103, 106, 109, 113 n. 17, 122, 128, 136, 159
visitor in a ritual 112 n. 15
visitor, to the lodge 35 n. 43, 50, 67, 78, 79, 80, 81, 88, 93 n. 15, 112 n. 15, 121
vocabulary 132, 146
vocalized invocation 103
voice recording 3
Voix, Raphaël x, 10, 26, 29, 111 n. 4, 135 n. 30
volatile adherence to the Būdshīshiyya 56 n. 24, 150
volume, in *dhikr*'s performance 98, 99
voluntarism 54 n. 9, 148
voluntary sector 66, 142
voluntary work 79, 87

walaya (*see also* blessing) 43
walī (*see also* saint, *awliyā'*) 34 n. 26, 35 n. 40, 45, 46, 56 n. 25, 80, 90, 92 n. 2, 104, 106, 112 n. 17, 121, 122, 130, 147, 156, 157, 159, 161
Wallis, Roy 11, 12, 56 n. 23, 114 n. 29, 134 n. 18, 141
war 112 n. 15
Ward, Patricia A. 34 n. 20
Warren, Carol A.B. 16 n. 6
water 80, 93 n. 5, 113 n. 21, 121, 123, 125, 133 n. 11, 133 n. 13, 134 n. 20
Waugh, Earle H. 9
waẓīfa (*see also ḥaḍra, waẓīfāt*) 41, 49, 98, 99, 100, 101, 102, 106, 113 n. 21, 147, 158, 161, 162
waẓīfāt (*see also waẓīfa*) 49, 79, 102, 103, 107, 113 n. 20, 161
wealth, devotee's 10, 106, 126
wealth, Hamza's 91, 94 n. 23
wealth, of *ṭuruq* 90
wealthy 103
web of meaning 147
web page (*see also* website) 3, 33 n. 12, 69
website (*see also* web page) 46, 48, 55 n. 20, 57 n. 34, 63, 65, 66, 68, 70, 71, 128, 134 n. 18, 144
weight 131
well-off member 44
Werbner, Pnina 8, 36 n. 46, 54 n. 7, 84, 88, 90, 94 n. 19, 102, 105, 114 n. 26, 120, 132 n. 2, 135 n. 24, 136 n. 32, 141
Werth, Lukas 134 n. 17
Wertheim, Margaret 63
West Africa 1, 135 n. 27, 159
West Asia 78
Westerlund, David 7, 29, 127, 136 n. 32
Westermarck, Edward 133 n. 6
Western Esotericism 145
Western Europe 1, 2 10, 14, 16 n. 1, 41, 55 n. 16, 65, 108, 111 n. 4, 115 n. 32, 131, 141, 143
Western Muslim 93 n. 10
Western Sahara 74
Western Sufism 11, 17 n. 15, 29, 34 n. 32, 35 n. 44, 64, 67, 75, 88, 93 n. 17, 111 n. 4, 113 n. 20, 129
western/er 9, 34 n. 32, 47, 48, 67, 69, 108, 111 n.4, 129, 137 n. 44, 145
Western' medicine 14, 130
westernization 145
Westernized 143
westernized version of Oriental doctrine
Weyel, Silja 54 n. 6
Wicca 137 n. 46
Wiccan 137 n. 46
Wiegers, Gerard Albert 133 n. 6
wife (*see also* wives) 50, 113 n. 20, 162
Willis, Michael J. 24, 25
witchcraft 125, 126
wives (*see also* wife) 35 n. 46, 50, 54 n. 7
workers, temporary 10
workplace 105, 135 n. 30
World Wide Web 63, 65, 67, 71, 75, 76 n. 8, 148
world-accommodating NRMs 12, 56 n. 23, 114 n. 29, 141, 142

World-affirming NRMs 12
World-rejecting NRMs 11, 12, 56 n. 23
worldview, Būdshīshiyya's 11, 54 n. 15, 64, 69, 103, 128, 147
worldview, Moroccan 145
worship 12, 56 n. 23, 112 n. 8, 137 n. 46, 158
worshipping, tomb 78
wuḍū (*see also* ablution) 113 n. 21

yā laṭīf 101
Yahya, Dahiru 32 n. 4
Yāssīn, 'Abd al-Salām 23, 24, 25
Yāssīn, Nadia 33 n. 12
Yoga 13, 111, 129, 136 n. 39
young devotee (*see also* young member) 47
young member (*see also* young devotee) 71
youthful, Būdshīshiyya's character 43
youthfulness 44
YouTube 63, 72
Yusuf, Hamza 59

Zaio 40, 45
Zaleski, Jeff P. 63
zāwāya 98
Zāwiya (*see also* shrine, *zāwiyāt*) 8, 15, 25, 28, 30, 42, 44, 45, 46, 47, 50, 54 n. 10, 80, 81, 82, 83, 85, 86, 87, 88, 89, 92 n. 1, 92 n. 4, 93 n. 14, 106, 122, 123, 131, 136 n. 36, 137 n. 47, 162
Zawiya, association 55 n. 20, 66, 67
zāwiyāt (*see also Zāwiya*) 23
Zebiri, Katherine x, 1, 17 n. 13, 55 n. 17, 59 n. 65, 115 n. 32
Zeghal, Malika 33 n. 9
Zindapir 8, 114 n. 26
ziyāra (*see also* pilgrimage, *ziyārāt*) 15, 78, 79, 80, 81, 82, 83, 84, 85, 86, 87, 88, 89, 90, 91, 92, 92 n. 1, 93, 93 n. 14, 94, 94 n. 21, 95, 96, 133 n. 6, 134 n. 20, 136 n. 31, 141, 159, 160, 162
ziyārāt (*see also ziyāra*) 88, 92 n. 1, 134 n. 20, 162
Zubaida, Sami 98